T0299580

"A testimony to the continued presence of the Devil among us [and] the victory of our Lord Jesus Christ."
—Father **LAWRENCE LEE**, STB, JCL, Exorcist of the Diocese of Hong Kong

"One of the most relevant books of our time!"
—Father **DANIEL J. REEHIL**, MA, MDiv, Exorcist of the Diocese of Nashville

"[Describes] the reality of spiritual warfare while giving hope and assurance that our Lord Jesus Christ—who has already won the battle—is at work."
—Father **LLOYD PAUL ELAURIA**, OFM, Exorcist of the Diocese of Ilagan

"Father Martins gives . . . accounts of the different ways Satan works to undermine human happiness. . . . I highly recommend it."
—Father **CHARLES GORAIEB**, MDiv, Exorcist Emeritus of the Diocese of Phoenix

"While the subject is harrowing, Father Martins' reminds us that greater is He who is within us than is within the world."
—**ABIGAIL ROBERTSON**, CBN

"This book will challenge, inspire, and make you ask yourself some tough questions."
—**RYAN BETHEA**, Producer and Co-Creator of *The Exorcist Files* Podcast

"[A] masterful blend of storytelling and explanation of how exorcism works will provide readers of all backgrounds with practical tips for finding freedom."
—Dr. **JOSHUA BROWN**, MD, PHD, Psychiatrist at McLean Hospital/Harvard Medical School

"Theologically astute and based on sound pastoral ministry."
—Father **STEPHEN V. HAMILTON**, STB, STL, Exorcist of the
Archdiocese of Oklahoma City

"[A] holistic approach to diagnosing the presence of evil—
using prayer, spirituality, and the best of the medical
sciences to minister to both body and soul."
—Dr. **DAVID D'SOUZA**, MD, CCFP, DTM&H, DCAPM, Assistant Professor
at Queen's University

"Father Martins reminds us that the Devil is too easily forgotten."
—Dr. **JASON WEST**, PhD, President and Vice Chancellor at
Newman Theological College

"Explains, in riveting detail, the vulnerability of the human person
when he or she is compromised by evil. . . . [T]he reader is left
encouraged that evil can be overcome with the power of God."
—Dr. **SUBHRA MOHAPATRA**, MD, CCFP(PC)

"[A] must-read book . . . [about] how demons enter and
how to make them leave."
—Dr. **CANDY GUNTHER BROWN**, PhD, Professor of Religious Studies
at Indiana University

"Whether believer or skeptic, Protestant or Catholic, I have no
doubt that readers will find Fr. Martins' approach to the demonic
both compelling and empowering."
—Dr. **KUTTER CALLAWAY**, PhD, Associate Dean, Fuller Theological Seminary

THE
EXORCIST
FILES

TRUE STORIES ABOUT THE REALITY
OF EVIL AND HOW TO DEFEAT IT

Father Carlos Martins

HODDER &
STOUGHTON

First published in Great Britain in 2024 by Hodder Faith
An imprint of John Murray Press

2

A CIP catalogue record for this title is available from the British Library

Hardback ISBN 9781399818902
Paperback ISBN 9781399818919
ebook ISBN 9781399818933

Typeset in Adobe Garamond Pro by Timothy Shaner, NightandDayDesign.biz

Printed and bound in Great Britain by Clays Ltd, Elcograf S.p.A.

John Murray Press policy is to use papers that are natural, renewable and recyclable
products and made from wood grown in sustainable forests. The logging and
manufacturing processes are expected to conform to the environmental regulations
of the country of origin.

Carmelite House
50 Victoria Embankment
London EC4Y 0DZ

www.hodderfaith.com

John Murray Press, part of Hodder & Stoughton Limited
An Hachette UK company

The authorised representative in the EEA is Hachette Ireland, 8 Castlecourt
Centre, Dublin 15, D15 XTP3, Ireland (email: info@hbgi.ie)

Mariis

in vita mea micantibus

ABOUT THE AUTHOR

FATHER CARLOS MARTINS' work in the ministry of exorcism has made him one of the most renowned experts in demonic activity and the supernatural worldwide. His blockbuster podcast, *The Exorcist Files*, has been downloaded by millions, drawing listeners to its suspenseful reenactments of his exorcist case files and the teachings that accompany them.

Once an atheist, Father Martins discovered Jesus Christ as an undergraduate. Now a Catholic priest and passionate evangelizer, he travels internationally as an itinerant preacher and is a renowned expert on Catholic saints and their relics, having received the ecclesiastical designation of *Custos Reliquiarum*. He is the Director of Treasures of the Church, a Vatican-sponsored evangelization ministry that uses relics of the saints to communicate the presence of the living God. A prolific ministry that travels internationally, it has attracted millions worldwide. Pope Francis has designated Father Martins as a Missionary of Mercy, with special faculties to serve as a papal delegate worldwide.

NOTE TO THE READER

This book contains actual accounts of possession and other demonic activity from my case files and notes.

To maintain anonymity for the victims and their families, I have changed the names of all involved. I have also changed other details where there was a reasonable chance the victims or their families could be identified.

Exorcists often use the term "the Devil" when referring to a generic demon. This is not because there is no difference between Satan and the demons under him, but because every demonic action is done under Satan's authority, regardless of whether Satan himself is the direct actor. Evil operates in a hierarchy. Satan sits at the top of that hierarchy and the other demons are his agents.

Exorcism is an ancient Christian practice. As an ordained Catholic priest, the theological explanations I provide in this book are grounded in the traditions common to both the Catholic and Orthodox faiths. Readers from other Christian traditions may find certain aspects unfamiliar or even contradictory to their own beliefs. I invite readers to consider the theology presented here with an open mind, knowing it is grounded in ancient Apostolic and Patristic traditions.

This book is intended for an adult audience and the topics discussed may be disturbing.

Unless otherwise noted, all Scripture references are from the Revised Standard Version.

The reason the Son of God appeared was
to destroy the works of the Devil.

—1 John 3:8

CONTENTS

FOREWORD

Throughout my priestly life, I have regularly encountered souls who, in one way or another, were afflicted by Satan and his fallen angels. I can confidently join my brother priest, Father Carlos Martins, in declaring that evil is real. Indeed, evil has not only a name but also a will—an unending drive to steal, kill, and destroy.

At the same time, I have personally experienced and witnessed in the lives of others the reality of the holy angels, including Guardian Angels. The words of daily prayers such as the *Angelus*, the *Angele Dei*, and the Prayer to Saint Michael the Archangel—

"The Angel of the Lord declared unto Mary . . .,"

"Angel of God, my guardian dear . . . be at my side to light and guard, to rule and guide," and

"Saint Michael the Archangel defend us in battle"—

are not figures of speech but references to purely spiritual creatures of God who are His messengers. They assist in our struggle to resist temptation and to live faithfully in Christ, with the help of the divine grace flowing immeasurably and unceasingly from His glorious-pierced Heart into our hearts (cf. Dan. 7, 10).

It is a sad truth that many today, including many within the Church, reject such claims or turn away from them as off-putting.

In recent times, a rationalist tendency has arisen that seeks to falsely reduce all reality to what is naturally explainable or to wholly emphasize a corollary of optimism about the Christian life, which takes no account of the ceaseless demonic activity led by Satan.

Christ, on the contrary, possessed no such delusions. With stark realism, He identified Satan as "a murderer from the beginning" and "a liar and the father of lies" (John 8:44). Similarly, the *Catechism of the Catholic Church* and sound dogmatic theology teach us to take seriously the reality of Satan and his cohorts while having confidence in Christ's ultimate victory over evil.

Satan's warfare against humanity is real and must be taken seriously. At the same time, man knows Christ's definitive victory over Satan, which he is called to share from the moment of his baptism and to not give way to cowardly fear and discouragement. The final chapter of the story of the battle between good and evil has already been written. It is the victory of Christ. It remains for us to make the intervening chapters stories of fidelity to Christ in the daily battle—stories of always remaining in the company of Christ through prayer, worship, and the devotional life.

In confronting the preternatural strength of Satan and his demons, one must not be beguiled by the sensationalistic presentation of demonic possession found in certain contemporary productions, beginning with the 1973 film *The Exorcist*, which reduces all of Satan's affliction to possession. The truth must rather guide us as it is announced in sacred Scripture and the perennial teaching and practice of the Church. A confrontation with Satan is never pleasant and has to do with the evil resulting from sin, but, at the same time, it is not terrorizing, as it is depicted in sensationalist films. If we are in the state of grace, we must always remain serene, knowing that the grace of the Holy Spirit always triumphs in the end.

With these considerations in mind, I am pleased to commend *The Exorcist Files* by Father Carlos Martins. Drawing upon his many years of administering healing grace to those afflicted by the Evil One, Father Martins describes how, in the various forms of demonic affliction, when Christ is invoked through prayer, He always triumphs. The struggle and suffering from the encounter with the mendacious and murderous devils are real, but Christ has forever provided the remedy that dispels their lies and thwarts their attempts to destroy. Father Martins's book is thorough and addresses the many questions surrounding the reality of demonic activity in the world, placing diabolical possession within the context of the entire spectrum of Satan's ploys in afflicting souls.

While his presentation of diabolical possession and exorcism is key, his descriptions of other forms of Satan's assaults are an essential help to the many Christians who do not experience possession yet still suffer from the forces of evil—for example, through the use of the Ouija board, occult activities, and witchcraft. Every chapter of *The Exorcist Files* constitutes an exhortation to the purity of heart that comes to us from the Sacred Heart of Jesus seated in glory at the right hand of the Father. The sevenfold gift of the Holy Spirit, which flows from the Heart of Jesus into the human heart, cleanses man of sin and fortifies him with divine love. While no Christian should look for encounters with the Evil One, he should be working daily and tirelessly to be pure of heart and thus to be prepared to resist, with the help of divine grace, the assaults of Satan.

Because the work of Satan is deceit and disorder—in short, sin—the accounts of the affliction of souls by Satan are always ugly. While it is necessary to acknowledge and confront unpleasant realities, Father Martins never presents the ugliness as inviting or enticing but, rather, as repugnant to a pure heart, as an incentive to respect and promote the good order with which God has created the world and which He has inscribed in every human heart.

It only remains to express deepest gratitude to Father Carlos Martins for his arduous work in presenting the reality of demonic affliction as accurately as possible, with fidelity to the perennial teaching and discipline of the Catholic Church. May his writing inspire us to recognize evil and be "fellow workers in the truth" (3 John 8), coworkers with Christ in battling evil with confidence in His victory. At the conclusion of our days on earth, as we look for the life which is come, may we be able to say with Saint Paul:

I have fought the good fight, I have finished the race, I have kept the faith. Henceforth there is laid up for me the crown of righteousness, which the Lord, the righteous judge, will award to me on that Day, and not only to me but also to all who have loved his appearing. (2 Timothy 4:7–9)

May God bless you and your home! May you witness ever more heroically the mystery of divine grace that casts out demons, heals souls afflicted by evil, and fortifies and increases purity in every human heart.

Raymond Leo Cardinal Burke
May 18, 2023
Solemnity of the Ascension of Our Lord Jesus Christ

DEMONIC POSSESSION, EXORCISM, AND MENTAL ILLNESS

One of my first encounters with the Devil occurred inside a house shortly after my ordination as a priest. A woman's home had been destroyed by fire, so she had moved into her uncle's house while he was deployed in Afghanistan. Before long, she began hearing voices calling her from adjacent rooms and scratching noises inside the walls. Appliances turned on and off by themselves, and objects sitting safely on a table or countertop would suddenly drop to the floor. The phenomena terrified her.

When I stepped inside the house, I felt an unmistakable tension, one I find difficult to put into words. It reminded me of playing hide-and-seek as a child when I expected my hiding place to be discovered at any moment. I had the intense feeling of being watched by something that didn't want me there. Even the air felt like it was against me. I was being warned: *Get out or else!*

That feeling, however, only deepened my pity for the woman and solidified my desire to help her. As I entered the living room, the ceiling fan began spinning. At first, it did so slowly—barely moving at all. In an instant, though, it was spinning so incredibly fast that its blades were scarcely a blur. The fan's copious wind scattered loose papers and small objects around the room. In a blink, however, the fan stopped and was perfectly still—only to begin slowly moving again a few moments later. Suddenly, it was spinning absurdly fast again, and just as suddenly, it began to spin in the other direction at the same speed.

I placed my bag on the dining room table and began to take out what I needed to make holy water. I asked the woman to fill a bowl from the tap and started the prayers when she returned. Just as I finished and began with the exorcism prayers for the house, I heard the chiming of a music box coming from upstairs.

"There!" she exclaimed. "That's the music box!"

When requesting my help, the woman had mentioned a music box as the creepiest of all the disturbances. It was in her uncle's bedroom and chimed randomly day and night, even though no one was winding it. She tried removing it from the house, but it wouldn't budge from its place on the dresser. It was as if the two were fused. She had even removed the winding key to ensure that it was not somehow being wound. The music box continued to chime, nonetheless.

I began sprinkling holy water around the home, moving upstairs after finishing the lower level. After blessing every other room, I moved into her uncle's room and saw the music box as it was chiming away. I reached down and picked it up without any trouble, and as soon as my hands touched it, it stopped chiming. I opened the lid to look inside it. To our mutual shock, the music box held nothing. There were no parts, no chimes, no wind-up mechanism, and no place for batteries. Nor was there any evidence it ever held any of these. It was an empty wooden box.

To borrow an overused saying, "Life is full of surprises." I never expected to be successful the day I walked into this woman's house, but I also never expected to be an exorcist. After I sprinkled the box with holy water, she never experienced diabolical phenomena again and lived peacefully within her uncle's home.

I also never expected to be in ordained ministry. In fact, until my conversion from atheism during my undergraduate studies, I never expected to believe in God. But now I write this book as a Catholic priest who is also an exorcist. Within the Catholic Church, exorcism is not a ministry to which a priest normally aspires. It is a ministry he is assigned . . . and accepts with great reluctance. If a seminarian or young priest shows a significant interest in the demonic, it is generally met with concern by his superiors or bishop, and he is told to direct his attention elsewhere. The only thing as bad as giving the Devil too little attention is giving him too much.

Rightly or wrongly, a certain "mystique" surrounds this ministry. People regularly ask exorcists, "Aren't you afraid of the Devil?" For my part, the answer is simple: no. If we fear the Devil, we have already ceded too much to him. I respect the Devil. I highly respect him. I do not, however, fear him. I fear God alone. I fear offending God; I fear abandoning His grace; I fear sinning against God. But I do not fear the Devil.

What is the difference between respecting the Devil and fearing him? An analogy might be helpful. You probably have a sharp knife in your kitchen. When you use that knife, you are careful because of what might happen if you are not. In other words, you respect the knife. Nevertheless, when you go to bed at night, as dangerous as your kitchen knife can be, you never worry about it or lose any sleep over it. If you did, you would agree that something is amiss with your mental state.

Though it is a joy to do this work, I have never enjoyed meeting the Devil and his minions. I would have been content with my life as a priest had I never encountered a single demon. Nevertheless, I do find this ministry a blessing and immensely meaningful. Through it, I assist Jesus Christ in rescuing souls He loves, souls for whom He gave His life but who are under the torment of His enemy. What could be more fulfilling than giving Jesus what He wants?

While it is the nature of an exorcist's job to combat demons, his primary focus is never evil, even though he may spend most of his time battling it. His primary focus is Jesus Christ, with whom he must be madly in love. This focus is crucial because it unites him to Christ and allows Christ to transform him into Himself. To borrow a term from Eastern Christianity, the exorcist's goal is to become *divinized*. His ministry is effective to the extent this has occurred.

I publish this work knowing there is always a danger in doing so. Many would rather read a book about the Devil than one about Jesus Christ. The human attraction to evil is an obstacle to many a person's growth in holiness. While in the following pages I discuss the nature and strategy of man's ancient enemy, I have done so only to highlight the victory of the Incarnate God, whose purpose is to "make all things new" (Rev. 21:5).

HAS NOT SCIENCE ELIMINATED THE NEED FOR EXORCISM?

We live in an age of contradiction. While virtually every human culture has stories of demons and demonic possession, many "scientifically minded" people dismiss the possibility of demonic activity out of hand. However, what if a person is unable to find relief from his symptoms through medical science, but experiences a cessation following exorcism? Wouldn't sound scientific reasoning and logic dictate at least a possibility that the symptoms' cause was, in fact, demonic? Rationality and good science demand that the existence of demons and their nefarious activity have their day in court.

Those who dismiss the possibility of demons fall victim to the demonic trap so succinctly put by the French author Charles Baudelaire, who wrote in his famous short story, "The Generous Gambler": *"La plus belle des ruses du diable est de vous persuader qu'il n'existe pas!"* ("The loveliest trick of the devil is to convince you that he does not exist!")

Sadly, many today—including Christians—falsely believe that the Gospel accounts in which Our Lord performs exorcisms are merely instances of Him curing people of a medical illness. Because the Gospel writers could not diagnose physical and mental illness, they attributed to demonic possession what is simply a medical problem.

Christianity has always believed in the importance of exorcism. Even during its fiercest persecutions, the young Church was aware that bringing souls into the Kingdom of God is, by its very act, a pillaging of the kingdom of Satan. Pope Cornelius, who reigned from 251 AD until his martyrdom two years later, left a fascinating personnel list. In his "Letter to Fabius," the bishop of Antioch, Pope Cornelius identifies the Church of Rome as having forty-six priests, seven deacons, seven subdeacons, forty-two acolytes, and fifty-two exorcists.[1] The fact that exorcists outnumbered the priests underscores the seriousness with which the early Church regarded the ancient serpent.

At the same time, the Church understands the need to distinguish between medical and spiritual illnesses. In 1583, the National Synod of Rheims decreed:

> *Before the priest undertakes an exorcism he ought diligently to inquire into the life of the possessed, into his condition, health, and other circumstances: and should talk them over with wise,*

prudent and instructed people, since the too credulous are often deceived, and melancholics, lunatics, and persons bewitched often declare themselves to be possessed and tormented by the Devil: and these people nevertheless are more in need of a doctor than an exorcist.[2]

In making this distinction, the Church follows the lead of the New Testament, which delineates between disease and demonic affliction in Mark 6:13: "And they cast out many demons, and anointed with oil many that were sick and healed them." Two additional Scriptures show that the ancient world recognized the distinction too. In both examples, the scribes accuse the Lord. In one, they declare He is out of His mind because He sets aside even eating in favor of preaching (Mark 3:21). In the other, they say He must be possessed by a demon because He claims to be able to lay down His life and take it up again (John 10:20). However, after the latter accusation, bystanders defend the Lord, saying His words are not the words of a demon because demons do not cure blindness (John 10:21).

Medical and spiritual illnesses are genuine, so any exorcist of competence will assert that each must be treated by the practitioner of its respective art: the physician or the exorcist.

DEMONIC ACTIVITY AND MENTAL ILLNESS

The presence of demonic spirits and mental illness is often not an either/or situation. It is possible to be under demonic control and be mentally ill simultaneously. Demons are predators, and—like a pack of lions on the hunt—they set their sights on those who are easiest to catch. Many who are mentally ill have scarring due to past trauma. They are often prone to forming friendships with the wrong people who can lead them into spiritually dangerous and morally sinful behavior. Mental illness can also cause severe depression, crushing all hope that a situation will improve and putting those who struggle with it at risk of being the target of demonic activity.

For their part, demons are adept at using the cover of mental illness to hide their presence. Just as an enemy will work to keep his presence secret, demons will work to blend into the conditions and circumstances of their host inconspicuously. Mental illness is often their perfect cover because family members and medical staff believe it—rather than the demonic—is the reason for the victim's aberrant behavior.

Still, there is no innate connection between mental illness and demonic oppression. An exorcist ought to insist that—*together* with prayer—a sober and proper examination be undertaken to confirm whether or not the suffering is from demonic oppression. *Exorcists begin with the presumption that the behavioral phenomena they observe are likely rooted in natural causes.* We take it for granted that odd or demonic-looking behavior is, in all probability, caused by some illness. We employ the services of medical staff and psychological experts to understand and diagnose the source of a subject's behavior. Thus, to assert that exorcism and science are at odds is, from my perspective, nonsense.

Modern Psychological Science and Exorcism

It's also fair to note here that modern psychology *acknowledges* the phenomenon of "possession." The American Psychiatric Association's *Diagnostic and Statistical Manual of Mental Disorders* (*DSM-5-TR*), sometimes referred to as the "psychology bible," regards possession as a state that lacks full explanation and is subject to cultural interpretation. While the *DSM* presumes such states are speculatively dissociative or psychotic in nature, and while it fails even to note Christianity's success in liberating persons from possession states

over the past two millennia, the *DSM* nevertheless contains fascinating and compelling remarks, among which is the following:

> *Possession . . . typically manifest behaviorally as if a "spirit,"*
> *supernatural being, or outside person has taken control,*
> *with the individual speaking or acting in a distinctly differ-*
> *ent manner. For example . . . an individual's behavior may*
> *give the appearance that her identity has been replaced by [a]*
> *"ghost."*[3]

If possession is "not attributable to the physiological effects of a
substance . . . or another medical condition"[4] then it bears asking:
if possession is not caused by drugs or illness, then what causes
it? Here we have modern science's hesitation to acknowledge the
possibility of spiritual evil, even though it cannot deny its clinical
manifestation.

Ours is an age of contradiction.

Why This Book and Why Now?

I've written this book to help readers keep the Devil out of their lives.
The West is quickly becoming de-Christianized and is embracing
paganism. This change has grave implications. Humans are spiritual beings. When someone no longer subscribes to the Christian
worldview—or believes in God, for that matter—spiritual instinct
still operates. It seeks satisfaction in the myriads of unhealthy pagan
and occult avenues flooding Western society. The witchcraft section
in many bookstores today is larger than the Christianity section.
Toy stores and online retailers market Ouija boards to children.
The acceptance and use of pornography has exploded, and the secu-
lar redefinition of sexuality and gender identity, aside from desta-
bilizing society, leaves those whom they purport to benefit in an

even worse state than they were before.[5] The overall religious literacy of people is so poor that many do not know the danger they are subjecting themselves to when they enter a spa offering Reiki treatments, use crystals that "raise" their energy levels, or consult a medium. Indeed, many Christians are unaware that they have a foot in two incompatible kingdoms—God's and the enemy's.

While I hope to present an understanding of the ministry in which I have engaged for years, my ultimate goal is to give readers a new appreciation of the victory of Jesus Christ and how He has empowered His Bride, the Church, to dispense the spoils of His victory for the liberation of all who believe in Him.

ONE

THE REALITY OF THE DEVIL

THE CASE OF
AN ODD THURSDAY AFTERNOON

Mark and Cheryl met in college and started dating after just a week of meeting. One year later, they married. They were both twenty-two years old.

Although they complemented each other well, their relationship became increasingly strained with each passing year. Both were eager for children, but for some reason, Cheryl could not get pregnant. She and Mark were tested medically, and the results always came back normal. Physiologically, doctors could find nothing wrong with them.

Cheryl became more and more depressed. She worked as a paralegal, but six years into the marriage, she could no longer focus on the details of her work. So she was fired.

Economically, the impact on the couple was minimal. As a college English professor, Mark made enough money to support his wife without her working. But he feared that, without a job, Cheryl would have more time to worry about being childless.

Mark was right. With the extra time on her hands, Cheryl did little more than worry. She was in a very dark period for a year and lived as a virtual shut-in inside their home.

Then there were new developments.

Cheryl suddenly began to buy baby clothes. At first, Mark didn't think much of these purchases, but eventually, they became excessive. She purchased large quantities of baby suits, bonnets, and baby blankets, along with large diaper "jumbo packs," cans of baby formula, and infant toys. She even bought a crib and an electronic baby monitoring system.

Then, more ominously, Cheryl began to collect insects. Dead insects. She made forays outside each morning and brought whatever she found to the house. Her collection included crickets, grasshoppers, hornets, moths, and butterflies. Initially, Cheryl put them in the guest room, which she had transformed into a baby nursery, lining them up, side by side, on the window ledges, on top of the dresser, and on the baby-changing table. When she ran out of surfaces, she began putting the overflow in the rest of the house.

Mark knew his wife was psychologically fragile. He trod lightly, casually asking Cheryl about the insects. The baby stuff, in a sense, he could understand. One could see it as a form of positive thinking. Cheryl wanted to be a mom, so she readied things for a baby. Her collecting of dead insects, however, was just bizarre.

"Honey," Mark said one night after dinner, "what are all the insects for?"

"Someone told me they would help me get pregnant," she said.

"How?" Mark asked.

"When they die, their spirits hang around their bodies looking for a place to form new life," she said. "Death releases life energy. I want that energy to make a baby happen inside my womb."

"Do you believe that?" Mark asked.

"I'll take all the help I can get," she remarked.

"Who told you to do this?"

"A friend," was her only response.

About two weeks later, Mark returned home from work, and as he was getting out of his car, the neighbor's cat approached him. It was carrying a dead squirrel in its mouth, which it laid at Mark's feet. The cat had an affinity for Mark and occasionally presented him with gifts. After petting the cat, he dropped the dead squirrel inside a trash bin next to the garage before stepping into the house. He noticed Cheryl was not home—she was doubtless collecting more insects—so he laid down for a nap.

He awoke after an hour. He could hear Cheryl preparing dinner in the kitchen. As he left their bedroom, he peeked inside the baby room. The squirrel he had discarded was on top of the changing table.

"Cheryl!" he called out. "Why the hell is this dead squirrel inside the house?"

"He's much bigger than an insect," she said. "He'll give off more life energy."

"Cheryl," Mark said firmly. "This has gotten out of hand. This dead thing is going to stink up the house. All of this dead stuff has to go."

"No!" she screamed. "Nooooo! I want to get pregnant. These things are going to get me pregnant. They're going to give me a baby." She threw the pot with their dinner across the room. It hit the refrigerator, leaving a significant dent on the metal door, and scattered their dinner across the wall. "You leave them alone," she screeched. "YOU LEAVE THEM ALONE!"

A shiver went up Mark's spine. Although Cheryl screamed the words, it was not her voice that came out of her mouth. The scream sounded like that of a burly man. Deep and low, it resonated off the cupboards and wall of the kitchen. Mark had an uncle with the most resounding voice he had ever heard. Cheryl's voice was even deeper.

Stunned, Mark got into the car and went for a drive. He was bewildered and unsure of what to do next. Cheryl had never made an outburst like this before. It was not in her personality to do so. After driving around for a while, he finally calmed down, picked up some dinner for the two of them, and headed back home. Cheryl was unwell. He planned to call their family doctor in the morning and ask him to recommend a psychiatrist.

Cheryl's behavior became even stranger in the week following the incident in the kitchen. Mark found a dead bird on the living room windowsill. Six times, Mark heard Cheryl speaking baby talk in the nursery—not just a sentence or two, but a conversation lasting five to ten minutes, as if she were interacting with an actual baby. Cheryl made cash withdrawals from their checking account almost daily—two hundred dollars a day for five days straight. Mark noticed their credit card also had recurring ridesharing charges on it. It was not unusual for Cheryl to use the service since they had only one car, which Mark used to go to work, but she never used it this much. He wondered what was going on. After what had happened earlier in the week, however, he was afraid to confront her.

One day Mark left the house at the same time he always did. Instead of going to work, he merely parked his car farther up the street, from a vantage point where he could see his house.

After about thirty minutes, a vehicle pulled into his driveway. Cheryl got in the car, and it drove off. When the driver dropped her off at the bank, Cheryl got out and went inside. Mark could see she withdrew two hundred dollars using the app on his phone. Soon she was back in the car, and it pulled away. Mark followed.

The car headed toward downtown and stopped in front of an old house with a large sign over the front door: PSYCHIC HEALER. This place had been here since Mark was in his early teens. He had never seen anyone go in before now. Although it was surreal, he watched his wife do just that.

"So, a psychic has been getting my money," he mumbled. "That's $1,200 just this week!" Cheryl stayed inside for slightly over an hour before another car arrived in front of the house. Cheryl walked out of the psychic parlor, got in the car, and it pulled away. The car stopped at a pet store, and Cheryl went inside. Ten minutes later, she walked out, carrying a paper bag, and the rideshare drove her back home.

After watching Cheryl walk into their home, Mark parked his car on the street a short distance from the house. He remained inside and planned his conversation with Cheryl. Her hoarding of dead animals, her speaking to an imaginary baby, the idiocy of visiting a psychic, none of this made any sense to him.

Just then, Mark thought of something else that was strange. Neither he nor Cheryl was very religious. They did, however, have a handful of religious frames and a cross hanging inside their home. The frames consisted of Scripture quotes received as wedding gifts, a picture of Jesus that had belonged to Cheryl's parents, and a picture of a guardian angel guiding two small children across a rickety bridge that Mark had possessed since childhood. He'd noticed the pictures had disappeared about three weeks earlier. He later found them in a cardboard box inside the garage.

At the time, Mark assumed his wife was redecorating. However, she had only taken down the religious items. *Maybe my wife is mad at God*, he thought. *Or maybe she's losing her mind.*

He entered the door that led to the kitchen, startling Cheryl with his early and unexpected entrance. It was Mark, however, who was more shocked. On top of the kitchen table were two dead bloody rats. A third one was on the counter, still in the process of dying. Blood oozed from a wound on its head, and it was twitching. Cheryl held a wooden tenderizing mallet in her hand, the end of which was splattered in blood.

"What the hell are you doing, Cheryl?" he screamed. Cheryl stood wordless. "You picked up rats at the pet store to kill them? What is the matter with you? Get those filthy things off the table."

Mark then heard the deepest voice he had ever heard in his life come out of his wife: "You keep the %&$# away from the rats!"

The voice made the ceiling and every cupboard door in their small kitchen vibrate. Cheryl never used vulgarity. In all the years he knew her, Mark had never heard Cheryl use a crude word.

"%&$# off!" she bellowed as she took a step closer to him and raised the mallet threateningly. Her moves were confident, self-assured, and aggressive—behaviors he had never seen her exhibit before. Suddenly, Cheryl seemed significantly larger and broader than he ever remembered. Her face was not her own. She seemed to take on the appearance of man, and a bodybuilder at that.

Mark knew that it was not his wife speaking. It could not be. He was interacting with something else.

He walked back outside and got into his car. All he could think of was to drive to a Methodist church two blocks away. It was the church he and his wife occasionally—but rarely—attended. Mark was not sure he believed in God. He believed in "something" but was just not sure what. Cheryl occasionally wanted to get up attend church on Sundays. Since this was her way of asking God for a baby, he always dutifully complied.

"I don't do Devil stuff, Mark," the minister said to him. "Scares the wits out of me." The minister had spent time in South America with the Peace Corps when he was a young adult. During that time, he saw many wild demonic manifestations among the superstitious indigenous communities he worked with, and the experiences left him rattled and disturbed. "You need to go to the Catholics for help with this. They're the only ones with a handle on this kind of thing."

Later that day, Mark called a Catholic church requesting help for his situation. The pastor referred him to me. As it turned out, Mark's house was less than five miles from where I was on that particular Monday, helping a friend clean out his garage. I agreed to meet Mark at a nearby coffee shop later in the day. Over coffee, he gave me details about Cheryl. We decided to go to his house together so I could meet her.

A priest typically wears distinctive clothing: a black clerical shirt with a white collar and black pants. However, on this particular day, I was wearing an old T-shirt and jeans because I had been cleaning out a garage. Cheryl had no idea I was coming. She had never met me before and I was wearing ordinary clothes, so she could not have known I was a priest.

Still, Cheryl sprang up from the couch as we walked in the front door. In a deep, booming voice, she turned to Mark and said, "Why did you bring this bastard priest here!"

"Who are you?" I asked her.

"You know who the %&$# I am."

GOD HAS A PLAN FOR YOU. SO DOES THE DEVIL.

In the first chapter of the Bible, God states His intention to create humans as the pinnacle of His creation.

> *Let us make man in our image, after our likeness; and let them have dominion over the fish of the sea, and over the birds of the air, and over the cattle, and over all the earth, and over every creeping thing that creeps upon the earth.* (Genesis 1:26)

Humans are the crown jewel of God's creation, the masterpiece that completed the divine work. After five days of creating, each assessed by God as "good," God created man on the sixth day and that creation was declared to be "very good" (Gen. 1:31). After man, God stopped creating. Nothing more was needed.

In charging man to rule over all other creation (Gen. 2:15), God reveals that all other creation exists for the sake of humans. That explains the unique friendship we can enjoy with God. Endowed with an intellect and will, man and woman exist as an image and likeness of the Creator.

God's love for humanity did not diminish even after Adam and Eve disobeyed God's commandment against eating the fruit of the forbidden tree. Their sinful betrayal provoked an outpouring of love as God immediately put into place a plan for redemption (Gen. 3:15). That plan included the covenants made with Noah, Abraham, Moses, and David, as well as the ministry of the patriarchs and prophets, through whom He revealed Himself to His people. In the fourth Gospel, God reveals that rescue plan in its splendor: "For God so loved the world that He gave his only Son, that whoever believes in him should not perish but have eternal life" (John 3:16). Indeed, Christ's last words on the Cross, as He endured the heights of agony, reference that plan's completion: "It is finished" (John 19:30).

Disobedience of God was not something engineered by humans. The Devil—described in Genesis as a serpent—presented evil as goodness in a powerfully attractive manner so beguilingly attractive that it made God's plan appear to evil (Gen. 3:6). The execution of the serpent's plan was impressive and ingenious. God's covenant with Adam was that Adam would till and keep the garden, and he had the freedom to eat from every tree he desired except the one forbidden to him (Gen. 2:15–17). The serpent, however, did not tempt Adam directly. He tempted Eve, who unwittingly became his agent.

Eve was created as a helpmate. She was just what Adam wanted, and he was ecstatic when he met her. "This, at last, is bone of my bones and flesh of my flesh" (Gen. 2:23).

In the joy Adam expressed, the serpent spotted a potential vulnerability: a weakness for his helpmate.

The serpent then approached Eve in a manner as alluring as it was cunning: he deliberately misquoted God, something Eve felt compelled to correct.

"Did God say, 'You shall not eat of any tree of the garden'?"
And the woman said to the serpent, "We may eat of the fruit
of the trees of the garden; but God said, 'You shall not eat of
the fruit of the tree which is in the midst of the garden, neither
shall you touch it, lest you die.'" (Genesis 3:1–3)

As the most "subtle" creature (Gen. 3:1), the serpent approached Eve with the wrong information. When he misquoted God, she corrected him. By conversing with the serpent, though, she made herself vulnerable. Because the fruit of the tree was appealing (Gen. 3:5), she succumbed to the rest of the temptation in short order.

Adam fell just as quickly. With his sin, however, something terrible occurs. "The eyes of both were opened . . ." (Gen. 3:7). In an instant, the world became a different place. Paradise is no more, and all of creation is affected by Adam's sin.

The destructive power of Adam's sin cannot be overstated. Because of the Fall, we have disease, hunger, addiction, penicillin, hospitals, pandemics, winter coats, life jackets, taxes, prisons, police precincts, armies, coffins, and cemeteries. Adam's sin confronts us constantly.

Stealthily, the serpent embezzled Adam's covenantal lordship over creation before Adam was even aware it was at risk. He did not overpower Adam and rob him of his blessing. He used cunning. Referring to the cunning nature of the Devil, Jesus later says, "The thief comes only to steal and kill and destroy; I came that they may have life, and have it abundantly" (John 10:10). The word "steal" here is the Greek *klepto*, which means "to thieve or steal in secret." That is precisely what the serpent did. He managed to get Adam to surrender the birthright himself.

Jesus also says the thief comes to "kill." In ancient times, this Greek word *thuo* was used in the context of religious observance to denote the sacrificing of animals. It means, "to sacrifice, give up, or surrender something dear and valuable." In contrast, *phoneuo* means "murder." Thus, when Jesus says the thief comes to kill, He does not mean murder. What the Devil does is worse. Through his wiles, he "reprograms" you so that *you* kill what you love. In allowing himself to be seduced by the serpent, Adam issued a death sentence to himself and the human race he later fathers.

The thief's third tactic is that he comes to destroy. The Greek word Jesus uses is *apollumi*, "to ruin or obliterate." If he cannot steal the blessing that God has imparted to you, and if he cannot get you to give it up willingly, he will seek to annihilate it so that you may not possess it.

Regarding Paradise, the serpent successfully thieved in all three senses: steal, kill, and destroy. Humanity has been paying the price ever since. These characteristics are in stark contrast to GOD, whose every action is truthful, life-giving, and abundantly creative.

The drama of human existence is thus two-fold. God plans to bless you with life and happiness. The Devil plans to rob you of that blessing and to impart his misery upon you.

ANGELS

Mark knew there was something wrong with his wife, Cheryl. He also knew that even though he was looking at his wife, something else was in control. Cheryl had struggled for years with depression, but something more than mere depression was afflicting her.

Whatever it was, it was evil. It was the most evil thing Mark had ever experienced. So evil, that for the first time in his life, he began to believe that the Devil might be real.

The Devil is a fallen angel, and demons are those angels who perversely followed him out of Heaven. Thus, one can only understand who the Devil is, or what a demon is, by understanding what angels are.

Angels are pure spirits (souls who lack material bodies). God created and endowed them with intelligence, free will, beauty, and great power to serve Him. Angels have remarkable properties, not the least of which is their name, which denotes an activity rather than a kind of being. The word "angel" means "one who brings a message." In the Gospel of Luke, for example, an angel brings word to Zachariah that his aged wife Elizabeth will bear a son, and identifies himself precisely as a messenger: "I am Gabriel, who stands in the presence of God; and I was *sent to speak to you*, and to bring you this good news" (Luke 1:19; emphasis mine).

Angels have distinct personalities. While Scripture doesn't distinguish or call out with specificity very many angels' names and characteristics, what it does say is fascinating.

- The angels "shouted for joy" when God created the earth (Job 38: 4–7).
- There are things angels do not know (Matt. 24:36), and they long to know them (1 Pet. 1:10–12).
- Angels dislike inquiries about their names. Scripture quotes one angel replying to the question that his name is too wonderful to share (Judg. 13:18). Another asked his inquirer, "Why?", didn't answer, then blessed him and left (Gen. 32:29).

- An angel in his glory is so magnificent that, if revealed, he would seem to a human to be God Himself (Rev. 22:8–9).
- If you feed a stranger, you may be feeding an angel in disguise (Heb. 13:2).

Modern culture often depicts angels as cute and fluffy-winged humanlike beings who blunder and annoy their way into our lives. A TV commercial for a cream cheese brand depicts an angel sitting languorously on a cloud, casually enjoying its product. Nothing could be further from reality. An angel is a holy and terrible reality (cf. Dan. 8:17). As agents of the Most High, angels act with God's very power. The least of the angels can destroy the universe and everything within it in the blink of an eye. The only limit to an angel's power is God's will.

Angels experience existence differently than humans. Because they are pure spirits—and, therefore, immaterial—the limitations of time and space are not binding. Angels take no "time" to travel between places. *In fact, they do not travel at all.* Without the limitations that a body imposes, an angel is as present to you and me as he is to the deepest part of the ocean, to the peak of the highest mountain on earth, and to the farthest edge of the universe. Every physical reality is immediately present to an angel.

The way that angels process knowledge is astounding. Without a physical component, angels lack a brain that could slow them down, which means the complexity of the physical and material universe does not slow them down either. While they are not omniscient (all-knowing), what they know, they know immediately by pure intuition.

What does this mean? Angels do not need to reason—do not need to engage in the act of drawing conclusions from premises. *All knowledge that an angel possesses, and the near-infinite causal implications about that knowledge, is known instantly by intuition.* When an angel learns something, he requires no time or effort to grasp its importance, meaning, ramifications, consequences, or side effects. Such abilities are dramatically different from the way humans acquire knowledge. While some of our knowledge is grasped immediately, such as when we look at a color, say blue, and immediately recognize it by the act of looking, our abstract or higher-level knowledge requires some cognitive processing. In other words, we learn through a gradual process of reasoning and analysis that takes time and effort.

To understand the sheer power of an angel's cognitive ability:

1. Imagine if it were possible to have every single mathematical calculation from every single textbook throughout time in front of us in one pile;
2. Add to that all the real-life mathematical computations that every individual has ever done since the beginning of time;
3. Add to that all the calculations that every computer has ever done, or ever will do, throughout all time.

An angel knows the answers for every one of these calculations. He does so, however, not because he has a super-fast processing ability (mathematical or otherwise). Angels require no process between a question and its answer. Instead, they have an intuitive and immediate connatural grasp of the correct solution, without any of the steps necessary for human intellect or for a computer. To call an angel a "supercomputer" would insult what an angel can do and how he does it. His ability is far superior to a supercomputer's (or even to all of them combined).

Another property of the remarkable and unique manner of an angel's cognitive ability is that he is incapable of forgetting. No matter how much time passes since an angel has learned a fact, he knows it always and it is immediately available to him.

Why do angels possess this level of intelligence? They require it to execute the work of God. The Book of Hebrews declares that angels are "ministering spirits sent forth to serve, for the sake of those who are to obtain salvation" (Heb. 1:14). Their work is accomplished so effectively that Scripture often equates their ministry with God Himself. There is a famous passage in the Torah, for example, which declares that no one can see the face of God and live (Exod. 33:20). In the Book of Judges, when an angel appears to Gideon, Gideon realizes it is an angel, and he is struck with sheer terror: "Gideon perceived that he was the angel of the LORD; and Gideon said, 'Alas, O Lord GOD! For now I have seen the angel of the LORD face to face'" (Judg. 6:22). In the next verse, the angel has to assure Gideon that his life is spared: "Peace be to you; do not fear, you shall not die."

DEMONS

Not all angels accepted the divine decree to serve creatures inferior to themselves. Lucifer refused to obey and convinced one-third of the angels to do the same (Rev. 12:4). How many angels did this comprise? While Scripture gives no exact figure, it states the number of angels is very significant (Dan. 7:10; Matt. 26:53; Heb. 12:22). Revelations 5:11 declares the total to be "myriads of myriads and thousands of thousands." Regardless, Scripture's description of the ensuing battle following Satan's rebellion is vivid and striking.

> Now war arose in Heaven, Michael and his angels fighting against the dragon; and the dragon and his angels fought, but they were defeated and there was no longer any place for them in Heaven. And the great dragon was thrown down, that ancient serpent, who is called the Devil and Satan, the deceiver

*of the whole world—he was thrown down to the earth, and his
angels were thrown down with him.* (Rev. 12:7–9)

Notice these three things about Satan and his demons. First,
they remain angels after the fall. That means, among other things,
they retain the tremendous angelic power of knowing and acting.
Even though a demon's fall has left him with a wounded nature that
limits some of his ability, that remaining ability, now turned against
mankind, makes them formidable enemies.

Second, just as the Fall of Adam wounded human nature, the
fall of the demons injured their angelic nature. The grace, beauty,
elegance, exaltedness, and goodness they once possessed were
replaced by effrontery, ugliness, vulgarity, crudeness, and wickedness. Demons are twisted and evil to unimaginable levels. They
exist to inflict and multiply evil to prevent human salvation.

Third, given the immensity of their angelic understanding and
the fact that they exist outside of time, their choice to follow God
or rebel against Him is eternal and irrevocable. Their very nature
makes them incapable of changing their minds.

As humans, we find this difficult to grasp. Demons hate God,
despite this decision causing them great suffering because they are
separated from Him. Is it not reasonable to expect one of them to
eventually see the error of his ways and switch sides? That is impossible since angels do not experience "the past" or a "future." They
exist outside of time and experience an eternal, ever-present "now."
In that ever-present now, Satan and his minions are forever blas-
pheming with their original rebellious "NO!" against God. Their
choice to rebel is not something they did in the past. It is an action
they are continually doing in the present.

For the same reasons, there is no chance that a good angel will
suddenly decide to join Satan and the demons. An angel's choice is

everlasting and unchanging. Jesus Christ refers to "the eternal fire prepared for the devil and his angels" (Matt. 25:41). If there were a chance that Satan and his demons could repent and convert, Christ would not have stated this. Demonic salvation is impossible.

Knowing that his choice entailed eternal misery, why did the Devil rebel? About this, Revelation is silent. Evil is a mystery, and there is no meaningful explanation for the Devil's behavior.

Profile of the Devil: What Makes Satan Tick?

While the Bible says much about the Devil's work, many find it surprising how little it says about the Devil himself. One must go to the final book of the Bible—the last one written—to read of the Devil being cast out of Heaven (Revelations 12, quoted just a few paragraphs ago). If Scripture discloses very little about Satan, it is certainly not quiet about naming him. Here is a sample of the names that identify him.

Satan *("Enemy")*—Job 1:6

Lucifer *("Morning/Day Star")*—Isa. 14:12

Devil *("Slanderer")*—Matt. 4:1

Beelzebub *("Lord of the Flies")*—2 Kings 1:2

Beelzebul *("Lord of Excrement")*—Matt. 12:24

Belial *("Worthless")*—2 Cor. 6:15

Tempter—Matt. 4:3

Father of lies—John 8:44

Murderer—John 8:44

Ruler of this world—John 14:30

Ancient serpent—Rev. 12:9

Accuser of God's people—Rev. 12:10

Adversary—1 Pet. 5:8

The fact that all of these possess negative connotations shows the state to which Satan has reduced himself, which is very different from the glory once his. The prophet Ezekiel inadvertently describes Satan when he writes about the king of Tyre.

> *You were the signet of perfection, full of wisdom and perfect in beauty. You were in Eden, the garden of God; every precious stone was your covering, carnelian, topaz, and jasper, chryso-lite, beryl, and onyx, sapphire, carbuncle, and emerald; and wrought in gold were your settings and your engravings. On the day that you were created, they were prepared. With an anointed guardian cherub, I placed you; you were on the holy mountain of God; in the midst of the stones of fire, you walked. You were blameless in your ways from the day you were created, until iniquity was found in you. (Ezekiel 28:12–15)*

The double meaning of his words is evident to the Christian who sees in them the fallen king being compared to the angel of Paradise whose iniquity has ruined him. Though the king's fall is great, there has never been a fall to match that of this angel. The prophet Isaiah also describes what led to Satan's fall:

> *"How you are fallen from heaven, O Day Star, son of Dawn! How you are cut down to the ground, you who laid the nations low! You said in your heart, 'I will ascend to Heaven; above the stars of God I will set my throne on high; I will sit on the mount of assembly in the far north; I will ascend above the heights of the clouds, I will make myself like the Most High.' But you are brought down to Sheol, to the depths of the Pit. (Isaiah 14:12–15)*

As in Ezekiel, Isaiah's describes the fall of a human—the king of Babylon—in comparison to Satan's. His expulsion from Heaven is the just retribution for his sin and now becomes what defines him. Our Lord Himself alludes to this when He says, "I saw Satan fall like lightning from heaven" (Luke 10:18).

The Devil's rebellion against God continues through his attacks on what God loves most: the beings He created in His image and likeness. Satan does this by doing what he did in Eden: tempting his victims to do his bidding. Satan's goal is to bring about his victim's eternal damnation by dying in a state of mortal sin. If this should happen, the Devil gains him—and God loses him—for eternity.

WHAT IS POSSESSION?

Between these two goals—tempting man and gaining him for eternity—there is another evil desire that the Devil aims to satisfy: the possession of his victim. Possession is the state where the victim is under demonic control *from the inside*. The demon takes over the body of the one he possesses. During possession, a victim's consciousness is suppressed, and the demon animates his body as his own.

Given that demons exist outside of time and space, how can a demon be "inside" someone during demonic possession? While a demon's lack of physicality frees him of the limitations to which physical objects are subject and gives him access to everything in the physical universe simultaneously, he does not have *power* over all things equally. When the Devil possesses a victim—and is now "inside" him—the Devil has gained legal jurisdiction over him in such a manner that he can bully and manipulate the victim from the inside. The legal control a possessing spirit has is so great that the body he possesses appears to be his own.

Thankfully, however, possession is rare. The renowned Fr. Gabriele Amorth (1925–2016), who was for decades the chief exorcist of the Diocese of Rome, wrote that although he had seen more than thirty thousand people over nine years, only ninety-three were cases of actual possession.[1]

However, if possession is rare, it is not because the demons do not desire it. They crave it with all their being. Because of His mercy, the Lord limits the ability of demons to possess.

One may ask, "Why do the demons desire to possess?" Christ Himself indirectly answers that in the Gospel.

> *"When the unclean spirit has gone out of a man, he passes through waterless places seeking rest, but he finds none. Then he says, 'I will return to my house from which I came.' And when he comes he finds it empty, swept, and put in order. Then he goes and brings with him seven other spirits more evil than himself, and they enter and dwell there; and the last state of that man becomes worse than the first. So shall it be also with this evil generation."* (Luke 11:24–26)

In his natural state, a demon is in agony. His experience of reality is even more painful and exhausting when he is not possessing, akin to the pain that a parched, comfortless desert offers to someone enduring it. Possession gives a demon a measure of comfort. How? Scripture does not say. Any explanation is pure speculation. During an exorcism, however, it is not uncommon for a demon to reveal that should he be cast out, he will be punished severely upon returning to hell for failing his mission. Thus, there seem to be at least two reasons why demons will do anything to possess a victim and then repossess him if he has lost his initial possession: seeking relief from reality as he experiences it and avoiding the torture inflicted in hell for failure.

A priest colleague of mine had an interesting encounter with a demon "seeking rest." The demon offered "peace" terms when it was clear his power was weakened, and he was on the verge of being cast out. He promised that if he was allowed to remain in his victim, he would reduce the tormenting of his host. This absurd "deal" came out of desperation, and the exorcist certainly did not accept it. Within twenty minutes, the exorcism was complete, the victim was free, and the demon was off to receive his just torment.

CHERYL'S LIBERATION

Cheryl knew I was a priest when I walked into her home, though there was no way she should have known, so it was clear I was dealing with a case of possession. I arranged for her first exorcism session about a week later, once I had time to learn more about her from Mark.

During the session, the demon inside Cheryl revealed he had gained the right to possess her from a pact she made with a fortune teller. Cheryl felt tortured by not being able to conceive. It affected her so acutely that she despaired of ever being happy.

Cheryl possessed a deep wound. She had grown up in a large family connected to a very large extended family. As a little girl, Cheryl often heard adults remark how children are life's greatest blessing. She also heard them lament the misfortune of her aunt, who, after giving birth to her first child, was unable to conceive any more. The sight of her aunt's bitter weeping haunted Cheryl. Thus, when Cheryl could not conceive, she believed she was destined for a misery even greater than her aunt's. She was willing to do whatever it took to avoid it, even accepting a deal offered by a fortune teller.

Cheryl required eight exorcism sessions for liberation. However, before release, the familial wound she carried had to heal, as it produced the fear that kept the demon within her. Not only did Cheryl have to embrace Jesus Christ as her personal Lord and Savior, she had to surrender her identity and future to Him completely. She had to accept God's plan for her, even if it did not include motherhood. Cheryl's acceptance was most difficult since she had defined her self-worth by motherhood. Unable to bear a child, she felt like a mere caricature of a woman.

In the end, it took the pain, humiliation, and powerlessness of demonic possession to convince Cheryl to look to God—rather than motherhood—for meaning. After several weeks of meeting with a psychologist, the exorcisms began to be effective at evicting the demon. The psychologist helped Cheryl see that her desire for motherhood was rooted in unhealthy expectations—in fantasy—and that her refusal to accept the circumstances life dealt her was the most significant factor contributing to her despair. After seeing the logic and rationality of the psychologist's counsel, Cheryl was ready to abandon her obsession with motherhood and trust that God would bring about her happiness in some other way, in a manner of His choosing.

THE DEVIL IS REAL. I HAVE BATTLED HIM.

People ask me what it is like to battle the Devil. My opponent is hatred himself. When I walk into a room to conduct an exorcism, the contempt and disdain of the ancient serpent, the one who refused to obey God, the one who caused our first parents to fall, the one who delights in every human misfortune and suffering, meets me head-on. The Devil knows that, as a priest, I continue the ministry of Jesus, a ministry that brought about the defeat of his kingdom. He hates a priest with all his being. He will do anything to avoid being cast out—including using violence, which he is more than capable of inflicting when God permits it.

On one occasion, when an exorcism of a middle-aged woman was about to begin, she locked arms with a man whose job it was to restrain her and threw him over her head as if he were a rag doll. The man was over six feet tall and weighed more than three hundred pounds. Doing a complete flip in the air, he landed on the floor ten feet in front of her. The woman then pointed her finger at the nearest light switch on the wall, about twelve feet away. One of the screws holding the switch's cover plate unscrewed itself and darted into her open right hand through the air. She drove it into her left forearm. Later, in the same session, she struck me in the face with such force that I needed two surgeries to repair the damage I sustained to my skull.

The Devil is real.

TWO

WHAT IS DEMONIC ACTIVITY?

THE CASE OF
THE ENGINEER AND HIS ABANDONED WIFE

Emma's house had a terrible demonic infestation. Photographs and artwork flew from the walls, and items regularly vanished without a trace. The lights often flickered on and off—but only in the room where she happened to be. The radio in her living room turned on and off by itself and even changed stations. However, the most bothersome phenomenon was a loud, mechanical hum like the sound inside a subway train. Emma could hear it at random times in the room next to hers. The rumble made the whole house vibrate.

Emma herself was in a ruined state. The slightest thing sent her into a rage: someone cutting her off in traffic; the mail arriving twenty minutes later than usual; even finding the napkin dispenser empty at a fast-food restaurant. Inconveniences infuriated her and caused her to curse, swear, grind her teeth, and even throw things. Such fits could last for hours.

Emma hadn't always been like this. She never had a temper, and no one recalled seeing her lose her cool in the past. But when Emma's husband, Robert, left her, she prayed hard for his return, which never happened. After a year, she stopped praying. "If prayer did anything, my husband would be back," she concluded. Emma was not sure she believed in God anymore.

Before losing Robert, Emma had treasured her relationship with God; her Catholic identity had been the most important thing to her. During the twenty-two years of her marriage, she had been very involved in her parish, volunteering in several ministries and contributing significantly to the parish's outreach to the poor. Her father died when she was six, and her mother had relied on her local parish's food pantry to help feed her five children. Since her parish kept them from going hungry, Emma expressed gratitude by dedicating hours to such work. After the collapse of her marriage, however, Emma's desire to volunteer diminished.

Emma once loved to entertain and she and her husband did so often. Now, her friends rarely saw her except for chance encounters at the grocery store or elsewhere in town. No one visited her home. Whenever friends called, she neither answered nor returned the call. Most had stopped reaching out.

Emma was a shell of her former self. The only thing that gave her energy was plotting revenge. She had her attorneys continually bring new litigation against Robert. Emma had dragged him into court six times since the divorce, demanding further concessions. The judge ruled in her favor each time. Her attorney fees cost more than what she gained. But her motive was to cause Robert as much grief as possible.

Robert was a respected diesel-electric engineer who worked on engine and transmission systems for one of the world's largest cruise ship makers. Robert was paid well for his talents. His salary had allowed him and Emma to live comfortably. Since they could not conceive children, they had few expenses. With their income, they'd enjoyed traveling, eating out, and supporting their favorite charities.

The divorce judge ruled that Emma should receive half of Robert's wages and keep their home. This was little consolation to her. His betrayal caught her completely off guard. He had simply left a note stating he was moving to France to be with someone else and that Emma could keep the house and everything in it. She felt humiliated, ashamed, and bitter. These feelings eventually gave way to just one: rage.

The disturbing phenomena in Emma's home prompted her to request the help of the local Catholic diocese, which contacted me. I found Emma pleasant and charming when I met her at her home. I asked questions to determine why these phenomena were occurring: "How long have you lived here?" "When did all this start?" She answered everything clearly, but her demeanor changed when I asked whether anyone else had previously lived with her. She began to tremble and shake.

"I hate him!" she screamed, baring her teeth. "May he rot in hell along with his mistress! We were married twenty-two years. I want Robert to suffer more than anyone has suffered before."

"When did he leave you?" I asked.

"Six years ago," she screamed.

The intensity of Emma's outburst and the anger exhibited in her body made me think he had left within the last few months. She was still displaying the reaction of someone who had just recently been injured. Her pain was too raw and fresh for the number of years since she was wounded. Time had brought no healing.

I had come to the house expecting to perform an exorcism of a place. The symptoms Emma described—falling picture frames, disappearing items, flickering lights, electronics turning on and off by themselves—though disturbing and unsettling—are all low-level demonic manifestations that can occur for various reasons. When they are that basic, inviting the occupants to repent, directing them to make a sacramental confession, and performing a simple house exorcism usually resolves everything. The only manifestation that was unusual was the loud mechanical hum.

I asked Emma to describe the hum in greater detail. She stated it was a loud rumbling that came from the master bedroom, the bedroom next to hers. "It used to be our bedroom," she said. "But when Robert left, I could not stand being in it any longer. I moved into the room beside it."

A thought came to me just then. I asked Emma whether she had a pair of earphones.

"What for?" she exclaimed, still emphatically exhibiting anger.

"I've thought of something." I pulled up a video of a cruise liner's engine room on my phone, plugged in her earphones, and without showing what the video was, I asked that she put them on. Then I hit play.

After about five seconds of listening, she gasped, "That's it! That's exactly the sound! What is it?" I informed her she was listening to the sound of an engine room on a cruise liner. Of all the demonic manifestations occurring in her home, this was the one specially meant to perturb her.

"That is the demons rubbing it in for you," I said. "It's a kind of ironic cry of victory. It's ironic because Robert has made a successful career producing this sound. And now, that sound is left behind in your marital bedroom—which he abandoned—to haunt you."

Emma tensed and made an animal-like scream. "That wicked beast!" she howled. "I wish I'd never met him! May he rot in hell forever!"

Emma was a victim twice over. She had loved Robert with an undivided heart, which he had coldly discarded. Then she became the victim of her own excessive rage, which kept her in bondage and prevented healing. This latter torture was worse than the first.

Exorcists look for the "door" that demons used to enter someone's life, the permission they were given to disturb and harass.
Emma's door was her demon-like fury. Emma's rage was an open
invitation to demons, who saw within her something of themselves. Their strategy was to kick her while she was down. I
explained all of this to Emma, pointing out that the diabolical
plan was successful because she cooperated with the strategy set
up to destroy her.

"Your attacking Robert allows his decision to inflict more harm
on you," I said. "The only way to stop it, Emma—and you have the
power to do it—is to forgive him."

Emma was about to blurt out something when the meaning
of what I had just said hit her. From her look, I could tell this was
the first time in a long time anything made sense. But her expression became passion-filled again. "I will never forgive that dog," she
screamed through clenched teeth. "NEVER!"

"Emma," I replied, "Jesus says that unless you forgive, you
cannot be forgiven."

"I will never forgive that dog," she said. "Just get rid of the
damn devils in my house," she added.

"Emma, as long as you refuse to forgive Robert, you are defying
God," I said. "That defiance is what will keep the demons here no
matter what I do. You are replicating the same defiance the demons
constantly commit with their whole being. Every action of theirs
is a defiance of God. Your life has become a mirror of theirs—you
live only to destroy Robert. It will be a waste of my time and yours
for me to do anything because, to put it simply, I don't practice
magic. I serve God. Only God's presence in this house and within
your heart can evict the evil occupying each. Without His presence
replacing that of the demons, I can do nothing because the demons
are simply dwelling inside what is theirs."

Emma stared at me pensively, analyzing what I said. There was an ever so slight softening of the muscles in her face. "Emma," I said, "can you and I say a prayer together, asking Jesus to give you the strength to forgive Robert? Can we put this in Jesus' hands and ask for His help?"

"My hatred of that dog is all I have," she snorted. "I have nothing else."

"That is not true," I replied. "You have your identity as God the Father's daughter. You say the word, and He will send His Son into your heart to rescue you. He will take away all your pain, bitterness, and hate. I mean that."

Just then, the diesel engine sound came on. The whole house rumbled with the loud noise.

"Emma," I said, "it's about time you became free of this. Let's ask God to bring it about. Can we say a prayer together?"

"God never listens to me," she said.

"He will listen," I replied. "You'll see. Can we just try it?"

Emma agreed to the prayer. I began by offering the Lord her immense pain and asking Him to give her the grace to be free of it. I asked that He give Emma assistance to forgive Robert. Though she could not bring herself to vocalize the words of forgiveness, she asked God for the grace to forgive, in her own words. Emma's willingness to request God's help showed that healing had already begun.

That night Emma's home had barely any disturbing noises. She slept peacefully, and for the first time in a long time, she felt like more than just an abandoned woman. Though Emma was not yet completely healed and still experienced a terrible temptation to rage, I was confident her healing would come in stages and time.

I met with Emma once a week over the next two months. In our fourth meeting, she was able to vocalize forgiveness toward Robert.

Her demeanor changed after that. She began reconnecting with friends and family and gradually returned to being her true self.

I directed Emma to do three things to ensure the permanence of her healing. First, she must start going to church and living out her Christian faith. Attending church is a divine command from which we cannot dispense ourselves. It is essential for our relationship with God. Second, she had to stop litigating against Robert. Litigating was a product of rage and would put her back into darkness. Third, she had to sell her home. Staying in it would bring back constant memories of Robert, and she needed a clean start. Living elsewhere was better for her psychological health.

Within a year, Emma was healed. She was happy, tranquil, and free of demonic harassment.

THE SIX TYPES OF DEMONIC ACTIVITY

Demonic attacks are not random or haphazard. They are deliberate. Demons use whatever they can—a sin, a trauma, or some other wound—to inflict the hellish existence they experience on their victims. Demons carry out this strategy through six kinds of activities.

1. Temptation

Temptation is the activity the Devil and his fallen angels preoccupy themselves the most. It is by far their most dangerous activity. The Devil can use temptation to make sin seem good and appealing, and our fall for his trickery can easily have deadly, eternal ramifications.

Many Protestants will strongly object to this last sentence and will stress the Protestant belief that salvation depends solely on God's grace and not on one's moral choices. In other words, once one is saved—once one accepts in faith that Christ is one's personal Lord and Savior—one is always saved. Paul's declaration that Abraham was justified (made right and just before God) by faith, not by works, in Romans 5:1 is an often-cited text Protestants use to prove that justification and salvation are "once and for all" acts. In other words, our sinful choices have no bearing on salvation once the gift of faith—God's justifying action—is received by the believer.

Like Protestants, Catholics hold that God's grace is necessary and indispensable for salvation, and it is given by God as a completely unwarranted gift.[1] This is the justification we receive in baptism and nothing more than this justification is needed for salvation. However, Catholics believe it is necessary for us to work to accept that very grace He freely offers (James 2:22). In Romans 5:1-2, Paul asserts that those who are justified by faith "have obtained access to this grace in which we stand, and we rejoice in our hope of sharing the glory of God." The word *hope* demonstrates that even after we receive justification, we are still left hoping for salvation precisely because it is possible to reject grace. We must work with the designs of God to bring about our salvation: "Working together with him, then, we entreat you not to accept the grace of God in vain" (2 Corinthians 6:1).

Catholics have always understood sin to be so powerful that it can drive God's very grace out of the soul. It is not uncommon for me to encounter a victim who has accepted Christ as his sovereign Lord and possesses robust Christian faith but is a victim of demonic activity. Because of the victim's sins of moral failures, the demon has attached itself to the believer. Certain sins, what Catholics call mortal sins, are actions so evil that they destroy our relationship with God and can result in eternal death. However, 1 John 8:9 states, "If we confess our sins, he is faithful and just, and will forgive our sins and cleanse us from all unrighteousness." With a repentant heart, we can be forgiven for our sins and renew our justification through prayer, reading Scripture, studying the faith, engaging in fellowship with the Christian community, and doing works of charity.

Feeling anger in response to betrayal is natural, but there is a world of difference between righteous anger and rage. The great philosopher Aristotle taught that every virtue is a mean between two extremes. The mean between excessive meekness and rage is righteous anger.

Jesus Christ demonstrated enormous anger when He whipped the money changers and overturned their tables in the Temple (John 2:13–22). His anger, however, remained rational and did not exceed the injustices that provoked it.

Emma was tempted to feed her anger, and it went from being righteous to becoming her god. She had abandoned God's worship and failed to keep His precepts. Thus, Emma's sin eventually became so grave that she abandoned her discipleship of Christ altogether; this occurred without her even perceiving it.

Not all temptations are the direct work of the Devil. Humans have three adversaries: the world, the flesh, and the Devil. The broken world and our sinful flesh exert their disordered desires upon us, just as the Devil does his. An alcoholic cannot blame his addiction on the Devil. Neither can we merely blame the Devil for the entertainment world's frequent disregard for God and goodness.

The solution for alcoholism is not exorcism per se. It is addiction treatment. And the solution for the entertainment world's paganism is a genuine conversion through an experience of God, not exorcism.

Everyone experiences temptation, which is *ordinary demonic activity*. Even Our Lord endured it. The next five types on the list are considered *extraordinary demonic activity*.

2. Vexation

From the Latin *vexare* ("to shake or disturb"), a vex is a demonic attack having a strength that goes beyond mere temptation. The vex can be either mental or physical. It can take on a variety of forms, such as the following:

- An outburst of impatience or anger over something that would not ordinarily be upsetting.
- A sudden prejudice and resentment resulting in a grudge.
- A sudden change from a positive mood to one of depression, sadness, or fear.
- An inexplicable loss of memory or memories about a good event or a good person.
- Repeatedly disturbed sleep caused either by frightening, depraved, or perverse nightmares or by suddenly waking during the night and being unable to get back to sleep.

A physical vex is a physical attack against the person, against that person's property, or against something connected with and valued by the person. The following are typical examples:

- Chronic clumsiness or accidents.
- Unexplainable persecution in one's workplace causing job loss or demotion.
- Sudden difficulty in a relationship.
- Chronic financial failures and misfortunes.
- Chronic mechanical malfunctioning of one's appliances or electronic equipment.
- Unexplained and undiagnosable chronic physical ailments.

- Repetitive and unending strife in the family, workplace, or church.
- A period where one's motives are chronically questioned and or misunderstood by those around us, such as by one's employer.
- Inanimate objects moving by themselves (e.g., books flying off shelves, portraits falling off walls, plates rattling in the cupboards).

Experiencing some of these realities does not necessarily mean one is vexed. But if there is a *pattern* such that symptoms occur with more regularity than coincidence or common sense would warrant, that may be a clue one is suffering from a demonic vexation.

Vexes are effective because they evoke responses in us that delight the Devil: aggravation, annoyance, discomfort, distress, disturbance, embarrassment, exasperation, frustration, grief, harassment, inconvenience, injury, ire, irritability, outrage, and torment.

A vex can do great harm by prompting its victim to make terrible decisions because of feelings of spiritual desolation, including temptation, sadness, a lack of confidence/hope/love, a feeling that one is separated from God or is unloved by Him.[2] Thus, until the vexation ceases, a person should avoid making significant decisions, such as changing careers, ending friendships or business partnerships, getting engaged to be married, ending one's marriage, and so on.

Emma was enduring vexation. Pictures flying off the walls; objects disappearing from the home; the flickering of the lights; the random turning on of the radio; and the overpowering roar of the diesel engine were all evidence of this.

Causes of Vexation

Vexes have three possible causes, each being unique and independent.

1. A vex may result from sinful activity, such as sexual sin, lying, theft, or any other violation of the Ten Commandments, or any violation of the commandments of Christ (e.g., failure to forgive one's enemies) or of His Church. Sins against the First Commandment (i.e., sins against God's sovereignty) seem to be among the most prone to causing vexation. These include consulting fortune tellers, clairvoyants, witch doctors, occult healers, practicing devotion to Santa Muerte, practicing Santería or voodoo, or engaging in séances or Ouija board activity.

2. A vex may also result from a curse, spell, or hex, which will be described in greater detail in the next chapter.

3. A vex may be retaliation for good and virtuous work that has annoyed the Devil. While vexes are always unpleasant, one should regard this vex as a compliment. If the Devil received so much injury from our work that he communicates his displeasure by vexing us, whatever we did to merit it is what we ought to keep doing. Relative to the other two kinds of vexes, this form is usually much less destructive and, like all demonic activity, only occurs with God's permission.

I believe every human suffers from diabolical vexations at some time or another. When we suspect vexation, we should morally examine ourselves to see whether sin has gained entry within us. If it has, we must eliminate it and reconcile with God. We also need to increase our prayer and offer up the suffering from a vex as a prayer, taking comfort that even the greatest saints experienced vexes. Prayer empowers, shields, and purifies.

3. Infestation

From the Latin *infestatio* ("to be overrun by pests or vermin"), an infestation is a multitude of vexations occurring within a specific location, e.g., within a room or home. Infestations do not directly attack people but rather property, places, and things. The symptoms of demonic infestation are the typical symptoms of a "haunted house" and may include:

- The sound of footsteps coming from a location where no one is present (e.g., in the attic).
- Hearing disembodied voices (e.g., singing coming from the closet) or random sounds (scratching or thumping from inside the wall; objects banging around in the basement).
- Doors opening and closing by themselves.
- The apparition of a person, animal, or some other figure.
- Objects moving by themselves or disappearing altogether.
- Lights, appliances, and electronics turning on or off by themselves.
- The repeated malfunctioning or breakdown of appliances, sewers, drains, et cetera.
- Strange and uncharacteristic behavior from the family pet.

While there was no question that Emma was being vexed, the sheer number of vexations occurring within her home had reached the point of infestation.

The most typical cause of an infestation is sin by one or more of the place's inhabitants. Its remedy requires the victim to reconcile with God, submit to His Lordship, and do everything possible to avoid sinning again. The person must commit to discipleship with Jesus and remove from his life whatever is incompatible with that discipleship.

After, the infested place must be cleansed. The most immediate, far-reaching, and lasting cleansing comes from an exorcism and a blessing by a priest. Because demons know a priest acts with the Church's authority, they respond to a priest's actions more so than anyone else's. The Roman Ritual contains a specific exorcism for places that is highly effective.[3]

Occasionally, even a combined exorcism and blessing will not end the infestation. In such cases, *assuming that the souls of everyone in the house are free of mortal sin*, the best remedy is for a priest to celebrate a Mass inside the house.[4] I do not recall an infestation surviving a priest's exorcism, blessing, and celebration of the Eucharist.

4. Oppression

From the Latin *oppressio* ("a violent seizure or overthrow"), oppression is a physical attack a victim experiences as coming *from outside his body*. The person may experience being touched, shoved, punched, kicked, scratched, cut, and even sexually violated. Some victims of oppression even endure the experience of being raped. These are not mere "feelings" but actual physical attacks. The blows received are real blows, as are the cuts. They are not self-inflicted. In some cases, the severity of the victim's injuries may require hospitalization and a lengthy recovery.

Oppression often includes an emotional or psychological component. For example, the enemy will make his victim depressed, anxious, and exhausted. He may also experience external problems, such as tensions with his employer, financial misfortune, and difficulties in his relationships (often suffering alone). It may also affect the body so that the victim suffers aches and pains and endures illnesses without apparent cause. Believing the troubles to be medically based, the victim will often go from doctor to doctor in search of a cure. The outcome is always the same: nothing medically wrong is found. The victim may even be suspected of lying or having a mental illness.

Ending spiritual oppression is more challenging than ending an infestation or a vex. The cause is usually habitual sin in the victim's life or even a single past sin of which the victim has not repented. Either one gives the Devil the right to oppress.

I once lived in a rectory within the downtown district of a large city. Sex workers walked the street in front of the rectory day and night. They were addicted to crack cocaine and supported their habit through prostitution. There was one in particular—Rose—whose behavior was bizarre. She attempted to solicit men even while they were walking with their girlfriends or wives; randomly yelled out blasphemies about Our Lord and the Christian faith; howled like a crazed animal; and engaged in erratic and aggressive behavior. For example, upon seeing a passing cyclist or motorcyclist, Rose would dart at him and push him off his vehicle, often resulting in serious injury.

Though Rose sometimes came to the rectory door requesting food, she never accepted spiritual help and fled when it was offered. One day, as I was discarding a bag in the trash bin behind the building, I saw her writhing on the ground next to the garage, violently moving her face as though an invisible fist was hitting her. Each punch left a mark on her cheeks and nose. Rose had demons, and their grip had now reached oppression: an invisible enemy was attacking her. She remains today one of the starkest oppression cases I have ever seen.

One day Rose just disappeared, and I never saw her again. She is another unfortunate soul who has a constant place in my prayers.

Thankfully, Emma had not experienced oppression. Though her house was infested, she was not physically tormented. Nevertheless, I believe she had at least the beginning of obsession.

5. Obsession

From the Latin *obsessio* ("a besieging"), obsession is an attack on the victim's mind *from the inside*. While the victim retains control of his body, the sovereignty of his person is partially compromised. For this reason, obsession is sometimes also referred to as *partial possession*.

An obsession consists of a series of intrusive and compulsive thoughts from which the victim cannot free himself. Examples include:

- Relentless thoughts about injuring or murdering someone.
- Severe and overwhelming anxieties, such as about the future, one's marriage, an event from the past (e.g., a sin or an embarrassing moment), or an impending decision (e.g., "Should I marry Sally?").
- Recurring suicidal thoughts.
- Infatuation with a specific person such that the victim cannot get the person out of his mind, perhaps even "stalking" that individual. (I am convinced some stalkers suffer from demonic obsession.)
- Compulsive temptations to commit a sacrilegious act, such as desecrating the Holy Eucharist or burning down a church.

- Extreme difficulty in falling or remaining asleep; the victim may experience constant compulsive nightmares that give him "clues" about some bogus mystery he needs to crack.
- An extreme addiction to religious matters such as desperation over one's sinfulness; obsessing about Christ's suffering on the Cross; constant and never-ending praying; severe and unhealthy fasting or other mortifications.
- Despairing about one's salvation, such as believing one has done an irreparable wrong and committed an unforgivable sin.

Oppressive thoughts are debilitating, and the victim believes these thoughts are entirely his own. The thoughts may come with corresponding emotions, sensations, and physiological responses. For example, a victim experiencing obsessive rage will also experience short and staccato breathing, increased heart rate, clenched fists, shaking, and other related symptoms.

The ever-present bitterness in which Emma lived was a case of obsession. Her hours-long tantrums along with the constant litigation she brought against her ex-husband gave her unhealthy and destructive energy.

Distinguishing demonic obsession from mental illness can be quite difficult. Even more challenging is distinguishing a demonic obsession from someone who *also* has a mental illness.

In my experience, there are three keys to discerning obsession from mental illness correctly.

1. Precedent

The thoughts often have no adequate antecedent cause nor prior history. They are generally new and fall outside the victim's normal baseline behavior.

One of my cases involved a man who was obsessed with his brother's wife. Carnal thoughts about having intercourse with his sister-in-law bothered him day and night. Years before, he was diagnosed with schizoaffective disorder that manifested in auditory hallucinations (compelling voices) and intense, aggressive behavior. Up until recently, he had never fantasized about her (or anyone else). Therein lies a crucial detail. If the obsession is entirely new and there is a point when it began, then that may well be a sign the cause is a demonic obsession rather than a mental illness. Even though the man had a diagnosed mental illness, the obsessive thoughts about his sister-in-law were a deviation from his normal, baseline behavior.

Some people object, saying, "The symptoms of mental illness also have to start at some specific time. So how does this distinguish mental illness from demonic oppression?" This objection is valid and reveals the difficulty in isolating one cause from another. The distinction can be extremely subtle and easily subject to error. To make things more difficult still, demons can—and often will—play on one's susceptibility to obsession. Nevertheless, one looks for a provisional point where one is comfortable in stating that the aberrant behavior has gone *beyond* what can be considered the individual's normal level of obsessive behavior (even pathologically normal).

2. Inciting Incident

Identifying the cause of the aberrant behavior is key number two. One asks, "Is there a reason why the obsession began at the particular time it did?" In the case of the man with the schizoaffective disorder, I discovered that his carnal thoughts began after he visited a psychic medium. Such an action is more than a sufficient spiritual cause for his affliction. However, even this identification is insufficient to establish a certain diagnosis.

3. Prayer

The employment of a third key is necessary: spiritual discernment. *One must pray.*

Prayer will reveal a proper diagnosis by producing a change in the spiritually-rooted obsessive behavior. When mental illness causes obsessive thoughts, those thoughts are unaffected by an exorcist's prayer, and the victim's behavior remains unchanged. This makes perfect sense. If the problem's root is a medical condition, why should prayers against the demonic affect it? However, when the root is some sort of demonic activity, prayer will always affect the outcome. The obsessive thoughts will at least diminish.

Unfortunately, for this man, the diagnosis of spiritual obsession and the subsequent prayer ministry by which it was broken took place after irreparable damage had already occurred. He was imprisoned for violating a restraining order his brother and sister-in-law took against him because of his aggressive and infatuated behavior. Neither wanted him in their lives any longer.

———

One further clarifying and important point: should prayer cause the obsessive thoughts to increase, although counterintuitive, *this is also evidence that the person is suffering from spiritual obsession.* The increase of obsessive activity is a simple demonic tactic: make it appear that prayer made things worse so that the victim becomes discouraged and desists from seeking it. Again, if the root cause of compulsive behavior is mental illness, there is no reason why prayers against the demonic should cause it to increase. But if it does, that is a sign that the exorcist's prayers have found their target—demons—who are using evasive strategies to protect themselves and to remain in place.

A key to discerning obsession from mental illness is change—any change—in the intensity of the victim's state after receiving prayer. A change means the exorcist's prayers have hit something demonic.

6. Possession

From the Latin *possessio* ("to be owned"), possession is the highest level of demonic attack and is the most powerful of the Devil's extraordinary activity.

A possessed person endures temptation, vexation, infestation, oppression, obsession, but the Devil now also controls the body and consciousness.

In possession, the demon animates the victim's body, which is how demonic possession reveals itself. Persons close to the victim witness a foreign personality such that it is clear the person they know is no longer in control of his or her body.

The demon uses the victim's body to engage in appalling behavior, such as:

- Inflicting severe self-injury through slashing, burning, beating.
- Physically and verbally abusing others.
- Marking the victim's home with demonic signs and symbols.
- Eating disgusting things: feces, insects, carrion, et cetera.
- Engaging in public nudity and actual or simulated sex acts.
- Disclosing the victim's sins to others and revealing embarrassing details about his life.
- Incontinence.
- Using speech that is caustic, combative, and scandalous.

The demon's manifestation within possession is not continuous. It comes in intervals. At times he animates the body; at other times, he retreats inwardly and leaves the victim free. Nevertheless, even when he is "quiet," the demon is always aware of what is occurring around his host. He is especially sensitive to the presence of anything holy—prayer, a crucifix, a sacred image, holy water, the sounding of church bells, Mass—and will manifest in a flash to remove himself from the danger. But he can manifest for any reason he desires. He delights in inflicting torture, which he does day or night.

When the demon is quiet, the victim can interact with his body. Persons familiar with the victim can tell it is him, but he exhibits the symptoms of someone who is tormented: anxiety, distress, confusion, and exhaustion. When possession recurs, the victim again loses consciousness and is pulled into an internal sleep, entirely unaware of what the demon is doing with the body. Nothing done during a demonic manifestation can be morally attributable to the victim.

Exorcists are often asked whether the demonic behavior depicted in the famous 1973 film, *The Exorcist*, is accurate. Except for one phenomenon—the three hundred sixty–degree head turn by the possessed—everything in the movie depicts what a possessed person might do. The following lists some typical phenomena an exorcist may witness.

Within the victim:

- Violent and unnatural bodily contortions and movements.
- Dramatic changes in facial features: expressions are twisted and contorted.
- Speaking with a course, guttural voice markedly different from the victim's.
- A near-constant uttering of insults, curses, threats, et cetera.
- Abnormal eye activity lasting continuously for hours, e.g., eyes rolling back into the head such that only the whites

of the eyes are visible, or the eyelids squeezed closed. Yet, although no light is hitting the pupils of the eyes, the demon sees everything around him perfectly.

- Complete rigidity of the body.
- Punching, kicking, and signs of great strength for hours without exhaustion, even though large and muscular men restrain the victim's limbs. This would exhaust even the most physically fit person. Yet, the demon can engage in this for hours without experiencing fatigue.
- Extreme contempt for, and aversion to, God, the Blessed Virgin, the saints, or anything religious.
- The appearance of wounds on the victim's body that vanish as quickly as they appear.
- Levitation.
- Making the sounds and movements of an animal and taking on its appearance, e.g., the victim may suddenly resemble a wolf or pig.
- Displays of knowledge of hidden matters, especially regarding something painfully embarrassing to another.
- Accurate predictions of future events, verified by their occurrence at a later time.
- Fluency in languages the victim has never learned.

Outside the victim:

- The room fills with foul odors.
- Sudden and extreme changes in temperature, either hot or cold.
- Furniture and other objects moving by themselves, breaking, being thrown by unseen forces, et cetera.
- Poltergeist phenomena throughout the home.

Emma was not possessed. Her demon had not been able to progress beyond obsession and infestation. I strongly suspect, however, that if her rage had been allowed to grow, the demon would make some compelling offer to assist her in taking revenge against her husband. Acceptance of that offer would give the demon the right to possess Emma and complete her takeover.

Emma's turning point was the invitation to forgive her ex-husband. She heard Christ's voice within that invitation and could feel His presence. It was a presence she had been familiar with since childhood but had not felt since her husband's abandonment and her relinquishing the Christian faith.

Forgiveness is the quintessential Christian virtue because Jesus Christ *is* the very mercy and the forgiveness of God. Stated differently, God's mercy and forgiveness is so great, it is a person, a person whose name is Jesus Christ. When we imitate Christ by forgiving those who have wronged us—even those who have sought to destroy us—we allow Jesus to incarnate Himself within us. That incarnation produces within the Christian a state of possession that is the exact *opposite* of demonic possession.[5] Rather than ensnaring and consuming, it liberates, heals, invigorates, and empowers. There is no greater weapon against evil for the Christian—and no greater gift—than the choice to forgive enemies in imitation of Christ. Evil is utterly powerless against it.

MAKING SENSE OF DEMONIC ACTIVITY

To understand both the interrelatedness and the hierarchical nature of demonic attacks, exorcists have long used the analogy of a fortified city under siege by an invading army.

It was common in the Middle Ages to fortify a city with a tall stone wall around its perimeter. Classic examples of such towns are Ávila in Spain and Corinaldo in Italy. The walls kept out the city's enemies and gave the citizens the advantage of height in their counterattack should the enemy lay siege. The walls were the city's most crucial defense.

When the Devil tempts, it is equivalent to an invading army's general knocking at the city's gates, asking its citizens to come out and parley. The Devil's vexations are equal to the army's destroying some of the city's external assets, such as the wells and the food supply and structures within the walls, by lobbing stones over them. During oppression, the Devil's attack is equivalent to the enemy battering the city's walls and gates with canons and battering rams. An obsession is when the gates have given way, and the invading army is taking over the city, block by block, working toward full control. Finally, in possession, the invasion is complete. The enemy suspends the freedoms previously enjoyed by the citizens and dominates them with oppressive rule.

—————

Demonic attacks are strategized and deliberate. While demonic possession is the most sensational of the Devil's works, it is also the rarest. Temptation is the most common. Possession, in and of itself, cannot condemn anyone to hell. However, should a person die in the state of grave sin, that person becomes one of the damned who will never see Heaven. Nothing worse is even imaginable.

THREE

WHAT IS EXORCISM?

THE CASE OF
THE POSSESSED FIREFIGHTER

One Saturday afternoon, I received a panicked call from a priest who lived a short distance away. Like most priests, he heard confessions. That day, a penitent began to roll around on the floor, growling and repeating over and over, "I'm not leaving!"

"I am sending him to you now," the priest told me.

I usually do not agree to see a case this immediately. I tell priests learning to be exorcists that there is no such thing as an "emergency" exorcism. "You are the exorcist. You pick the time and the place for the exorcism. Never let the Devil dictate either to you."

There are reasons for this. First, a person under the Devil's power and control may not want liberation. Many who request an exorcism do so under the direction of the Enemy himself. Why? To waste the exorcist's time and deplete his energy so that he is rendered less effective. Without a victim's cooperation and desire to be free, the exorcist's efforts are useless. As strange as it may sound, people have the right to belong to the Devil if they choose. A great many do! God endowed us with free will, and He respects our choices, no matter how bad they are. Thus, part of an exorcist's discernment is to determine whether the victim truly desires to be free of the Devil.

Exorcists have busy schedules, and they are often parish priests as well. It is impressive how the Devil will find the worst time to make a case "flare up." An exorcists must learn to reject being arbitrarily pulled away from regular schedules. If the Devil is there now, he will be there next Tuesday at 2:00 p.m. I teach my trainees to schedule an appointment to meet the demon at a time convenient to them, not to the Devil.

Besides, there are other people's schedules to consider. An exorcist never works alone. He needs a team to both assist and protect him. Demons are powerful and will manifest that power during an exorcism. An exorcist needs stout men who can restrain the victim. Having someone trained in psychology and another trained in medicine, such as a doctor or a nurse, is invaluable. He also needs a secretary to record events. If the victim is a woman, other women must be present. Finally, he needs intercessors, people praying for the session's successful outcome.

On this day, my team happened to be with me already. We were meeting to review our cases. Because of this, I agreed to see the man immediately.

Four people arrived at the church offices a short time later: Jeremy and his wife and parents. Jeremy was in his late twenties and was tall, barrel-chested, and very fit. Large muscles bulged from his body. I thought, *If he gets violent, there will be no stopping him.*

When he introduced himself, I found Jeremy to be polite, soft-spoken, and gracious—the epitome of a gentleman. By his demeanor, no one could guess anything was wrong with him. Then again, neither did I presume there was. The only knowledge I had was that another priest *believed* Jeremy manifested demonically. An exorcist, however, must make his own assessment.

The Catholic Church's ritual for exorcism is called the Rite of Exorcism. The ritual requires moral certainty that an individual is possessed before an exorcist may perform it. "Moral certainty" is understood as the conclusion any intelligent and rational person would reach given the evidence gathered. It's not to be confused with absolute certainty, the type of certitude offered by mathematics in which any mathematician will reach the same objective and unchanging result. That kind of certainty is seldom available in real-life situations. Thus, the Church looks for *signs* that evidence a demon is present.

The classic signs of possession are:

- The ability to speak and understand languages one has never studied.
- Knowledge of events that are impossible for the individual to know through natural means.
- Displays of superhuman strength (strength beyond one's natural human abilities).
- A "vehement aversion to God, the Most Holy name of Jesus, the Blessed Virgin Mary, the Saints, the Church, the Word of God, sacred things and rites, especially sacramental ones, and to sacred images."[1]

Given my priest friend's proximity and the evidence he provided by phone, I believed an intervention that very day was wise. So, when they arrived, I led Jeremy and his family to a room where we could meet. Jeremy's story and that of his wife and parents concurred with that of the priest. The four had gone to the parish where Jeremy intended to make his confession. As a Catholic, Jeremy knew that to receive the Eucharist, he had to confess his sins and receive the Lord's forgiveness in the form of the priest's absolution (cf. John 20:23). While he had not practiced his faith in twenty years, a recent conversion experience made him desire to reconnect with God. However, when he stepped inside the confessional, he fell to the floor.

Jeremy had no memory of what happened in the confessional. He recalled walking toward it, then being inside the car on the way to see me. This "skip" in memory is typical during possession. When the demon takes over the victim's body, he also takes over his consciousness, such that the victim has no recollection of the possession or the events during it.

I excused Jeremy's wife and parents so that only he, my team, and I remained in the room. I wanted to give him as much freedom to speak as possible without his family being privy to details he may not like them to know. He described an experience when he was eight years old. His older brother's friends brought a Ouija board to the house and invited him to participate. He remembered the planchette moving in response to various questions the group posed.

That night, when he turned off the lights and got into bed, he recalled seeing a dark figure in his room. The figure was so black that, although the lights were off, everything else in the room looked like it was in broad daylight. Besides being intensely black, the only additional detail he recalled was that it had a human body but a cat's head. The figure spoke to Jeremy, promising to make him very strong if he gave him something, and it named a strange word Jeremy had never heard before and which he could no longer recall. For reasons Jeremy did not know, he made the terrible mistake of accepting the offer. The figure leaped into the air and jumped into his body through his chest.

From that moment, Jeremy recalls being the strongest kid in the school. He could lift more than anyone else. Even his teachers were amazed at his strength. He developed an astounding athletic ability and dominated every sport. But with these, Jeremy experienced an increase in aggression as well and became easily upset. He frequently got into fights against much older and bigger kids. He never lost.

His strength and aggression increased through high school, and he gained a reputation for being the toughest kid around. No one was willing to fight him. But something else that frightened him deeply began to occur: blackout periods where he lost consciousness and memory. These came without warning. Jeremy would suddenly find himself in a completely different place, having no idea how he got there. There was also a long lapse of time, usually from one to seven hours. He recounted an occasion when he was shopping at a hardware store. His next conscious awareness was walking down a sidewalk ten miles away, having no idea how he got there, but with $258 more in his pocket than he had earlier. He had no clue from where it came.

Jeremy always wanted to be a firefighter. He enrolled in the fire-fighting academy after completing high school. Although he had to work hard at academics, he breezed through the athletic components, shattering the academy's records. He was hired immediately upon graduating.

Around this time, Jeremy began dating Rachel. Rachel was attracted to his physique, and Jeremy was elated that she was willing to put up with his temper. As time went on, the relationship became serious, and they married. Shortly afterward, Jeremy began having terrible rages. Suddenly and without warning, his personality would change. Though he never struck his wife, he threatened to do so, and Rachel began to fear for her safety.

Additionally, Jeremy's blackout periods had grown to encompass multiple days. He "woke up" in a completely different town on one occasion. He was shirtless and shoeless, his knuckles were scraped and bloody, and his body was covered with bruises, cuts, and scratches. Two days had elapsed. He had no idea where he had been or what he had done.

The blackouts had always frightened Jeremy, but now that he lost whole days and found signs of trauma on his body, he was terrified. There was something inside him over which he had no control, but he did not know what to do about it. Each time he disappeared and went missing, at least once every two months, Rachel called the fire department and reported that Jeremy was ill. Somehow, he managed to keep from getting fired.

Around this time, Jeremy's parents rediscovered their faith. The critical event was a retreat at their parish that affected them deeply. Although Jeremy's parents were raised Catholic, they had become only nominal Christians who, aside from Christmas and Easter, never attended church. After he moved out on his own, Jeremy never thought about God. Even Christmas and Easter held no religious significance for him.

After the retreat, everyone who knew Jeremy's parents could see a dramatic difference within them. They had never been bad people, but now they were extraordinarily good people. Love flowed out of them, and they radiated peace and joy.

Rachel noticed her in-laws' joy and began participating in a weekly prayer group held in their home. In time, she began to experience the transformation and peace she saw in her in-laws. Eventually, Rachel broached the God question with Jeremy. "Jeremy," she said, "we're not kids anymore. It's about time we started going to church."

"You're right," Jeremy agreed. "It is about time." That conversation was the impetus for Jeremy's desire for the Sacrament of Confession on that Saturday afternoon.

I performed a diagnostic test on Jeremy. As my team members asked him questions, I walked to a bookcase, grabbed a stack of books, and placed them on the table in front of him. While some books concerned spiritual topics, most were on random and unrelated topics, such as *How to Drywall a Basement*, *The 2012 Baltimore Orioles Yearbook*, *Programming in C++*. I continued making trips to the bookcase and retrieving stacks of books on random topics. The point was to control Jeremy's eyes. I knew he would scan the titles of each stack, looking for a clue as to why I was doing this.

I did not want Jeremy to notice me doing one thing. On one of my trips to the bookcase, I dipped my finger in a glass filled with water that I had placed on one of its shelves before Jeremy's arrival. It was holy water. There was no way Jeremy could tell. I barely touched the tip of my finger to the water. I returned to Jeremy, carrying a stack of books with my other arm. While still behind him, I flicked the holy water onto his back. Since the amount of water was minuscule, there was no way Jeremy could perceive it as it fell on his clothes.

With startling speed, he shot up out of his chair and arched his upper body backward—behind himself—such that, though our bodies still faced the same direction, he was now face-to-face with me, though his face was upside down. At the same time, he hissed violently and bared his teeth—which suddenly appeared to be two inches long—in the manner of a threatened cat. His pupils were rolled into his head so that only the whites of his eyes were visible.

This simple test clearly and firmly established demonic possession. Though the amount of water I placed on Jeremy was extremely minimal, it caused agony to the demon and flushed him out. Humanly speaking, there is no way Jeremy could have known he was sprinkled with holy water. Only a demon would have known. The illusory lengthening of Jeremy's canine teeth was just icing on the cake.[2]

"Demon, who are you?" I asked.

"%&$# you, priest!" he responded. "He is mine. He gave himself to me. You will never have him!"

"Demon, I want to speak to Jeremy," I said.

He responded with a slow, mocking laughter.

"In the name of Jesus, I command you to bring forth Jeremy," I declared.

The name of Jesus is terrible and frightening to the demons, and they are not free to disregard a command attached to it. There is no other name in heaven or on earth like it.

> God has highly exalted [Jesus] and bestowed on him the name
> which is above every name, that at the name of Jesus every knee
> should bow, in heaven and on earth and under the earth, and
> every tongue confess that Jesus Christ is Lord, to the glory of
> God the Father. (Phil. 2:9–11)

Most people are surprised to know that even demons respect the name of God. I have never witnessed them trash-talk the Name. I have seen demons claim to be God. I have seen them show disdain for the things God loves. I have seen them ridicule and lie about God. But I have never seen them disrespect His Name. That is a realm where—evidently—even demons will not tread.

By commanding in Jesus' name, I am compelling the demon to comply with the one who has already defeated him. Christ is the victor of the great cosmic battle of good and evil. As such, He *already* holds the demons on a leash, and they can only act with His permission.

Though I commanded him in the name of Jesus, there was no obvious sign of the demon's compliance. Demons are annoyingly legalistic. They often obey an exorcist's command without indicating they have done so. Then, when the exorcist repeats the command and utters prayers to compel its compliance, the demon suffers no injury from them because he has *already* complied. But in the process, the exorcist spends needless energy. It is all part of the demon's plan: to drain the exorcist and make him believe he has no authority and power. If he falls for it—if the exorcist places more faith in the demon's ability than in his own as a priest of Jesus Christ—all his subsequent commands will be less effective because there has been a detrimental lessening in his faith.

One detail in Jeremy's story indicated the demon's hold on him had been waning even before he came to see me. Jeremy had already decided to get his life right with God. He had decided to confess his sins and return to his Christian faith. What is more, *he was following through with those decisions.*

Someone may retort, "I'd be ready to get rid of the demon in five seconds." It is not as simple as that. A demon offers his victim something that pleases him in exchange for hospitality. Demons keenly study us throughout our lives. They know what makes us tick. They have identified our strengths, noted our weaknesses, and devised strategies to defeat us. The Devil knows us better than we know ourselves.

When the Devil makes an offer—for something sinful, for some supernatural ability, or some other demonic "gift," such as success in life—there has been careful engineering put into it to make it maximally tempting. Furthermore, a demonic gift's nature makes the victim dependent on it, like an addict to a drug. It is often unbearable for the victim to give it back once he has accepted it.

In Jeremy's case, the Devil offered him extraordinary strength. Jeremy loved the gift. He delighted to be stronger than anyone else and win every fitness and endurance contest he entered. At heart, however, he knew it was all fake. His strength did not come from self-discipline, training, and hard work but from a pact with a monster that held him in bondage. Jeremy had the freedom to win every strength contest, but he was not free to be himself. He felt like both a liar and a prisoner.

Having commanded in the name of Jesus that the demon bring forth Jeremy, I knew he was not free to disregard it. He behaved as if disobeying, but I knew Jeremy would hear me if I spoke. "Jeremy, I know you can hear me," I said. "You need to tell the demon, 'I renounce you. I choose Jesus and the life He gives. Leave me.'"

The demon's power appeared to partially abate, as I could now see Jeremy's pupils again. Jeremy turned his head slightly toward me, looking confused and bewildered.

"Jeremy, you need to renounce the demon and claim Jesus as your Lord," I repeated. As I said this, Jeremy's eyes rolled into his head again, and once more, all I could see were the whites of his eyes. "Switching out" during an exorcism is common. The demon will retreat when he needs a reprieve from the prayers. Besides my prayers, he had to endure those of my team members who were reciting the Rosary, asking for the Blessed Mother's intercession.

"Tell those idiots to shut up!" roared the demon, referring to my team members praying the Rosary. Their praying had the desired effect. It was grinding the enemy down.[3]

"Jeremy, I know you can hear me," I repeated. "You can stop this. Tell the demon to leave."

Jeremy's eyes changed from looking like they belonged to an alert, ferocious animal—a manifestation of the demon—to those of someone struggling to fight off tremendous grogginess and fatigue.

"So sleepy," he managed to stutter.

"Jeremy, you need to fight this. The enemy won't leave without your cooperation. It depends on you."

Jeremy slumped over. The demon put him to sleep to prevent his cooperation.

"Jeremy, wake up. You need to fight this," I yelled as I shook him firmly.

"So tired," he responded, barely able to pronounce the words.

"Jeremy, repeat after me, 'Come, Lord Jesus.' Invite the Lord into this battle. Say, 'Come, Lord Jesus.'"

"C-c-c-c-come . . .," he stuttered, and his voice trailed off.

"Jeremy, just say 'Jesus.' Just say the Lord's name."

He slumped into his chair and was asleep again. As I shook him, the glass of holy water on the bookshelf was hurled past me and smashed against the wall, breaking into pieces. It came so close to my face that I felt the air it displaced as it sailed past. Doubtless, this was the demon's retort to my using it to diagnose his presence. He was showing disdain for the tool I used to flush him out.

"In the name of Jesus, I command you demon to stop manifesting. I bind you in the name of Jesus. You have no authority here. All authority belongs to Christ, and those baptized in His name."

"%&$# you, priest! You %&$#ing ignorant &@%$^$!" thundered the demon.

"Demon, in the name of Jesus, be silent. Jeremy, say *'Jesus!'*"

Faintly—but distinctly—Jeremy managed to stammer the word, "Jesus." There was an immediate lessening of the demon's grip on him. Some of the grogginess left his face. He straightened up in his chair and was now able to hold himself up.

"Keep saying 'Jesus,'" I told him.

"Jee. Jeeeees. *Jesssus. JESUS!*" By this last time, Jeremy was able to say the Lord's name with all his strength in a roar that was befitting a man of his physique and stature. It was piercing.

"Jeremy, repeat after me. In the name of Jesus."

"In the name of Jesus!" he replied.

"I renounce this demon and everything he gave me: strength, power, and ability beyond my means. I give them all back to him."

He repeated, "I renounce this demon and everything he gave me: strength, power, and ability beyond my means. I give them all back to him."

"I choose Jesus Christ and the life He offers, and I choose to belong to His kingdom."

"I choose Jesus Christ and the life He offers, and I choose to belong to His kingdom," he repeated.

"I renounce using the Ouija board, and I ask God to heal me of any connection I still may have with it."

Jeremy repeated it.

Even the air in the room was now different. A heaviness that had been there was gone. Jeremy was alert, at peace, and smiling. The demon had departed.

I invited Jeremy to make his confession, which he'd tried to make earlier in the day but could not. I asked everyone else to leave the room, and Jeremy received the Sacrament from which he had been away for over two decades. I also gave him the Blessed Eucharist to further heal and strengthen him.

I reminded Jeremy that the demon will reenter him if he fails to live his Christian identity. Having claimed the victory of Jesus, he must have Jesus as the center of his life. It was clear from his demeanor that he was eager to do just that. I scheduled a follow-up appointment with him and presented him to his family, who were still praying in the adjacent room. For the first time in their marriage, his wife, Rachel, could experience life with her husband apart from any demonic influence.

THE SIX STEPS TO LIBERATION

Most people think the task of an exorcist is to cast out demons. That is a dreadful understatement.

The job of the exorcist generally involves six steps:

1. He must diagnose whether demons are present or the issue is due to some other cause (mental illness, physical sickness, an overactive imagination, or simply fraud).

2. If demons are present, he must uncover the rights they have gained over the victim.

3. He must guide the victim to revoke those rights.

4. He must lead the victim to conversion. (Scripture warns in Matthew 12:30 that no one can be "kingdom neutral." One either belongs to Christ, or one is against Him.)

5. Using the Church's authority, he must cast out the demons, who have now lost their right to possess. Depending on the level of the demonic hold, this process may necessitate multiple exorcisms.

6. He must provide ongoing pastoral care to the victim to prevent the enemy's return.

Step 1. Investigation and Diagnosis

Diagnosing possession can be slow and tedious. While the diagnosis happened quickly for Jeremy, his case is an exception. *Rarely does the exorcist possess certainty of possession before beginning prayers of exorcism.* Most of the time, he works with probability and his gut feelings. There is a good reason why this is so: the Devil does not want to be discovered. He is coy, secretive, and clandestine. It is not because the Devil is timid or meek—Satan hasn't the slightest trace of meekness or humility. He is consummately discreete because, like a prowling lion, he accomplishes more by lurking and hiding among the shadows than by exposing himself.

Many people contact me claiming they are possessed and in need of an exorcism. I have never found a single *self-diagnosed* case to be genuine in the years I have been an exorcist. While some claims were due to someone's overactive imagination, most were rooted in mental illness.

The first tip-off that someone is *not* possessed is the self-certainty that he is. I have found such certainty more consistent with mental illness than with demonic attachment. Mental illness can control someone's thinking and leave him robbed of his connection to reality. For example, many with schizophrenia struggle with hallucinations, disordered thinking, and destructive behavior. Many describe hearing "voices" originating from "God," and very often their message is negative, violent, and harmful. (e.g., "I, Jesus, am furious at the man who lives across the street. He is working against My plans to save the world. I want you to convince him to change. If he doesn't listen to you, kill him.")

The Catholic Church's rules governing exorcism warn the exorcist to use "the utmost circumspection and prudence" in diagnosing the need for exorcism.[4] He is advised against both extremes: gullibility and excessive skepticism.

An exorcist begins by paying close attention to the symptoms identified by a claimant. Genuine demonic activity reveals itself in patterns. The symptoms recur and repeat themselves, there was usually a discrete point when they began, and there is typically an event that set it off. But there are other things to note.

Demons reveal their presence through a lack of freedom in an area where someone ought to be free. For example, if someone is suddenly unable to walk into a church or read a spiritual book without feeling nauseous, agitated, or exhausted—and yet, he can go anywhere else, or read anything else, without issue—an exorcist would take keen notice of such symptoms.

People with evil spirits often ascribe the evil they experience to themselves and will speak in contradictory terms: "I did X, but it wasn't me. But I know that I did it." The use of contradictory language is one of the main differences between an affliction caused by demonic activity and one caused by mental illness. Someone with mental illness typically describes the "evil" afflicting him as something external to himself, saying, for example:

- "Demons follow me."
- "The Devil tries to run me off the road when I drive."
- "I can see the demons standing beneath that tree over there. They are laughing at me."
- "The demons hover just above my head. Sometimes I can see their movements."

Generally speaking, there is no spatial distance between the victim and the demons. They are internal to his person and are so intimately connected with him that he finds it difficult to distinguish his being from theirs. While he experiences their "interference" with his choices, it blends itself so naturally within him that he often believes he is the cause, even though he would ordinarily *never* make the choices he is making. In contrast to the mentally ill, who often insist they require an exorcism, those who do need an exorcism often insist they are mentally ill.

The symptoms of demonic affliction worsen over time. When uncertain whether someone has a demon, I will patiently wait and observe what happens over time. A demon cannot help himself: he will increase and expand his hold over the victim, who will report increased or additional symptoms. However, the Devil is subtle and will do anything to avoid detection. Many victims of demonic affliction have suffered because they could not find someone who believed them or who was able to diagnose their affliction.

The surest test for a demon's presence is the victim's reaction to the exorcist himself and the prayers he offers. A demon finds an exorcist's physical closeness and prayers unsettling and painful. The exorcist looks for a reaction, looking for *the three classic signs of possession* mentioned earlier in this chapter. When an exorcist encounters even one, he has the proof required to proceed with a complete exorcism, as nothing in the natural order can produce it.

However, demons do not gratuitously display these three signs simply because the exorcist is looking for them. While I have witnessed demons produce these signs often, I have only seen them do so *after* I have begun prayers against the demonic. In other words, I pray deliverance prayers as a way to provoke demonic manifestation, even before I am confident that demons are present.

Another manifestation may be a fourth sign: a person's extreme aversion to holy things and prayer. It occurs as in Mark 5:6–7, where the mere sight of Christ tortures the demon. While *this is an authentic supernatural sign and* one of the easiest signs for an exorcist to test, it requires caution.

False positives are a possibility when testing for aversion to the holy. When they see the exorcist doing something exorcistic—such as sprinkling holy water or holding a crucifix in his outstretched hand—those who are mentally ill, the imaginative and emotional, and even frauds—may react in a manner that resembles aversion. Mental illness is unpredictable and can produce what appears to be a demonic reaction. Highly emotional people and those with active imaginations can have difficulty differentiating what they feel or imagine from reality. The sight of a priest praying can be so arresting at an affective or sensory level that they can interpret the experience as being caused by demons. And frauds see a religious gesture on the priest's part as the cue for them to begin playacting. Avoiding such reactions means the priest must test for this sign in a manner that is not obvious.

Avoiding false positives is why I applied holy water to Jeremy discreetly. On a physical level, there is no way he could have known I did so. Thus, his reaction was a clear sign that he had a demon. Exorcists develop numerous covert ways to test for aversion to the holy.[5]

There are many manifestations a victim can exhibit that, though not supernatural, can help an exorcist diagnose the presence of demons,[6] and the exorcist carefully notes what symptoms he sees that may include violence (Acts 19:16), screaming (Mark 5:5), muteness (Luke 11:14), body contortions (Mark 9:8), self-injury or attempting suicide (Mark 5:5 and 9:22), sudden and intense nausea, body wounds that suddenly appear and disappear, and spontaneously falling asleep. An increase in symptoms when he clandestinely prays more intensely means it is more probable that the victim has demons.

Why was Jeremy's demon unable to hide more effectively? Why was a small amount of holy water so effective at exposing him? Jeremy's desire to be free had already caused his demon to lose much of his hold. Jeremy had already decided to reconcile with God, which opened him to grace. By the time Jeremy reached my office, his demon was already in pain.

Step 2. Determine the Rights to Possess

When a demon attaches himself to someone, it is because a "door" has been opened, and once a demon's presence is known, the exorcist must uncover *why* he is present.

Many people think that exorcism consists merely of using the Rite of Exorcism to overpower demons: that demons are hit on the head with the prayers of the ritual until they leave. That is not accurate.

The exorcist must not engage in a contest of willpower against a demon. Demons are incredibly strong, extraordinarily cunning, and mercilessly antagonistic. Even if the exorcist is successful at pitting his strength against the strength of weak, low-level demons, not all demons are of this sort. More powerful demons are formidable opponents. If an exorcist's strategy is to pit his strength against the demonic, he will quickly find himself worn down and exhausted. This faulty approach is often at the heart of the discouragement felt by novice or poorly trained exorcists. Their energy becomes so depleted, and their exorcisms take so long, that they begin to believe they should not be in this work. The demons gain a long-term victory if such priests, believing they are useless, completely abandon the ministry.

An exorcist must focus not on the demon *but on why the demon is present*. Stated differently, if a demon inhabits someone, he has been granted the right. Demons live and breathe legalism. As long as the demon enjoys the legal right to possess, he is not required to leave *because he is inside a dwelling that is his*. Just as someone who owns a deed to a property cannot be evicted from it, an exorcist cannot evict a demon from a victim over whom he has gained the right to possess.

Uncovering demonic rights is challenging and can be the most difficult part of an exorcist's work. A victim himself often does not know how he has acquired demons. In the case of Jeremy, this was not the case. He knew exactly why he had a demon: he had agreed to a pact with him. But it is often not that easy. An exorcist will probe a victim's experience, personal history, and psyche to locate the legal claims a demon may have. The demon will do everything he can to remain hidden.

If a victim is unsure why demons are harassing him, I will typically show him this list of dysfunctions and ask if any apply. If any do, I begin the next step.

COMMON DOORWAYS DEMONS USE
TO ACCESS HUMANS

- Engaging in impure sexual activity: fornication, adultery, pornography, masturbation, contraception, homosexual acts, perversion, et cetera.
- Bearing false witness: lying, deception, breaking promises, oaths, contracts, covenants, and so on.
- Irreligiosity: refusing to practice religion as God desires it; excusing oneself from observing the precepts of religion and morality; relegating oneself to being merely "spiritual."
- Hardness of heart: refusing to forgive others, refusing to forgive oneself, prolonged rage, prolonged sadness, entertaining suicidal thoughts.
- Use of blasphemous language.
- Enjoying profane or perverse entertainment.
- Practicing Wicca, sorcery, witchcraft, black magic, white magic, voodoo, divination, et cetera.
- Casting spells, sending curses, et cetera.
- Practicing Freemasonry, New Age, Reiki, et cetera.
- Using Ouija boards, horoscopes, tarot cards, et cetera.
- Consulting "healers," curanderos, mediums, fortune tellers, psychics, practicing necromancy, and the like.
- Engaging in role-playing games, and violent or sadistic video games.
- The effects of past trauma—e.g., excessive fear, rage, arrogance, vengefulness—which can often lead the victim to make poor choices.

Step 3. Lead the Victim to Claim the Lordship of Jesus Christ

Every exorcism is done in Jesus' name. Jesus is the one mediator between God and man (1 Tim. 2:5), the one who came to destroy the Devil's labors (1 John 3:8). He is the victor who will reign forever (Rev. 11:15). His authority is supreme.

But for an exorcism to be effective, the victim *must accept* Jesus Christ's victory and *place* himself under Christ's Lordship. He must decide to move from the kingdom of darkness to the kingdom of light.

The Acts of the Apostles tell us about seven Jewish exorcists who, having witnessed how Paul performed extraordinary feats in Jesus' name, attempted to exorcise demons by doing the same, but without being Christ's disciples. Their actions merely exposed them to the demon's fury.

> *Then some of the itinerant Jewish exorcists undertook to pronounce the name of the Lord Jesus over those who had evil spirits, saying, "I adjure you by the Jesus whom Paul preaches." Seven sons of a Jewish high priest named Sceva were doing this. But the evil spirit answered them, "Jesus I know, and Paul I know; but who are you?" And the man in whom the evil spirit was leaped on them, mastered all of them, and overpowered them, so that they fled out of that house naked and wounded. And this became known to all residents of Ephesus, both Jews and Greeks; and fear fell upon them all; and the name of the Lord Jesus was extolled.* (Acts 19:13–17)

Not everyone who requests exorcism believes in Christ. Many of them—perhaps even most—do not. Thus, proclaiming the Gospel to the victim is the exorcist's first task. I do so by assuring the victim that Christ has already triumphed over evil, and His victory is immediately available. We merely need to accept Christ as Lord and Savior. I invite victims to do so by repeating the following or similar words:

> *I choose Jesus Christ as my personal Lord and Savior. I choose to be His disciple and follow Him as my Lord. I claim the life He offers me and give my life completely to Him. I ask that His grace and power set me free from all evil. Amen.*

When I elicited this response from Jeremy, the demon inside him attempted to render him unconscious so that he could neither hear my words nor respond to them. The demon knew Jeremy no longer wanted anything to do with him, and this was his last-ditch attempt to maintain his possession. Fortunately, he could not stop Jeremy from accepting Christ.

Step 4. Lead the Victim in Rescinding the Rights Surrendered to the Demon

Jeremy's case illustrates how crucial it is to nullify a demon's rights. It is insufficient for the victim merely to desire that the demon leaves. The rights a demon holds are equivalent to a contract. Just as a contract signed by parties is binding until it is rendered null, demonic rights require nullification before a victim is freed. The best way to accomplish this is through *renunciations*, statements that legally "cancel" his relationship with the demon.

Jeremy had to renounce his opening the door to evil by using the Ouija board, his agreement to the pact that the demon offered him in his bedroom, and the superhuman strength he received through that pact. These three open doors were keeping Jeremy ensnared. Freedom meant all three needed closing.

I asked Jeremy to repeat after me:

In the Name of Jesus, I renounce using the Ouija board. I no longer want any part of it. I renounce agreeing to the pact the demon offered me. I want nothing to do with it. I give back everything that came to me through it—strength and power, and I claim back for myself everything and anything I surrendered to the demon. Amen.

It is not enough to dissolve the connection between the victim and the demon. Jeremy had to *replace* the broken relationship with a relationship with Jesus. When a demon leaves, he leaves a spiritual vacuum. Just as *nature abhors a vacuum,* so does the spiritual world. That vacuum cannot remain but must be filled with what ought to be there (cf. Matt. 12:43–45; Luke 11:24–26). Following his renunciations, I led Jeremy through the following "claim" statements:

I claim You, Jesus Christ, as my Lord and Savior. I give myself completely to You and submit to Your will for me. I accept whatever You desire. I ask You to send Your Holy Spirit to fill the space the demon occupied within me.

Step 5. Cast the Demon Out

Once the demon's rights are canceled, he must be cast out. This step is vital since he has no obligation to leave on his own. Again, demons *are legalistic,* and if the exorcist does not evict him, a demon may remain behind as a squatter.

The demon's power will determine the method to get him to leave, and that can be difficult. I use anything and everything that will assist me. There is more power in the Sacraments than in anything the exorcist can do. They impart God's very life. I invite the victim to reconcile with God in the Sacrament of Confession. Next, I offer him the Lord in the Blessed Sacrament. Finally, I administer to him the Sacrament of the Sick. Each of these Sacraments offer healing, the precise medicine the victim requires. The prayers I proclaim from this point onward will have an even greater effect.

Once the other steps listed above have been completed, I cast out the demon using these or similar words:

> *In the Name of Jesus, I bind you demon and all others that may be connected to Jeremy and render you powerless to do anything except what I order you to do. Upon my command, you must leave Jeremy and go immediately and directly to Jesus Christ, the Son of God and Savior of the world, to Whom I chain you until He Himself sends you elsewhere. You must leave wholly and completely, leaving behind no residue or trace of you or your works. You must not contaminate anyone or anything else as you depart nor retaliate in any way. And you must never return.*
>
> *I command you to leave as I have directed . . .NOW!*

My steps for ordering a demon to leave include the following:

1. I order any and every demon connected to the victim to depart and to be helpless to do otherwise.
2. He is to leave when I say—neither before I have commanded nor at a time of his choosing later.
3. I direct him to where—or, rather, to Whom—he must go.
4. He must leave nothing of himself behind.
5. The possibility of retaliation is removed.

I add these caveats because of the legalism of demons. In one of my earliest exorcisms, I commanded a demon to leave but did not add the word "now" at the end of my command. The demon never left. I could not figure out why. After pummeling him with prayers, I ordered him to tell me why he was still present.

"In the name of Jesus, tell me what rights you still have?" I asked him.

"None," he replied.

"What further do I need to do to get you out?"

"Nothing," was the response.

"Then why haven't you left?"

Very politely, he responded, "You didn't tell me *when* I had to leave."

"NOW!" I bellowed.

Step 6. Provide Ongoing Pastoral Care

It is one thing to drive demons out. It is an entirely different thing to keep them out. To protect the effort at accomplishing the former, an exorcist must invest in the latter.

A post-liberated victim requires guidance in his discipleship with Christ, centered on four areas: human, spiritual, intellectual, and pastoral.

1. Human Formation

Human formation seeks to ensure that the liberated victim is integrated and self-directed on a human level. It aims to help him to develop self-awareness, self-discipline, emotional well-being, and a healthy self-image. It also seeks to help him foster healthy relationships, build affective maturity, and fulfill his vocation.

Many victims have poor human relationships. Their "friends" often had something to do with their being possessed. Such friends need to be replaced, or the liberated victim risks being pulled back into a dysfunctional and unhealthy lifestyle. But merely telling the victim that he needs to get new friends is easier said than done and, without assisting him, is cruel. Most victims are unaware of how to do so. They will benefit from being "plugged" into a solid group of Christian friends who patiently incorporate him into their lives and encourage him to live in a Godly manner.

2. Spiritual Formation

Spiritual formation seeks to aid the liberated victim in deepening his relationship with Christ and His Church. Signs of a healthy relationship include:

- Dedication to daily prayer.
- Adherence and obedience to the Church's teachings.
- Regular reception of the Sacrament of Confession and the Sacrament of the Eucharist.

The exorcist needs to assist the liberated victim in developing a spiritual plan of life. Connecting him with a spiritually mature layperson to serve as a "buddy" is helpful. Such a person walks with the victim on his journey to wholeness, guides him through the steps to spiritual growth, and regularly checks on him. Having such a person ensures the victim does not feel alone. It's helpful to have someone on whom he can count.

3. Intellectual Formation

Intellectual formation seeks to aid the liberated victim in cultivating learning as a lifelong pursuit. Its goal is to empower him with the theoretical and practical knowledge needed for effective living and decision-making.

An exorcist must ensure the victim is engaged in adult faith formation, including those covering Scripture, catechesis (i.e., teaching and instruction), and discipleship.

4. Pastoral Formation

Pastoral formation seeks to integrate the liberated victim in the Church's life and ministry. It aims to promote his growth by incorporating him within a local Church community.

A liberated victim receives healing when he participates in at least one Church ministry. This participation can be as simple as pouring coffee at social gatherings and other Church events. Participation in such charitable works gives him a sense of belonging and purpose, enabling him to feel needed and appreciated.

USING THE RITE OF EXORCISM

At this point, the reader may ask, "But none of these six steps involve the Rite of Exorcism . . . when is it performed?" The answer to that question is, *it varies.*

The six-part structure I have laid out above is the overall strategy for liberation. To ensure the victim's freedom from demons, an exorcist must accomplish all six.

However, the order is fluid. Of the steps mentioned above, Steps 2 to 4 are listed in the order in which I most often accomplish them. But they may be done in a different order, depending on a case's circumstances. For example, if someone is afflicted with a curse, it may not be obvious how it took effect and why. That may only be revealed in Step 5 when the demons are ordered to depart (i.e., the demons themselves may reveal they cannot do so until the curse is broken). Similarly, if someone was abused in a satanic cult, he may not be able to claim the Lordship of Jesus, especially if symbols and images of Jesus were used in the abuse he suffered. In this case, I may have to return to Step 3 once I have proved to the victim that he has been lied to about Jesus.

The Rite of Exorcism is a tool at the exorcist's disposal, and he can employ it anywhere—and as often as he likes. However, most exorcists I know resort to using the Rite only when renunciations and other prayers have not produced the desired effect. In other words, they use it if demons are preventing the victim's cooperation (i.e., suppressing his natural abilities to do so) or because demons are making it impossible for the exorcist to communicate with the victim altogether.

The Rite itself is not used as frequently as many suppose. In Jeremy's case, I did not need to use it. Using it would have added unnecessary labor and time. The demon was managed well enough without resorting to it.

An exorcist is not a gunslinger. The Rite has a well-defined place and purpose, and its instructions are clear. It is a powerful weapon against demons the Church has provided to exorcists. When I elect not to use it, I do so simply because I have judged it is not required. Nevertheless, I do not presume to possess a method or technique better than the Church's in this matter. Nor should other exorcists. I do not hesitate to use the Rite when I deem it advantageous.

———

Many believe exorcism to be a Catholic magical spell that when prayed—poof!—demons magically disappear. Such is not the case. Exorcism is a process. The role of the exorcist is to aid the victim in switching the Kingdom to which he belongs. The victim must move from the Kingdom of Darkness to the Kingdom of Light. However, without the victim's active participation and consent, the exorcist cannot cast out his demons, as the place they inhabit is theirs by right.

FOUR

DOORWAYS: HOW DEMONS ENTER A PERSON

THE CASE OF
LINDA AND CHARLIE

A woman named Linda called one day to ask me to bless her home.

The house blessing is a familiar ritual for Catholics in which a priest asks God to expel any evil attached to the home and invokes God's grace and protection on it. There does not need to be "a reason" to have one's home blessed.

However, I always ask why the person is requesting the blessing. It is my way of starting a conversation about where people are at with God.

Linda's answer to my question was, "Because weird things are happening inside it."

"What kinds of things?" I asked. She reported the following:

Self-relocation of objects. Linda, her husband, Charlie, and their three young boys lived in the home. All five observed the same strange phenomenon. When they placed an object down—like a set of keys on the kitchen counter or a newspaper on the living room coffee table—and turned away—say to get a glass from a cupboard, the object moved to a new location, usually across the room. No one moved it, but it was relocated. Though spooky and disturbing, this phenomenon was harmless enough: nothing was damaged, just moved.

As time progressed, the occurrences became more malicious. For example, one day, the TV remote control went missing. All five family members went through the house looking for it, each blaming the next for its disappearance. After thirty or so fruitless minutes, they abandoned their efforts and went outside to sit in the backyard. When they returned, the remote control was sitting in plain view on the coffee table.

Manipulation of the lights. When someone turned on a room's lights, the lights in another room turned off. Or, if the lights were turned off, the lights somewhere else turned on.

Self-movement of furniture. The family lived in a small two-bedroom home. All three of the boys slept in the same room. Charlie tucked his boys in at night in a bunk bed they shared: the two youngest boys, aged seven and five, slept on the top bunk, and the nine-year-old slept on the bottom. Charlie often horsed around with his boys at bedtime, shaking and pulling on their metal-framed bed and threatening to throw it across the room. The boys loved it.

Long after the children had fallen asleep one night, Linda and Charlie heard the kids' bunk bed twisting and shaking, followed by their eldest son's screaming. They ran to the kids' room, and turning on the lights, they witnessed the bunk bed in a flurry of autonomous twisting and shaking. The eldest boy looked frantically, now that the lights were on, for who was shaking the bed. He was baffled when he saw no one.

Equally bizarre was that all through the commotion, the two youngest boys in the upper bunk never woke from their sleep.

Strange night sounds. From the time he was a toddler, the eldest boy had a habit of shaking his right leg as he slept. One night, as Linda was reading in bed, she heard his leg shaking in the next room. But it was doing so more rapidly and more agitated than usual.

Curious, Linda got up and looked inside the boys' room, only to find them sleeping soundly. Her eldest was perfectly still. After returning to bed, the same agitated shaking began again. She rechecked the room, only to find everyone perfectly still. After returning to bed a second time, the movement started again. She went back to check the kids' room and, like before, found no one stirring. However, a growl came from the dark corner of the room.

A shadowy figure. Some weeks after the first manifestations began, the family members began to see a kind of translucent shadowy figure—about the size of a child—walking in the house. It appeared peripherally, only at the edge of one's vision—until one tried to look at it directly—then it quickly vanished.

However, as time went on, the figure lost more and more of its "shyness" and ceased to disappear when looked at directly. It walked throughout the house but was especially fond of the children's bedroom, walking in and out as if it belonged there.

The figure's presence terrified the family, and the children were scared to enter their bedroom. All three now slept with Mom and Dad.

Disembodied footsteps. As Charlie walked toward the front of the house to leave for work one afternoon, he heard the footsteps of a child walking toward the back of the house, followed by the back door opening and closing. No one else was at home. Thinking it was an intruder, Charlie ran toward the back door. A tall wooden fence enclosed the backyard: whoever stepped outside had no way out. He opened the door only to find the yard empty.

I asked Linda the questions an exorcist might ask. *How long have these phenomena been occurring?* About five months was her reply. *How long have you lived in the home?* About three years, she said. *Do the phenomena occur anywhere else, at work, at the kids' school, or in your relatives' homes?* No, was her reply.

Linda's answers established key facts:

- They did not inherit a harassing spirit (i.e., from the home's previous owners).
- Her family is the spirit's explicit target.
- The demonic phenomena were contained to her home; though there was no guarantee that it would not, at any moment, extend to other sectors of their lives.

Linda impatiently asked, "When can you get this thing out of our home?"

Her impatience was understandable, but it needed correcting nonetheless: "Linda, you don't understand. This thing is not in your house. You're in *its* house." She began to cry.

I needed more data. "Linda, evil does not harass a family out of nowhere. It needs to be let in. A door was opened to it, allowing it to enter your lives. We need to find what that door is."

She surprised me with her reply. "I think I know what the door is."

Exorcists spend a great deal of time looking for "doors." They probe and question, attempting to uncover how evil has managed to gain entry. The process can be lengthy because people often do not connect their sinful behavior with the harassing evil. Or, if they do, they are often silent—and even dishonest—about the connection to avoid the embarrassment of revealing their sins.

Linda again surprised me with her honesty. "About six months ago, I had an affair," she admitted. Adultery violates one of the Ten Commandments and is what Catholics call a **mortal sin**: a sin so grave that it cuts us off from God's grace. Such mortal sin more than qualifies as a "door."

With tears and sobs, Linda expressed regret and sorrow for her choice. She communicated that Charlie knew of the act and forgave her. "At around the same time," she continued, "Charlie started using hard drugs again." A second mortal sin. Aside from breaking civil law, using drugs is a form of killing oneself. Drugs do violence to the body which, by our baptism, becomes the temple of the Holy Spirit (1 Cor. 6:19).

I told Linda I wanted the entire family to be present when I exorcised their home so that the children could witness the Church ridding the spirit that terrified them. I also wanted to speak with Linda and Charlie to explain in greater detail why all this occurred. Such a conversation was crucial because it is one thing to expel evil, but an entirely different matter for it to stay expelled. Linda and Charlie opened a door, giving a demon a legal right to harass their family. It had to be closed. Only Linda and Charlie could do that. While an exorcist can command a demon to depart, that demon will only obey if his right to access has been revoked by the ones who opened it. And should the door be reopened later, he will return, and with a vengeance. Linda and Charlie needed to understand this.

I went into our rectory chapel to pray before the Eucharist. I asked Our Lord to give me an insight into the demon affecting this family. "Imitation" is what I heard in my heart, over and over. To imitate is to simulate or copy, which perfectly described the demon's activity.

- A family member puts an object down *here*. The demon moves it over *there*.
- Someone turns on a light, and the demon turns off a light (and vice versa).
- Dad shakes the bunk bed. The demon shakes the bunk bed.
- The children walk in and out of their bedroom. The demon does the same.
- The eldest boy shakes his leg at night. The demon imitates him.
- Dad walks out the front door. The demon walks out the back door.

All this mirrored the essence of Linda and Charlie's sins. Linda left the happiness of her marriage and chose an "imitation marriage" by way of an affair. Charlie left the joy of his family and chose an "imitation happiness" offered by drugs.

We have all heard the adage that art imitates life. The same applies to evil: *demonic attachment imitates one's sinful life*. The harassment afflicting Linda and Charlie reflected the behavior by which they allowed it into their lives.

When I went to the family's home, Linda introduced me to Charlie and the children. Since most of the conversation was going to be about their parents' moral failures, I suggested the children go to another room. I described to the adults how their sins were the cause of the demonic attachment. Though Linda accepted my explanation, Charlie was unsatisfied.

"Linda and I came from living bad lives," he interjected. "Yes, we made mistakes this past year. But even with her mistakes and mine, we've lived better than we ever have before."

I appreciated Charlie's perplexity. In our call, Linda shared that from adolescence to their early years together, she and Charlie lived godlessly. It is not that they wanted to be evil. They just acted, morally and ethically, as they had been raised.

When the children were born, however, each underwent a process of maturation and conversion. They made a conscious decision to be good parents and good Christians. In their defense, they lived dramatically different from how they had in the past.

I explained that good intentions are insufficient to keep one's life demon-free, a point against which Charlie protested: "But no demons ever latched on to us before when we committed those sins. Why now, when we are better people than we have ever been?"

"Charlie, I have no answer to that question," I admitted. "What I do know is that God permitted it, and if He permitted it, then it is part of His plan for your eternal salvation. If it takes a demon moving into your home for you to get on board with that plan, then so be it. Your response to what God wants is important—not just to be free of the demon—but to live a life that will transform you into what He wants you to be. You may have become a better person than you were. But He wants you to become better still."

Loud bangs came from the dining room in which the children were playing. Charlie got up to settle them down. Shortly after his return, the noise started again, only louder. Once again, he left to restore order. On his return, an enormous thud came from the dining room, so loud and startling that it sounded like a refrigerator had tipped. It caused the whole house to shake. Charlie jumped out of his chair and darted toward the dining room. When he emerged a minute later, his disbelieving look revealed he had not found the sound's cause.

As Charlie sat down in his chair, his face revealed exasperation at being powerless in the face of the evil tormenting him in his own home. Leaning back in his chair, he repeated his previous complaint that the demonic harassment they were experiencing was grossly unfair. Just then, his cell phone—by itself—flew out of his pocket and, flying through the air as if some invisible hand had lobbed it, landed six feet in front of him. Charlie drew in a long breath, about to explode.

"Charlie," I interjected, "focus on me. The demon knows his time is short. His only hope is to distract you from what I am telling you. The doors that you and Linda opened must be closed. I know you regret opening them in the first place, but that alone is insufficient. Your sins must be sacramentally confessed and renounced so that the demon loses his rights.[1]

After hearing each one's confession privately—wherein each made a heartfelt reconciliation with the Lord—I absolved each of their sins.[2] Then I led them through formal renunciations of their actions by which the demon gained rights over them. Both are necessary despite some erroneously believing that confession and renunciation are equal. They are not. The former restores our relationship with God and His Church. The latter severs the "legal" connection demons have with us.

There is no set formula for such a renunciation. Nevertheless, however one chooses to word it, I always recommend it be done in the name of Jesus, the name which Scripture states is so far "above every name," that it will make "every knee bow, in heaven and on earth and under the earth, and every tongue confess that Jesus Christ is Lord" (Philippians 2:9). Jesus' name is God's power.

Linda's sin was adultery. "Linda, repeat after me. In the Name of Jesus, I renounce, repent, rebuke, and reject my adulterous act. I want no part of it. I choose to follow God and His commandments and recommit faithfulness to my husband, Charlie, giving myself entirely and exclusively to him. Amen."

Charlie's sin was indulging in drugs. "Charlie, repeat after me. In the Name of Jesus, I renounce, repent, rebuke, and reject drug use. I no longer want any part of it. I choose to put my family first and accept them as God's gift. Amen."

Linda and Charlie had "closed the doorway" and canceled the demon's rights. All that remained was to cast him out.

In the Name of Jesus, I take authority over you, the harassing spirit or spirits present in this house. I bind you in His Holy Name, and upon my command, you will leave this house and this family and never return. You must go immediately and directly to the foot of Jesus and remain there until He sends you elsewhere. You must leave wholly and completely. You must not retaliate nor contaminate anyone or anything else as you depart. I command you to leave . . . now!

I made holy water and gave sprinkling rods to the two youngest children, directing them to splash holy water throughout each room. They loved it and went straight to their bedroom to begin. I gave a thurible to the oldest child in which I had placed incense on lit charcoal. His job was to swing the thurible and make the house as smoky as possible. I wanted the children to have the satisfaction of being part of the cleansing, and I wanted them to experience their home smelling like the inside of a church.

The ritual took just under ten minutes, after which I departed. The family never experienced any manifestations again.

THE RIGHT TO HARASS, OPPRESS, POSSESS

The case of Linda and Charlie illustrates a vital fact regarding demons: they require permission—"a door"—to enter someone's life.

Doors allow things in. They keep things out. People do not get demons by making peanut butter sandwiches. Nor do they get them by riding the bus, using public washrooms, or living next door to someone possessed. Demons are acquired when people open the door to them.

Linda and Charlie's good intentions and much-improved Christian living were not enough to keep the Devil away. In fact, their decision to reform their sinful living may have been why the Devil was so interested in them.

When someone lives a morally disordered life, moving from sin to sin, without regard for God and His commandments, the Devil usually pays little interest. Why would he? Such a person already belongs to his kingdom. However, if that person tries to leave his kingdom, the Devil will become very interested.

Demons are legalistic. They look for ways to attach themselves to someone, gaining the equivalent to a legal right to demonize, harass, and oppress. Demons have a voracious appetite for gaining those privileges and will do anything to preserve them.

Attaching himself to a host is merely a demon's first step. His second and most pernicious step is manipulating and exploiting his host's wounds: taking advantage of whatever is unhealthy, dysfunctional, injured, or hurt. Merely attaching himself to a host does not enable a demon to thrive and flourish. For that, he must parasitically infest his host's wounds.

In a word, demons *need* wounds. Just as in nature, a theological organism needs a habitat to thrive, so a demon needs the same in the spiritual realm. Wounds provide demons with the conditions to flourish and propagate.

Wounds have two sources: trauma and sin.

TRAUMA

By trauma, I do not mean slight hurts or injuries, but what psychology might call "super trauma": an experience so intense and damaging that the victim's well-being is prevented from fulfillment in a lasting way.

Tim

Tim was a man in his fifties who suffered from terrible anxieties. He had a debilitating fear of death, was afraid of making friends, and was too anxious to hold a job. He survived by collecting social assistance and living with his elderly mother, who still cared for him.

Tim's phobias began when he was nine and playing with his friend, Joey. When Joey missed a catch, he chased the ball into the street where a car slammed into him, mangling his body horrifically and killing him. Tim witnessed it. In that instant, the world became a different place for Tim. It was no longer a safe world. It was a world in which a nine-year-old could die horrifically, just by playing catch.

Trauma is significant because it alters our view of reality, causing us to see things in a false and distorted way. In other words, it
causes us to believe a lie. In Tim's case, that lie took on several forms:

- "I asked Joey to play with me. It's my fault he died."
- "Joey was hit by the car because of my bad throw. I am a
  terrible friend."
- "Death is horrific. Nothing can stop it."

Tim could not recall whether he had an explicit belief in God
when the accident occurred. Nevertheless, his "religious" understanding of reality—his most fundamental beliefs regarding what
holds reality together—was affected by his trauma.

I met Tim in a hospital after his mother injured herself in a
fall. She was in a room adjacent to that of someone I was visiting. I
popped my head in, said hello, and offered to pray with her, which
she accepted.

As I stepped into the room, I smelled the pungent odor of
vomit. Tim was so traumatized by being in a hospital that he had
vomited in the trash can. After praying with his mother, I offered to
pray with him. He never gave a reply, but his mother yelled, "Yes,
he needs it! He's afraid of everything!"

I placed my hand on Tim's head, and, among other things, I
petitioned the Lord to free him from the spirit of fear. For an instant,
I saw Tim's eyes squint with an expression of fury. I attributed this
to embarrassment at his mother's intervening on his behalf. He then
began a prolonged fit of coughing. When I finished praying, I left my
card, assured them I would continue to pray for them and departed.

A week later, Tim and his mother visited my office. Tim reported
his life was "completely different" after I prayed with him at the
hospital. He no longer had the paralyzing fears that began after

Joey's accident. Tim was so free that he suggested to his mother they drive to see me, something previously unthinkable. Tim's terrible phobia of cars, which caused him to vomit continuously each time he rode in one, was gone.

The trauma of seeing his friend horrifically killed had left Tim with a deep wound, and a demon was able to control him by manipulating it. Following his deliverance, Tim possessed freedom he had never previously known. While he still lacked some normal abilities, such as social skills, a by-product of living as a recluse most of his life, he was functional to a level unimaginable before his deliverance. He even obtained a part-time job at a grocery store.

Linda

Linda had been unfaithful in her marriage to Charlie, which became one of the factors that led to demonic harassment of her family. That choice to commit adultery was itself conditioned by a traumatic wound. The effects of adultery marred Linda's childhood. Chronic infidelity destroyed her parents' marriage when she was nine years old. She and her five siblings were separated and raised in the homes of extended family members since neither her mother nor father could afford to do so. Her father was already paying child support to two other women, and her mother had two children fathered by different men. These extramarital relationships had occurred while her parents were married to one another.

Linda believed cheating was part of spousal behavior. The distortion led to her infidelity and enabled a demon to bond himself to her and her family.

There is evidence that Tim had a demon: he exhibited a chronic lack of freedom in areas where people are usually free; the demon manifested when I prayed a deliverance prayer; Tim experienced dramatic freedom following the prayer. While Tim was not possessed, a demon found a way to use his trauma to bond to him. How? The demon likely exacerbated his pain to make Tim believe that life was hopeless and that happiness was unattainable because he was responsible for Joey's death. While the accident was unfortunate and tragic, the demon proposed a distortion of the truth. But the moment Tim accepted that distortion, a demon created a bond with him. While it was not strong enough to give the demon rights to possession, it did give him powerful authority over him. Unfortunately for Tim, everyone in his life believed his issues were purely psychological ones that had been occasioned by Joey's accident. No one guessed that they might have had a spiritual cause. Being delivered by prayer sooner might have saved Tim years of needless suffering.

There is no evidence that a demon attached himself to Linda during childhood as the one did to Tim. Nevertheless, as soon as Linda acted on her distorted belief—that the marital bond is not permanent—the demon wasted no time establishing his bond.

The examples of Tim and Linda show the importance of proper spiritual formation for young people. In those appropriately formed, it is more difficult to believe a demon's lie. We also see how helpful counseling and psychological therapy can be to someone suffering the effects of trauma. These could have brought healing and correction to both Tim and Linda's distorted views and prevented them from becoming entrenched. Unhealed wounds are the target of demonic manipulation.

To demons, trauma is low-hanging fruit, an easy way to latch onto a person and feed off his injury. While people do not become possessed by trauma directly, trauma makes one prone to dysfunctional choices by causing one to believe a lie. Those choices can then occasion demonization, as the examples of Tim and Linda both demonstrate.

SIN

The other type of wound that creates conditions for demons to thrive is sin. Sin has three species: personal sin, generational sin, and transferred sin.

1. Personal Sin

Every soul is God's direct creation. However, the moment it is created, a soul becomes the property and jurisdiction of the Devil. Such is the tragic inheritance left by Adam and Eve's Original Sin. Their disobedience of God was so destructive that it forfeited the immortality of the human race. Through Original Sin, the Devil gained jurisdiction over each of their descendants. In addition to owning us in this life, an eternity with the enemy awaited one in the next. Rather than a blessing, Original Sin ensured that life was the opposite: a never-ending curse.

Although some Christians find accepting this reality challenging, one cannot deny it without destroying the essence of the Christian faith: humanity needed a Savior to liberate it from sin.

Before Christ's resurrection, all humans—both righteous and unrighteous—were consigned to hell at death. Being human, Jesus was subject to the same penalty. That is why the Apostles Creed states He "descended into hell." However, because He paid the penalty for sin in full, "it was impossible for death to keep its hold on him" (Acts 2:24 NIV), and He emptied hell of every righteous soul who had died since the beginning of the world, an act referred to by Christian theologians as the Harrowing of Hell.

Christ instituted the Sacrament of Baptism to remove Original Sin and keep us from hell. But it does even more. Baptism bestows a new identity. It transfers our legal ownership from Satan to God the Father, who makes us His sons and daughters. It gives us Jesus Christ as our Savior, who delivers us from Satan's dominion and gives us an eternal inheritance. It gives us the Holy Spirit who makes His dwelling within us and gives us His very life.

When one commits even a single mortal sin, however, the effects of baptism cease to be operative.[3] All sins are offenses against God, but Scripture distinguishes between deadly and nondeadly sin (1 John 5:16–17). A deadly—or mortal—sin is an action so evil that it destroys our relationship with God. The *Catechism of the Catholic Church* defines mortal sin as: "a grave violation of God's law; it turns man away from God, who is his ultimate end and his beatitude, by preferring an inferior good to him."[4]

Mortal sins meet three conditions:

Concerns grave matter. For a sin to be mortal, the action must involve something serious. Stealing a paper clip from the library does not constitute grave matter. Stealing someone's identity to deplete a bank account does. At the same time, violations and losses are relative. Stealing five dollars from a millionaire does not involve grave matter as the harm he suffers is trivial. Stealing five dollars from an indigent does, as his loss is significant.

Sufficient knowledge of the evil involved. Mortal sin involves awareness by the sinner that his act is sinful. For example, pulling the trigger on what you believe is an unloaded gun is not an action done with full knowledge, even if someone is shot.

Deliberate consent. A mortal sin necessitates that the sinner freely choose the action. Consenting to sexual relations with a person to whom one is not married is gravely sinful. Submitting to rape because one is threatened with death is not.

Mortal sins are not "accidental." They require premeditation: the agent knows he is committing serious evil, has accepted this fact, and was free not to do so.

————

Many today downplay sinfulness, deify personal freedom, and presume God's "automatic" mercy and forgiveness even when they have no intention of stopping their sinful behavior. However, I would be amiss if I did not repeat what the Catholic Church has proclaimed from its beginning: *should a person die in mortal sin, he forfeits salvation and incurs the penalty of eternal hell.* God's Word promises that death comes as a thief in the night (1 Thess. 5:2). Should it find one unprepared, the fate received will be the same as that meted to the Devil and his minions: eternal torment and everlasting anguish (2 Thess. 1:7–9).

Mortal sin gives the "legal right" to the Devil to possess a soul, and all lesser rights besides: the ability to hound, harass, burden, oppress, and torment. It is removed only through confession and repentance.

So if the Devil obtains the right to possess when someone commits even a single mortal sin, why does he not always do so, since mortal sins are often committed without resulting in demonic possession? The Devil's rights are always subject to God's ratification. Fortunately for us, God holds the Devil on a leash and does not allow him to act on his rights without His divine permission.

Mortal sin is the single most significant cause of possession and demonic harassment. When someone comes (or is brought) to an exorcist for his ministry, it is this type of wound—a personal mortal sin—that he looks for first. A turning away from God is a turning toward the Devil.

The tragedy, however, is that a sin does not always have to be mortal to lead to possession. I know an eight-year-old child who

became possessed after participating in a Ouija board session organized by his older siblings and their friends. The boy had no idea of
the spiritual danger and had no notion it violated divine law. Nevertheless, none of his siblings or friends became possessed—only the
eight-year-old. The nature of the occult activity in which he was
involved was all that was necessary for a demon to attach to him.

2. Generational Sin
Each person is responsible for his own sins.

> *The soul that sins shall die. The son shall not suffer for the iniq-
> uity of the father, nor the father suffer for the iniquity of the
> son; the righteousness of the righteous shall be upon himself, and
> the wickedness of the wicked shall be upon himself.* (Ezekiel
> 18:20)

Nevertheless, the family line of a sinner inherits his sin's effects.

> *I the LORD your God am a jealous God, visiting the iniquity of
> the fathers upon the children to the third and the fourth gener-
> ation of those who hate me.* (Exodus 20:5; echoed in Exodus
> 34:7)

Exorcists refer to this type of inheritance as *generational sin*. It
consists of the continuation of a sin's adverse effects upon one's descendants. The most well-known example is Original Sin. Though Adam
committed it, each of his descendants inherits it (Gen. 3:14–19).[5]
Exorcists encounter families that exhibit generational patterns
of dysfunction. For example, I recall one family where the grandfa-
ther was an alcoholic, his son was an alcoholic, and his grandson was
an alcoholic. Then, on his fourteenth birthday, his great-grandson

was given his first beer, and, before an hour passed, he consumed five more. The boy had never had a drink before. But he exhibited an alcoholic's behavior.

A biologist may assert that the behavior is genetically induced because the boy has a genetic predisposition to alcoholism. A psychologist or addictions counselor may argue the cause is societal and environmental, a by-product of the boy's exposure to alcoholic behavior.

While genetics and societal dynamics can produce repetitive behavior, Scripture suggests some dysfunctional repetitions have spiritual causes.

A woman called my office requesting assistance against a recurring pattern of suicide in her family. Her father had taken his life. Two of her brothers had taken their lives. Her brother-in-law, who had never suffered from suicidal thoughts, attempted suicide three times within four years after marrying her older sister. Another man who recently married the woman's younger sister experienced intense suicidal thoughts since his wedding day.

However, one detail indicated demonic causation: every suicide attempt *occurred on a Thursday*. Such a pattern cannot be ignored. Five persons had at least attempted suicide—three of them successfully—always (and only) on a Thursday.

When the woman called, I was out of state but promised to meet and pray with her upon my return. By the time I did, another of her sisters had taken her life . . . on the previous Thursday.

Helping victims overcome generational sin is a regular part of an exorcist's ministry.

3. Transferred Sins: Curses, Hexes, Spells, Demonic Blessings, and Jinxes

By transferred sin, I mean any evil that is spiritually willed by another. It is usually called a curse, a hex, a spell, a demonic blessing, or a jinx. Curses are sent, either by pronouncement or using a physical object over which a ritual has been performed (e.g., a voodoo doll).

Curses are real and can serve both divine and evil purposes. While a blessing is a desire for another's well-being, a curse is its opposite: an explicit wish that someone receives misfortune, harm, or injury.

Scripture is replete with examples of curses. God threatens with curses as retribution for wickedness and infidelity (Gen. 12:3, Deut. 28:15, Prov. 3:33, et cetera). When it produced no fruit, Jesus destroyed a fig tree through a curse (Mark 11:12–25). Saint Paul invoked a curse on the Jewish sorcerer Elymas, striking him with blindness (Acts 13:4–12). Chapter 9 explains *why* curses are effective.

Benedict was a graduate student I met years ago while serving as a chaplain at a university. He experienced a period where he found it impossible to engage in his studies. When reading, he recalled nothing by the time he had reached the end of a page. His class lectures made no sense, and he could not find the motivation to complete assignments. Devoid of energy, Benedict slept over twelve hours a day. Were it not for a roommate who brought him food, he would not have even eaten as he found leaving his room exhausting. The only commitment Benedict undertook—no matter how weary he felt—was to attend daily Mass, a habit he had maintained since childhood. Upon returning, however, he felt so depleted that he slept for hours.

It was only after a year of this debilitative state—with no doctor able to diagnose a cause—that Benedict shared what was happening with his mother, as he could no longer continue school. Without telling him, his mother arranged to spend a night of intercession for him along with a friend. During the night, each woman had a vivid image of a multitude of snakes slithering from beneath Benedict's shirt during the vigil.

When Benedict awoke the following morning, things were dramatically different. Everything was physically brighter. He described it as being like sunglasses he was unaware he had been wearing were suddenly removed. He found himself with his old energy and zeal. The lectures he attended made perfect sense, and when he read, he retained everything. He could function normally again.

After three days, however, the dimness returned; Benedict could not read, lectures were incomprehensible, and he was fatigued. He informed me of the new turn of events. Placing my hand on his head, I prayed a simple exorcism prayer, asking God to remove whatever was afflicting him.[6] When I finished praying, the darkness was no longer present, and by day's end, he confirmed the other malevolent symptoms were also gone.

Two weeks later, the symptoms returned. Benedict was a devout Catholic, and his morality was beyond question. I was confident he was not mentally ill or given to exaggeration and he was doing nothing to invite evil upon himself. When I asked why he thought these things were occurring, he told me an unusual story.

Benedict was from Eastern Europe, the youngest of six children. When he was seven or eight, an old lady named Borya—a distant relative who lived near his family—arrived outside their home screaming. Some misfortune had befallen her, and she attributed it to Benedict's family. Reaching into a bag, Borya pulled out a live chicken and, while slicing off its head, declared that Benedict and his siblings would fail in whatever they undertook. The family chased her away and never gave her words another thought. Less than two years later, rebel soldiers killed her and dismembered her gruesomely.

As the years progressed, Benedict's siblings moved out of the country one by one to attend university. Each dropped out of his academic program and never graduated. Later, each one experienced problems such as difficulties involving infertility, a partner's infidelity, a sudden and unexpected divorce. Frequent job losses and financial struggles also plagued them.

Benedict fared the worst by far. As an undergraduate, he experienced none of the struggles of his siblings during their bachelor's degrees. However, as soon as he began graduate school, they started with a vengeance, and he experienced them worse than his siblings. "She put a curse on us, Father," Benedict declared. "I am sure of it."

I began another simple exorcism on Benedict, still uncertain that a curse was behind his affliction. While praying over him, I observed something I had never before seen: Benedict's face looked like an angry older woman's, bitter and full of resentment. He was perfectly still and was not contorting his face. It was as if someone else's face was superimposed over his.

I took it as a sign that there was indeed a curse, and I began to meet with Benedict to pray for its breaking. Benedict also began his rigorous prayer regimen for the same. While both our efforts helped, they merely seemed to manage the curse's symptoms. While the "darkness" and the academic afflictions never returned, new symptoms took their place.

For the next three years, efforts against the curse felt like a frustrating process of moving two steps forward but one step back. Benedict suffered from loss of appetite, emotional instability, spontaneous and unjustified resentment against those closest to him, and "bad luck." This last symptom was especially uncanny. Since Benedict was an international student, he regularly interacted with the government concerning his immigration status. Without fail, every government document issued to him contained numerous errors (his name, address, immigration status, country of origin, medical records, et cetera). No matter how often he corrected them, the subsequent documents issued contained new errors. Twice, his file's errors were so severe that his visa was canceled, and he received notice to depart the country. Last-minute reversals only came after proving the government agency had made the errors.

It took over three years and many prayers—both on my part and Benedict's—to bring him liberation from the curse's most crippling effects. There was never a dramatic moment where the curse completely broke, just a slow grinding down of its worst effects. Every so often, a new symptom manifested, setting off new rounds of prayer. His case remains the most debilitating curse I have ever encountered and illustrates how pernicious curses can be.[7]

———————

Doors are wonderful: they allow things in; they keep things out. Demons require a door, an entry by which they receive the legal right to demonize, harass, and oppress. They do not attach themselves to people arbitrarily. They must either be let in or sent in.

Attaching himself to a host is only a demon's first step. His second step is to access his host's wounds, exploiting and manipulating his victim's injuries, hurts, illnesses, or dysfunctions.

The above cases show how wounds are necessary to demons and how strong their hold on the victims may be once they secure them. If people only knew the suffering and anguish a demon can produce, no one would ever again open a door to one.

FIVE

AN EXORCISM SESSION

THE CASE OF
THE DISAPPEARING EIGHTH GRADER

"Get away from me, you pervert! You filthy priest!" Lena screamed as I went to sit in the chair next to her.

Lena was thirteen years old. The accusations of impropriety her demon was screaming at me are why exorcists have witnesses present when they work with minors. Aside from fulfilling their assigned tasks, my team members also serve as witnesses. I also have at least two female team members present to ensure credibility should accusations of misconduct be leveled against me.

I insist that at least two family members be present when I exorcise a minor, and one family member must be a female.

The fact that an exorcist has a team of witnesses and a policy requiring the presence of family members would speak loudly in a legal case regarding his credibility and professionalism. Demons are cunning, and an exorcist needs to protect himself from the false accusations they would be happy to engineer against him. Demons can convince their victim that the priest has done something inappropriate by planting false memories or creating bogus mental images.

"Get away from me, you pervert!" Lena screamed again.

The journey that landed Lena in my office started with an argument with her mother, Rita, over her eighth-grade class photo. Lena was Rita's only child, and her mother had a tradition of hanging her class photos in the hallway of their home. After getting a print elegantly framed, she would indicate where Lena was in the picture with loving, though intentionally loud and gaudy, scrapbook decorations. It was a tradition that Rita started when her daughter was a child.

But when Lena's latest class photo arrived in the mail, Rita was angry that her daughter was not in the picture. Aside from spoiling her tradition of having the class photos in the hallway, she had purchased Lena a new dress for the occasion.

When confronted, Lena insisted she had been present at the photoshoot. However, when she looked at the picture, she was as surprised as her mother to find herself missing. Lena remembered where she had been standing at the picture taking, but there was an empty gap at that spot. Rita accused her daughter of skipping school and demanded to know where she had been. Lena indignantly exploded in response to her mother's accusation.

Lena had never felt close to her mother. She found her mother overbearing, bossy, and self-centered. She worried about things like money, safety, and keeping things under her control. When Lena was ten years old, her father, Dave, left her mother. Two years later, Rita married Mike, whom Lena detested, finding him too much like her mother.

Lena dearly missed her father and worshipped his memory. He was fun, spontaneous, and greeted her at her bedside each morning. He had taken Lena on long walks, wrote her poetry, sang to her while playing his guitar, and stayed up late talking with her. The day he left was the worst day of her life. He left a note saying he was going to pursue a singing career on the West Coast and that he would come back for her. Lena believed his leaving was caused by her mother's contrariness and was therefore her fault.

Rita loved her daughter but found her impossible to please. When Dave abandoned them, she had mixed feelings. On the one hand, Rita had never loved him and was free to find someone else. On the other, Dave had been Lena's full-time babysitter.

Rita and Dave had dated briefly during their sophomore year in college. When Rita got pregnant, they moved in together but never married. Rita dropped out of school after Lena was born. Dave stayed in school another semester before dropping out himself. He never held a job, nor did he ever look for one. In all the years they were together, Rita was the breadwinner. Dave was the epitome of laziness in her eyes: he strummed his guitar all day, writing songs that would never bring in any income. Ever the dreamer, he fantasized about a music career that would never happen.

Besides watching Lena, the only initiative Dave ever showed was growing marijuana in the basement, which he smoked throughout the day in the attic. After he left, Rita heard from him only once: he emailed asking for a $500 loan to get an apartment. He also asked her to tell Lena he loved her, though he never called to tell her himself.

After Dave left, Lena lived as a shell of the happy child she had once been. For a year she struggled to eat and sleep, and cried frequently. She never called her friends anymore, said nothing in class, and avoided her mother, shutting herself inside her room whenever she was home.

Lena took up reading. She started with novels she received as birthday presents. She then borrowed books from the library and began reading them immediately upon arriving home from school, stopping only when called for dinner. After dinner, she would go right back to reading. Rita was concerned at the amount of time Lena was spending alone, but she was glad that her daughter finally had the energy to do something other than grieve her father's absence. Besides, she too liked to read, and she saw in Lena's love of reading something of her own genes.

Lena began using her birthday and Christmas money to buy books. She loved a series of fantasy novels that chronicled the adventures of a group of young friends who stumbled upon magical hats inside a thrift store. The hats enabled them to exit reality and create a new one, like the Holodeck on *Star Trek*. The series' author had a vivid imagination and a powerful gift for storytelling. One novel centered on the group discovering buried treasure and using it to buy airplanes, massive playhouses filled with games, a zoo, et cetera. In another novel, they went back in time to be present at the signing of the Declaration of Independence, secretly adding their names to those of the other signatories, which then became immortalized in history.

The ability of the characters to create whatever reality they desired enthralled Lena. That was just what she wanted—to escape her current life and create a new one. She read through the series, reread them a second time, and then a third.

Lena daydreamed about going back in time to when her father still lived at home. She imagined making a mom-proof plan with him before he left, so he could come and take her to live with him without anything stopping it. She would give him a private email address so he could contact her, which her mother did not know about and could not monitor.

Lena painstakingly created fantastical daydreams. In one, she imagined her father organizing an enormous eleventh birthday party at which musicians sang Lena-themed songs and poets recited Lena-themed poetry. The party took place on an ocean marina her father now owned, complete with a dolphin nursery he'd named after her.

In another daydream, she accompanied her father with a team of scientists to Canada to save a rare species of eagle from extinction. Their job was to collect the eggs from the last known nests in the wild to breed them in captivity. While traveling to a remote nest, they chanced upon a man from a native tribe trapped after slipping into a ravine. He led them into a series of previously unknown stalactite- and stalagmite-filled caverns in gratitude for being rescued. The caverns had beautiful pools of blue, green, and red waters, each filled with unique species of fish.

In Lena's alternative reality, her father had become a world-famous singer, but he only sang songs about her. She was world-famous as a result, receiving crates of fan mail each week. Some fans complimented her looks, others expressed how much they longed to be her, and still others sent gifts and asked for advice about everything from school and homework to relationships and how to become famous. World-renowned, Lena and her father needed protection from the paparazzi. They became masters of disguise and employed a team of professional actors and undercover security agents who facilitated their sneaking into the next live show her father was to perform.

Lena lost herself in creating fantasies, and it felt to her that she lived through each one, experiencing even smells and sounds. At first, Lena wrote out the details so that nothing would be forgotten. But she soon discovered she could relive a particular episode whenever she desired and modify it with new information and experiences.

Before, Lena had read to escape reality, but now she stopped reading altogether. She obtained that escape from the stories she was creating in her mind.

Rita was still fuming about Lena's absence from the school picture. She called the school and demanded to know why she had not been notified of her daughter's absence on picture day. The school's records showed Lena as present the whole day. Rita then inquired with Lena's homeroom teacher. She recalled seeing Lena in the auditorium during the photo taking and even remembered Lena's dress.

Lena had a dentist's appointment, so Rita picked her up from school. It was a tension-filled drive, with each still smarting from the confrontation about the school picture. Once they arrived at the office, Lena sat in one of the empty waiting room chairs while her mother reported her daughter's arrival to the receptionist. While standing at the counter, Rita looked at the receptionist's security monitor displaying a live video of the waiting room. She saw herself standing in front of the counter, but Lena was nowhere to be seen. All the chairs were empty. Believing Lena had bolted, Rita turned around, ready to bound for the door, when—to her astonishment—she saw her daughter sitting in the same chair as before. Lena looked relaxed, with her eyes closed, and a slight smile was on her face. Puzzled, Rita turned to look at the security monitor again, but the dental assistant, who had just stepped into the waiting room, called Lena for her visit. Lena got up out of her chair and walked into the examination room. Rita followed.

On the drive home, they stopped to pick up takeout for dinner. When they arrived at the house, Lena wanted to shower before eating. Rita placed the food in the oven to keep it warm, poured herself a glass of wine, and sat in the living room next to Mike. Then she heard a piercing yell.

"Where the hell is it?" Lena screamed from upstairs. "What did you do with it?"

"What are you talking about?" Rita called out with a start.

"My bath towel. It's not here, dammit!" Lena screamed.

"I put it in the wash this morning. And don't use that tone with me," Rita retorted as she started walking upstairs to confront her daughter.

"You have no right to touch anything of mine!" Lena roared back. "My dad gave me that towel," she added. "Don't ever touch it again!"

Just then, Mike joined them. "Lena, stop acting like a brat and be kind to your mother for once," he admonished.

"Get lost, jerk," Lena fired back. She closed her eyes and leaned against the bathroom wall. Her mother was about to raise her voice when the anger left Lena's face, replaced by a look of total relaxation. A slight smile began to form on her face. Then, faintly, Rita heard Lena say, "Hi, Daddy."

"Lena," Rita called, "Lena, look at me." Lena's face remained transfixed. Rita found her sudden change in demeanor creepy, and she turned toward Mike with a bewildered look. But Mike was looking at the mirror over the bathroom sink.

"Michael," Rita called.

Without taking his eyes off the mirror, Mike lifted his hand and pointed to it. Rita looked in the direction of his finger. All three of them were standing in the bathroom. The mirror, however, only displayed reflections of Mike and herself. There was no reflection of Lena.

Unnerved, Rita called out Lena's name, which produced no response. She put her hand on Lena's shoulder to give her a shake. Without the slightest change in her expression, Lena shoved her mother. Rita flew out of the bathroom and crashed into a desk that stood in the hallway. Mike stepped toward Lena, and she punched him so hard that he fell windless to the floor. It was minutes before he could even stand up. Lena stood in the same place in the bathroom, transfixed and smiling.

Mike was stunned. The force of Lena's punch was beyond that of which a thirteen-year-old girl was capable. Far beyond. It was as hard a hit as any he had ever taken, and he had grown up with four brothers. He stood and attempted to lift Rita, who was whimpering and favoring her left hip, which had hit the desk's corner.

Rita was unable to stand. Her hip was fractured, and she would be unable to walk for weeks. The punch Mike received herniated his abdomen and necessitated surgery. For her part, Lena acted as if nothing had occurred and, when asked about it, claimed she did not recall the violence but only the confrontation about the towel.

Rita knew something was not right with Lena. She feared Lena might react violently again. She was now afraid of her daughter.

Two weeks later, while Rita was still convalescing after hip surgery, she heard Lena arrive home from school as she sat in the living room.

"Sweetie," Rita called out. "Sweetie, can you please bring me some water. I need to take my pain pills." A moment later, Lena arrived with a glass of water. "Thank you, sweetie," Rita said. "How was your day?" Rita asked.

"Fine," Lena replied as she began to walk away.

"Can we chat a moment, Lena?" her mother asked.

"Um. I have lots to do."

"Lena, please sit down," Rita said. "I just want to ask you a couple of questions." Lena remained standing. "The day of my accident, you said that your bath towel was a gift from your father."

"It was."

"But that's impossible," Rita replied. "Your father lives on the other side of the country."

"He comes to see me," Lena replied. "He picks me up and takes me places—every day." Lena looked baffled at her mother's look of incomprehension.

"What do you mean?"

"He comes to see me."

"He comes here?"

"Yes. And takes me where he lives."

Rita was at a loss. She did not want to say anything that would set off Lena's temper. Mystified, all Rita could think to say was, "What's it like to see him?"

"Oh, it's wonderful," Lena answered. "He takes me to different places, and I've met so many new people. I just love living with him."

Living with him . . .my baby has lost her mind, Rita thought to herself, grief-stricken. As much as she tried to prevent it, a tear ran down her cheek. Anxious to not appear upset at what was evident happiness for Lena, Rita said, "I miss seeing him," almost gagging on the words but hoping the tear might pass for sorrow at Dave's three-year absence.

"You do?" Lena replied, astonished.

"I do," Rita answered. "How does he look?" she added.

Sitting down in the easy chair across from her mother, Lena replied, "He looks wonderful. He's writing the best music ever. He has a band he sings in that . . ."

Lena wanted to cry. Her baby was mentally ill, and this realization caused terrible anguish inside her, sending tears down her cheeks. As she listened to her daughter's accounts of her father's nonexistent visits, Rita silently turned to God in the most earnest prayer she had ever managed. *Dear Lord, help my baby. Please, help her. Please heal her . . .*

"Stop that!" Lena yelled.

"I can't help crying, baby," Rita answered.

"It's not your crying," barked Lena.

"Then what?"

"What you were doing."

"What was I doing?" Rita asked. Lena was silent. After the pause got awkward but unsure of what made Lena displeased, Rita said, "I'm sorry, Lena. I'm just upset. Please continue."

Lena began to relate a nonsensical experience in the most elaborate detail. As she did so, Rita planned to get Lena a referral to a mental health specialist, thinking, *Maybe if we intervene in time, Lena can snap back to her normal self.* She began to pray again silently. *Oh please, God, she's been through so much. Please don't let this happen. Please heal her . . .*

"STOP THAT!" Lena screamed.

"Stop what?"

"You were praying."

Rita was dumbfounded. She wondered why praying bothered Lena. But more than that, she wondered how Lena even knew she was praying—something Rita occasionally did but never openly. "I'm sorry, sweetie," Rita replied. "Go on with your story."

Rita listened attentively to Lena's relating of her imaginary experiences, trying to appear more attentive, to mask what she was honestly thinking. She tried to express interest in Lena's stories and delight in hearing the details. Here and there, Rita even asked a question of clarification or two to show she was paying close attention. When Rita was confident she had proved her attentiveness, without changing her body language, she began silently reciting a Hail Mary. *Hail Mary, full of grace . . .*

"%&$# YOU! I TOLD YOU NOT TO DO THAT," Lena shouted as she picked up a vase and threw it against the mantel smashing it to bits. She then stormed out the front door.

Rita was shocked and wondered how Lena identified the exact moment she was praying three times. It's as if her daughter could read her mind. *Mental illness doesn't cause that,* she thought.

Rita called her parish priest, who subsequently put her in touch with me. Because many of Lena's symptoms appeared to be consistent with mental illness—periods of disassociation from reality, vivid hallucinations that have no extramental reality, sudden outbursts of violent rage—all beginning after the period of depression following her father's leaving, I asked her mother to take Lena to a psychologist for a mental assessment. Sure enough, Lena was diagnosed with psychosis, a condition in which a person cannot differentiate the real from the imagined.

The doctor wrote a thorough report that assessed Lena's symptoms scientifically. However, there were symptoms the psychologist could not explain. The first was the strength behind Lena's attack on her mother and stepfather. Lena gave her mother a push from a standing position—she had no running start—and the momentum sent her mother flying out of the room. Lena weighed 87 pounds, while Rita weighed almost twice that at 162 pounds. Likewise, the punch Mike received, which ulcerated his stomach, was delivered without any "windup," yet it sent a fit 205-pound man to the emergency room.

The other unexplained symptom was Lena's ability to know when her mother was secretly praying. While it is sometimes possible to accurately guess what someone is thinking, there is no natural way Lena could know all three times the precise moment her mother engaged in silent prayer. There was also no reason why her response should be one of instant fury. Thus, even though Lena was diagnosed with a mental illness, an assessment by an exorcist was warranted.

Rita and Mike brought Lena to see me on a Saturday afternoon. Lena was cooperative and answered each question I asked straightforwardly. By this time, she had seen the psychologist for two months and accepted that she had a mental illness. He had convinced her it was unreasonable to believe her experiences were real and that they were common signs of psychosis. He did this by breaking down Lena's hallucinations into their parts.

He pointed out that her "experiences" were always preceded by a burst of anger and resentment brought on by her father's absence and usually directed toward the cause of his leaving—her mother. Lena had reported a second sensation that followed the anger: mild pleasure that steadily increased until it became so intense and euphoric that Lena felt powerless to resist it. When she consented to it—an act she described as "letting it take over"—Lena would suddenly find herself living a false experience with her dad, but one that felt so real she took it for reality. In time, she discovered she no longer required anger as a springboard to enter this delusional state but could cause it directly just by willing it.

Allowing the psychologist to examine Lena helped because by the time I met with her she already knew her experiences were hallucinations. The psychologist proved to her that these three occurrences—the losing of her temper, the euphoric feeling, and her consenting to that feeling—were manifestations of an abnormal mental state. He noted, for example, how there was no time lapse between her "consent" and the beginning of a new experience with her father. She would be in her home one moment and then on the other side of the country the next, with no travel between.

While her episodes were so vivid that Lena took them for reality, the psychologist made her realize that she never physically left the place where she was before the hallucination began. In other words, her father was not visiting her and taking her to where he lived. Lena came to accept that and recognized there was something wrong with her belief that he did. This meant that Lena was still rational—and not delusional—even though she was prone to occasional psychotic hallucinations.

What I had to discover was whether there was anything demonic afflicting her. As I have mentioned, prayer is the surest way to find out. I explained to Lena that I wanted to ensure that her hallucinations were due to psychosis alone and not to anything demonic. To that end, I asked her whether it was okay for me to pray with her, asking God to remove anything that was not of Him from her life, especially if it was present in these experiences. She agreed. I asked her permission to place my hand on her head as I prayed. She again agreed. I only got as far as standing up . . .

"Get away from me, you pervert!" Lena screamed as she shot out of her chair. "Stay the %&$# away from me!"

Lena had a demon. Just anticipating my moving closer was enough to cause his manifestation.

"I am %&$#ing out of here," snarled Lena as she headed toward the door.

"In the Name of Jesus," I said, "I command you, demon, to stop harassing Lena and to depart from her. Lena, sit back down in the chair!"

The look on Lena's face suddenly changed from one of contempt and disgust back to the neutral appearance of the thirteen-year-old with whom I was speaking moments earlier. She turned around and started walking back to her chair, but her feet would no longer move. It was as if they had become glued to the floor, even while the rest of her body was still moving forward. Amazingly, although the bottom of Lena's feet were still flat on the floor, her body was leaning forward at a forty-five-degree angle, with her head only some three feet off the floor. She turned her head up to look at me and screamed: "What's happening to me?"

"Demon," I called out, "in the Name of Jesus, I command you to unbind her feet." Lena fell to the floor. Her face once again contorted, and her eyes rolled into her head so that only the whites were visible.

"The pig is mine," the demon derided. "She gave herself to me."

"Her baptism made her the daughter of God the Father," I replied. "In the name of Jesus Christ, Savior of the World and Son of that same Father, I command you, and any like you, to depart from her!"

"Go %&$#yourself, priest," the demon belted. "I am her father. She asked me to be her father."

"Only because you deceived her," I replied. "And for doing that, God will increase your punishment."

"%&$# you, priest. The pig is mine. She'll have lots of fathers in hell. As many as she wants."

I reached into my bag and pulled out a relic of Saint Joseph, the foster father of Jesus. It contains a fragment from a piece of his clothing—his cloak—venerated from ancient times in the Basilica of St. Anastasia in Rome. I placed it up against the back of Lena's head. The demon howled, "Get him off me! Get him off me!"

HEALING FROM ALL MANNER OF WOUNDS

Lena needed eight exorcism sessions before she was free of the demon, who confessed in the third session that he entered her shortly after her father left when she abandoned all hope of ever being happy. Anyone would be depressed at losing one's father. Still, Lena's *prolonged* state of depression was demon-induced, and it was all part of a plan to make the deceptive euphoria of her hallucinatory experiences that much more convincing.

Lena's liberation required a four-part healing process. The first part was that she had to accept that her father had abandoned her, which was difficult and traumatic. But once she recognized that her experiences were hallucinations, the cold reality of her father's decision became obvious. Though it caused her tremendous anguish, she accepted it as reality.

The second part was that Lena needed to forgive her mother for the defects—actual and imagined—that she held against her. She had to accept her perception of her mother as inaccurate and her anger as unjustified.

The third part was that Lena needed to forgive herself for having a father who abandoned her. While objectively speaking, she committed no wrong, the human psyche is peculiar. It will often hold itself responsible for the misfortunes and disappointments that come its way, even though it had nothing to do with causing them. Lena had to release herself from the symptoms she felt at having a father who coldly abandoned her, including:

- thinking that his abandonment and subsequent lack of communication were somehow "her fault."
- believing that if she had been a better person he would never have left.
- believing she was worthless.

Finally, Lena had to claim her identity as a daughter of God and renounce having accepted the demon who deceivingly presented himself as her father. Lena's mental illness made this a challenge. When reality became difficult, psychotic imaginings made her naturally gravitate to disassociation. Yet, the fact that the demon entered Lena proved she had enough psychological and moral freedom to choose a lie. When hallucinating, she knew at least partially that she was exiting reality. For example, the "go-getter" personality her father exhibited within her hallucinations was different from how he had always conducted himself. Her opting for this lie—a father who dramatically changed for no reason—was a door by which a demon accessed her. Lena may struggle with schizophrenic hallucinations her whole life and will fight the temptation to exit reality when life gets difficult.

Lena remains, for me, one of the starkest cases of someone who became possessed because of a traumatic wound. Hers is a textbook case of how the Church's ministry of exorcism and the psychological sciences can work together to resolve an unfortunate person's suffering.

THE GIRL NOT IN THE MIRROR

So why did Lena's image not show up in her class photo, the monitor at the dentist's office, and the bathroom mirror? In other words, what made Lena "disappear"?

Demons can manipulate the physical world. While a demon cannot remove a person from physical reality, he can manipulate light. Sight is possible because light serves as a medium of physical reality. When we see a tree, for example, what is visible is the light reflected off the tree. In the case of Lena, the demon manipulated the light she reflected, preventing her image from appearing in the class photo, the dentist's video monitor, and the bathroom mirror.

The second issue still unresolved is why the demon produced that particular phenomenon—her lack of reflection—since it is the very thing that led to his expulsion. Mike's observation that Lena did not cast a reflection in the mirror had led to the violence that ultimately ended with her receiving an exorcism.

This question is more difficult to answer. Exorcists often find it challenging to understand why a demon acted in *this* manner rather than another or what the purpose of *this* phenomenon might be. It was only after some years that I felt confident in explaining the disappearance of her image. My explanation requires understanding what the demon was trying to do with Lena.

Demonic activity flows from the sordidness of a demon's will. Lena's demon was out to destroy her. He sought first to have her believe—through her father's abandonment and what she perceived as an overbearing mother and a cold, distant stepfather—that she was forever condemned to misery. The evidence is the debilitating depression she experienced after he left: she was hopeless and empty. Then the demon offered Lena a way out: he facilitated a fantasy world where she could produce her own reality. While the fantasy world brought her out of depression, she became dependent on entirely illusory experiences.

These two moves were designed to get Lena to change her belief about reality. If the demon could alter her perception of the real, he could control her—which he did. The ultimate expression of that control was to make Lena's very image disappear. Her image not showing up was the demon *proudly* boasting, "Lena's not here anymore. I've got her somewhere else."

Why would the demon risk his plan's success by causing her image not to appear since that is what indicated his presence? That is an example of a demon's broken nature. Just as a person who is in a blinding rage or is severely intoxicated is intellectually blinded, so demons are often blinded by their own vices and rage. Lena's demon was executing an effective plan, but he was too prideful, arrogant, and smug to keep it discreet. He could not resist proclaiming his machinations as if he were already raising a hand in final victory. Saint Thomas Aquinas, one of the greatest theologians who ever lived, described one of sin's main effects as follows: concupiscence darkens the intellect.[1] Put simply, sin makes you stupid. Lena's impetuous demon proves Aquinas' point.

The demon's bragging prevented the success of what I believe was the third part of the demonic plan. Had the demon remained in Lena, he would have dragged her deeper into the world of illusion. Then, after she was entirely dependent on it—emotionally and mentally—he would collapse the fantasy and expose everything

Lena treasured as the worthless product of make-believe. That collapse would be more crushing than even her father's leaving, producing abject hopelessness. The demon's goal would then be to convince Lena to take her life.

After the demon's eviction, Lena's image appeared normally in mirrors and on screens, just as before she became possessed.

————

The job of the exorcist is to discover the rights the Devil has gained that enable him to attach to his victim. Once he knows the demonic rights, the exorcist can aid the victim in rescinding them. This annulling of rights is what freed Lena from the monster who was afflicting her. It is also what frees everyone who is suffering from the same.

Lena's liberation was greatly aided by the work of a skilled psychologist whose scientific training identified detrimental wounds in her psyche. The therapy he provided her for these wounds—supplied in conjunction with the exorcism ministry she was receiving from me—facilitated her liberation.

While it is common today to hear of the alleged incompatibility between science and faith, in my experience the truths of faith and science are harmonious. The same God gave each us both gifts, so one does not contradict the other any more than God can be in contradiction with Himself.

In exorcism, science and faith work harmoniously to bring about liberation. While faith, of its nature, is above reason, any perceived dissociation between them does a disservice to the victim and risks leaving him bereft of lasting healing.

SIX

HEAVENLY BACKUP

"Not him, you %&$#n priest!" the demon roared. "I %&$#n hate him."

The demon was reacting to an image of Alessandro Serenelli I was attempting to position over the shoulder blades of its possession victim. When I went to slip the same prayer card down his shirt-sleeves, the demon thrashed with such violence that the men helping hold him could barely restrain him. It took two stout men per arm to restrict each appendage.

When the first card was in place in the sleeve, the demon turned toward it and spoke to it as if it were a person.

"I %&$#n hate you!" it bellowed. "Get off me!"

Alessandro Serenelli is the infamous murderer of an eleven-year-old girl whom he mortally wounded in a botched rape attempt in a small Italian village on July 5, 1902. She died of peritonitis the following day after the bacteria from her intestinal tract leached into her bloodstream and ate her alive. As she lay in agony, she uttered some of the most heroic words ever spoken: "I forgive Alessandro Serenelli, and I want him with me in Heaven forever."

The twenty-year-old Serenelli was unremorseful, declaring at his trial that he wounded the girl while defending himself from *her* sexual attack. He was sentenced to thirty years in prison.

Six years into his prison sentence, Maria appeared in his cell, handing him fourteen white lilies, one for each time he stabbed her. Her gratuitous forgiveness filled Serenelli with contrition. Whether Maria's appearance came in a dream or a vision, one thing is certain: the event touched Serenelli so profoundly that, in an instant, he changed from being a violent, unremorseful murderer and would-be rapist to a gentle and humble Christian.

After serving twenty-seven years of his thirty-year sentence, he was released, the last three years being commuted because of his exemplary behavior after Maria's apparition. Nevertheless, his release began perhaps an even more difficult period of his life.

Though some would hire Serenelli for odd seasonal jobs, the pay was low, and the work was always temporary. Even when hired, the money was never enough for him to obtain a dwelling, and almost no employers were willing to shelter him, fearing for their safety and that of their families. One farmer, knowing of Serenelli's past and ready to look beyond it, accepted him as a farmhand. Since Serenelli had been a farmer before the murder, he greatly appreciated the job. Not long afterward, however, even this opportunity ended abruptly: the man's wife approached him in the field, lay down on the ground, pulled up her dress, and commanded Serenelli to take her. Over the years, other women who, knowing of his past and craving an encounter with a "bad boy," echoed her scandalous offer. Serenelli took such proposals as his cue to leave town.

The former convict's restlessness, poverty, and troubles went on for years. His need eventually led him to the door of a monastery of the Passionist fathers, where he offered his services as a laborer in exchange for room and board. The priests accepted him, assigning him a room and giving him charge of the vegetable garden.

In a short time, another hired hand reported that a large sum of money—4,000 lire—had been stolen from his room.[1] The police were summoned, and Serenelli was taken to jail where the marshal repeatedly exhorted him to confess his crime and give back the money.

"But I have nothing to confess," Serenelli declared.

After fifteen days, it was discovered that the gardener had feigned the theft to be rid of Serenelli, whose work ethic he feared would cause him to lose his position. Upon Serenelli's release, however, the Passionists refused to allow him back at the monastery.

Eventually, Serenelli was accepted by the Capuchin Franciscans, a religious order noted for their embrace of poverty and austerity. He spent the first years as a gardener, but by 1945, due to his advanced age, he became the convent's porter, answering the door to its many visitors.

Serenelli remarked that he often prayed to his victim, whom he regarded as his protectress. He lived in the certainty of Maria's forgiveness and the hope it offered him. He never doubted that she was praying for him and desired his company in Heaven. But the thought of his crime never left him.

Once, as one of the Capuchin priests was lamenting that it never rained, Serenelli exclaimed, "If only it rained so much that it washed away even the bloodstains of my life. I still have to atone, but if the water of the Tronto River that passes near here had the power to wash the hands of criminals, I would submerge myself in the current day and night."[2]

Everyone who knew him agreed that Maria's forgiveness was the pivotal moment in Serenelli's life. Who knows the extent of the darkness that would have been his without that forgiveness? Until the day he left the earth, Serenelli repeated over and over, "Maria's forgiveness saved me."

As significant as Maria's forgiveness was, something else was equally as important: Serenelli had to accept that forgiveness. After becoming aware of the full weight of his crime's gravity, he had to choose to release himself from guilt. Such an act requires humility and courage. It would have been tempting and far easier—as Judas who betrayed Jesus demonstrated—to walk away from the offer of forgiveness and to accept the bogus notion, "What I have done is too big and too ugly to be forgiven." Serenelli took up the long and heroic battle against those thoughts, and he faced the world squarely on with the identity of being the murderer of a little girl he brutally killed in a rape attempt, a girl whom the Catholic Church canonized a saint on June 24, 1950, the youngest in its history.

Serenelli lived the rest of his days humbly and prayerfully. He embarked on the path to Christian perfection, and his holiness became evident to all who knew him. A priest who lived with him once remarked, "If I wished to describe in two words Alessandro's spiritual form, I would say that he is a 'penitent saint.'"[3]

Using Serenelli's prayer card in exorcism is how I learned the extent of his "sainthood." I produced the prayer cards myself in 2015 after Pope Francis proclaimed an extraordinary Jubilee Year of Mercy, a year of focus on the virtue of mercy and forgiveness. To prepare the United States for the occasion, the Vatican asked me to bring the major relics of Saint Maria Goretti, the Little Saint of Great Mercy, on a pilgrimage of the country, and over 250,000 people came to visit her mortal remains.

To mark the occasion and provide pilgrims with a memento of the pilgrimage, I produced a prayer card of Saint Maria that was given to each pilgrim. I touched each to her relics to make them into what Catholics call third-class relics (see Acts 19:11–12). However, I also gave each pilgrim a prayer card of Alessandro Serenelli in hopes of initiating a devotion that might lead to his eventual canonization. I touched each of Serenelli's cards to a letter that he handwrote.

Printing cards of someone who is not yet beatified or canonized is an informal but common practice in the Catholic Church. The cards show an image of the person, a prayer asking God to grant his or her glorification, and a petition that some request be granted through the individual's intercession. Such cards are a means to promote popular devotion to the cause.

Sacred images connect us with Heaven. They move the heart, facilitate intimacy, and help build faith. Enter a Catholic church and you will find it is adorned with such images on the walls and windows—in virtually every sacred space. The veneration of holy images is to religion what the treasuring of photographs of deceased relatives is to any family. After family members pass away, photographs are often our closest connection with them. In humans, the heart is unceasingly fed by the eyes.

That is why, if an exorcism cannot take place in a church or chapel, as a minimum, the Rite of Exorcism calls for images of Christ crucified and of the Blessed Virgin Mary to be prominently displayed. Most exorcists have multiple saints images on hand, even if they are just prayer cards, which he touches to the demon, noting any saint toward whom the demon displays particular contempt.

Occasionally I will hold a sacred image up to the demon, but my preference is to slip them inside the victim's shirt at the spine, where the neck meets the shoulders, and inside each sleeve. Why these locations? When a demon manifests, he often does so from the back toward the front: as if he "stepped" into the person from behind. Thus, I have found demons especially sensitive to holy objects applied to the spine and back of the neck. Since demons communicate their rebellion through their arms (flailing, striking, et cetera), these are effective locations to place holy objects.

I have used various prayer cards during exorcisms, but the demon's response when I used the Serenelli cards in the above case was the most visceral I have seen. Later in the session, the demon revealed his name as "Murder." It all fit perfectly. The onetime murderer proved himself to be a formidable weapon against this rebellious angel, who made no secret that he was disgusted with him. Once Serenelli became infused with the light of Christ following his conversion, his presence became torturous to the enemy.

In every exorcism since that occasion, I have placed a Serenelli card inside the back of the victim's shirt and inside each sleeve. They have become my preferred weapon. The demons never fail to express hatred of him as they thunder orders that I remove them. In one recent case, the demon departed as soon as I touched the victim's neck with the first card. He never returned.

Serenelli is an effective heavenly backup against the demonic precisely because they recognize him as one that "got away."

THE TOOLS OF THE EXORCIST

An exorcism is a process of acts to cast out demons. Though they may not know it, Christians do many things that are exorcistic. A pious recitation of the Our Father, with its petition, "deliver us from evil," is one example. Another is applying holy water, either on one's person (e.g., crossing oneself with it) or on one's property or possessions (e.g., in the home or car). Any act of faith (a prayer, a pious action, an act of charity done for the love of God and neighbor, et cetera) is exorcistic since it moves one closer to God—our ultimate Good—and away from Satan and his kingdom. All these acts of faith are caustic to demons.

When someone is possessed, his demons usually prevent him from doing anything exorcistic, such as praying or using holy water, and he requires the Church's intervention to attain freedom. This intervention is called solemn or major exorcism. An exorcism for anything short of possession is called minor or simple exorcism or deliverance prayer.

The Church prescribes several tools to aid the exorcist in conducting a major exorcism.

The Rite of Exorcism

The Rite of Exorcism consists of prayers and rituals in which the Church uses its unique, Christ-given authority to attack possessing demons.

No official ritual existed in the first fifteen centuries of the Catholic Church. Each diocese had its methods for combating evil. However, during the reign of Pope Paul V (1605–1621), a standard ritual reflecting the "best practices" of the ages was issued. The *Ritus Exorcizandi Obsessos a Daemonio* (*Rite of Exorcism of the Possessed*) was published as part of the *Rituale Romanum* (*Roman Ritual*) in 1614 and an abbreviated Rite was issued in 2004. The latter has been subsequently translated into various languages, enabling exorcists who cannot read Latin to perform an exorcism.[4]

The first rule governing the use of the Rite states that only a priest may use it.[5] There is a good reason for this. Exorcism is dangerous, and one who is uninitiated can quickly find himself in trouble.

The exorcist's task is to place himself in the "breach" between the demon and his victim. If he is unprepared for such a confrontation, he can become a victim himself. If his faith is weak, he may be overwhelmed when he discovers the Devil's power. If he is inexperienced in demonic tactics, he may end up as the plaything in the Devil's mind games and may find himself worn out and exhausted in short order. If he is morally impure—if he has sin on his soul—he loses all protection that grace affords him and opens himself to being possessed. While in the earliest centuries the Church entrusted the ministry of exorcism to laypersons, for reasons of safety, it has appointed exorcists only from among her priests. By virtue of his sacramental, apostolic ordination, a priest "possesses the authority to act in the power and place of the person of Christ himself."[6] In form, authority, and holy tradition, the apostolic priest is the Second Person of the Trinity. When the demon looks at a priest—any priest—he sees Jesus.

However, the Church does not permit every priest to exorcise. An exorcist must receive delegation from his bishop, who does so only when convinced of the priest's "piety, knowledge, prudence, and integrity of life."[7] Without possessing his bishop's permission, it would be dangerous and foolish for a priest to attempt an exorcism, as he would be working outside the unique authority Christ granted to the Church to destroy the gates of hell (Matthew 16:18). Not only would his commands lack power, but the priest would lack the protections he needs against the demons' attacks.

This does not mean that priests who are not exorcists cannot cast out demons. Any baptized individual can perform simple deliverance on someone or something under his authority, if he does so with faith, e.g., parents can command demons to stop harassing their children; spouses can command the same regarding one another; a proprietor can command demons to vacate his business, et cetera. However, in cases of possession, the demonic hold on the victim is so strong that the Church has wisely reserved that ministry to specially trained priests whom it empowers to exorcise.

Another exorcist once told me about his first encounter with possession. He had not yet been appointed an exorcist by his bishop, and his diocese did not have one at the time. A man called, claiming his wife had a demon. She spoke in strange voices and became violent when any prayer was said near her. The priest went to the house and, upon entering, a masculine voice bellowed from inside the woman, "What the %&$# do you think you're going to do, priest? Your bishop hasn't even appointed you." The woman was not a Catholic, and did not know about Catholicism, yet she recited the law of the Church that required him to obtain delegation to perform the exorcism. Even if she had learned that fact, she could not have known that the bishop had not authorized him to exorcise. But the demon inside her knew. As long as the priest lacked authority, the demon knew he was safe. Safe enough to boast and openly challenge the priest.

Before beginning an exorcism, the exorcist prepares himself through prayer and fasting. He purifies himself through the Sacrament of Confession and receives the Holy Eucharist during the celebration of Mass.

———

The Rite begins with the **Litany of the Saints**, a prayer invoking the intercession of the entire heavenly Church. The exorcist pays special attention to the demon's distress or annoyance when a particular saint is named. The exorcist will invoke that saint's intercession throughout the Rite since the demon has already revealed that the saint wounds him.

After the Litany of the Saints, the recitation of different prayers, of Psalm 53 and of various Gospel passages, recall God's love and His incomparable strength and sovereignty. Only then do the deprecatory and imprecatory prayers of exorcism follow.

Deprecatory Prayers

While the parts of the Rite where the priest directly commands the demon are the most renowned—made famous by such movies as

The Exorcist—the deprecatory prayers are, in fact, the most important. The word "deprecatory" comes from the Latin *deprecatio* ("an
invoking prayer"). These are prayers of supplication in which the
priest begs God for the victim's liberation, for efficacy to be given
to his commands, and for success in casting out the demon. God
is the true exorcist, not the priest. The priest appeals to His mercy
because if the exorcist is to be effective, it will be because God has
deemed it so. This is why deprecatory prayers always precede any
direct commands against the demon in the Rite.

The following is an example of one of the deprecatory prayers.
(The symbol ✠ indicates where the exorcist makes the Sign of the
Cross.)

*God, Creator and defender of the human race, who made man
in your own image, look down in pity on this your servant,
(name), now in the toils of the unclean spirit, now caught up
in the fearsome threats of man's ancient enemy, sworn foe of
our race, who befuddles and stupefies the human mind, throws
it into terror, overwhelms it with fear and panic. Repel, O
Lord, the Devil's power, break asunder his snares and traps,
put the unholy tempter to flight. By the sign ✠ (on the brow)
of your name, let your servant be protected in mind and body.
(The three crosses which follow are traced on the breast of the
possessed person). Keep watch over the inmost recesses of his
✠ heart; rule over his ✠ emotions; strengthen his ✠ will. Let
vanish from his soul the temptings of the mighty adversary.
Graciously grant, O Lord, as we call on your holy name, that
the evil spirit, who hitherto terrorized over us, may himself
retreat in terror and defeat, so that this servant of yours may
sincerely and steadfastly render you the service which is your
due; through Christ our Lord. All: Amen.[8]*

Imprecatory Prayers

The word "imprecatory" comes from the Latin word *imprecatio* ("calling down of curses"). Rather than petitions made to God, these are commands made directly to the demon, such as the following:

I adjure you, ancient serpent, by the judge of the living and the dead, by your Creator, by the Creator of the whole universe, by Him who has the power to consign you to hell, to depart forthwith in fear, along with your savage minions, from this servant of God, [name], who seeks refuge in the fold of the Church. I adjure you again, ✠ (on the brow) not by my weakness but by the might of the Holy Spirit, to depart from this servant of God, (name), whom almighty God has made in His image. Yield, therefore, yield not to my own person but to the minister of Christ. For it is the power of Christ that compels you, who brought you low by His cross. Tremble before that mighty arm that broke asunder the dark prison walls and led souls forth to light. May the trembling that afflicts this human frame, ✠ (on the breast) the fear that afflicts this image (on the brow) of God, descend on you. Make no resistance nor delay in departing from this man, for it has pleased Christ to dwell in man. Do not think of despising my command because you know me to be a great sinner. It is God ✠ Himself who commands you; the majestic Christ ✠ who commands you. God the Father ✠ commands you; God the Son ✠ commands you; God the Holy ✠ Spirit commands you. The mystery of the cross commands ✠ you. The faith of the holy apostles Peter and Paul and of all the Saints commands ✠ you. The blood of the martyrs commands ✠ you. The continence of the confessors commands ✠ you. The devout prayers of all holy men and women command ✠ you. The saving mysteries of our Christian faith command ✠ you.

Depart, then, transgressor. Depart, seducer, full of lies and cunning, foe of virtue, persecutor of the innocent. Give place, abominable creature, give way, you monster, give way to Christ, in whom you found none of your works. For He has already stripped you of your powers and laid waste your kingdom, bound you prisoner and plundered your weapons. He has cast you forth into the outer darkness, where everlasting ruin awaits you and your abettors. To what purpose do you insolently resist? To what purpose do you brazenly refuse? For you are guilty before almighty God, whose laws you have transgressed. You are guilty before His Son, our Lord Jesus Christ, whom you presumed to tempt, whom you dared to nail to the cross. You are guilty before the whole human race, to whom you proffered by your enticements the poisoned cup of death.[9]

The language and style of imprecatory prayers are dramatically different from deprecatory prayers. Imprecatory prayers address the demon authoritatively, and the truth of his misdeeds are thrown at him in a heap of abuses. He is reminded of his sins not because the demon has forgotten them, but because the truth is itself exorcistic.

Exorcism is the act of replacing the demonic spirit inhabiting the victim with that of Christ. It is not Catholic "magic." Exorcism always weakens a demon, though expelling him may take multiple sessions. There also may be multiple demons inhabiting the victim that may need to be exorcised individually. In which case, the exorcist prays the Rite again, either on the same day or at another time. While some cases of possessions are, thankfully, finished in one or a few sessions, sadly, others can last many years. In my personal experience, as well as that of most of my colleagues, the average case of possession lasts around nine to fifteen months, with an exorcism being performed at least once a week.

Location for Exorcisms

The Catholic Church insists—whenever possible—that an exorcism occur inside a church or chapel. There is good reason for this. Just as in the old covenant, Yahweh resided in the Temple in Jerusalem, so in the new covenant, Christ is truly present in the Tabernacle of every Catholic church and chapel where the Holy Eucharist is reserved.

The Eucharist is a great strength to the exorcist. When a demon inhabits a person, he subjects himself to the conditions of the physical world. The Eucharist's physical nearness is itself the demon's silent opponent, whom it attacks and weakens before the exorcist even does anything. The demon will attempt to avoid this by preventing his victim from entering the building, causing him great pain if he should try to do so. It is not unusual that a victim must be carried to his exorcism.

If a victim is too incapacitated to travel, the exorcist may have to conduct the ritual in the victim's own home. Regardless of where it occurs, for the sake of the victim's dignity, the Church demands that the location chosen be discreet and private, void of spectatorship and any possibility of eavesdropping.

The Imposition of Hands and Exsufflation:
Touch and Breath

The Rite calls for the imposition of hands: a gesture found numerous times in the New Testament symbolizing both the touch of Christ (Mark 10:14–17; Luke 4:40) and the imparting of the Holy Spirit (Acts 6:14–17). Symbolically, it makes the priest's role as a conduit of God's grace real and visible. I do not recall laying my hands on a victim during an exorcism where a demon did not recoil while angrily screeching, "Get off me!" or "Don't %&$#n touch me!"

The Rite also calls for the exorcist's most unusual action which is exsufflation: blowing in the face of the demon. The gesture recalls the act of Creation when, after forming man out of dust, God breathed into him His life-giving spirit (Gen. 2:7). It also recalls Christ's breathing the Holy Spirit upon His Apostles following His resurrection (John 20:22). One could describe exsufflation as the Church imparting the Holy Spirit upon the victim to refashion him after an evil spirit has marred him.

I recall the reaction—the level of which amazed me!—when I performed exsufflation on a demon for the first time. The demon had threatened to kill the victim if I did not cease with the exorcism, and he had been so violent and combative that the men restraining the victim were exhausted. When I blew into the demon's face, he stopped all his movement and laid motionless for several moments. It is as effective a weapon at stunning a demon as I have seen.

The Priestly Stole: An Attire for Exorcism

The exorcist's attire is simple. On top of his clothing, he wears an alb (a white robe symbolizing the purity imparted by Baptism), or if he is wearing a cassock, he wears a surplice over it (basically, a short alb). Regardless of which garments he chooses, the rubrics for exorcism call for him to wear a purple stole. Purple is the ecclesiastical color associated with healing. That is why, for example, a priest wears a purple stole when he hears confessions.

The stole is perhaps an odd-looking garment. It is a strip of material some four inches wide and typically six to seven feet long. The priest hangs it around his neck, with the ends draping down over each shoulder and hanging over each breast—as if he were wearing an upside-down letter U. But for how it is worn, it might appear similar to a scarf, although it is not. The stole symbolizes the authority of the priesthood and of the priest himself. When a priest acts with that authority—celebrating Mass, baptizing, marrying a couple, forgiving sins, blessing an object, et cetera—he wears a stole. A stole's odd shape is due to what it symbolizes: the yoke worn by beasts of burden. A driver commands his beast and wields authority over it. However, the beast possesses the driver's authority to go where it is commanded. It is a perfect analogy for the priesthood. A priest has no power of his own but receives it from God under whose authority he remains. The priest, however, possesses the authority to do what God commands. When a priest acts *as priest*, he has the authority of Christ. Demons are the first to attest to this.

Several years ago, one of my mother's friends found out I would be visiting my mother for a week. An excellent seamstress, she decided to make me a stole as a gift. She purchased purple material at the fabric store and, within two hours, had sewn a purple stole.

On this visit, a local priest asked for my assistance in diagnosing a case he thought might involve a demon. I drove to his office, bringing along the stole I had just been given. We interviewed the man in question. Afterward, I asked whether I could put my hand on his shoulder and pray with him. As I was doing so, I picked up the edge of my stole with my free hand and lightly touched him on the shoulder, next to my other hand. The touch was so light I doubt he could have felt it. He shot out of the chair, blurting, "What did you do? My shoulder is burning!"

Twenty-four hours earlier, that purple fabric was on the shelf in a store. Were the man touched by it at that time, he would have felt nothing. However, having been sewn into a stole and used by one vested with Christ's authority, it was a conduit of Christ's power.[10]

The Crucifix

The crucifix—a cross with the image of Christ crucified on it—is a symbol of His victory. To the Christian, the crucifix is a reminder of the depth of God's love. To the demons, it is a reminder that their future will consist of everlasting defeat. How Christ achieved His victory was one that not even the demons could have imagined with all their incredible intelligence. Jesus, the Son of God-made-man, willfully submitted himself to torture and murder, not out of weakness, but out of the invincible strength that comes from love. Paul calls Christ crucified "the power of God and the wisdom of God" (1 Cor. 1:24).

The Rite of Exorcism calls for the priest to bless the victim with a crucifix. The demons find it abhorrent, and its touch afflicts them. During one of Lena's exorcism sessions, I held a crucifix to her shoulder for an extended period. I uttered no prayer—I just kept it against her shoulder. At one point, the demon stopped his struggling, turned to me, and asked, "Why are you torturing me?"

Holy Water and Blessed Salt

The use of holy water is a well-known Catholic practice. Holy water fonts exist at the entrances of churches. A priest sprinkles an object with holy water after he blesses it. Catholics preserve holy water to bless their homes and family members. Less known today is blessed salt, but its use is as ancient—and its effect as formidable—as that of holy water.

Because it explicitly produces a weapon to combat evil, the rite for making holy water in the 1952 *Roman Ritual* is something with which every exorcist is familiar. It calls for blessed salt to be added to holy water. Before each element is blessed, the priest invokes an exorcism prayer to remove any demonic authority attached to it. There is a good reason for this. Satan became the prince of this world and everything within it when Adam fell. Since ordinary water and salt are to be employed as weapons against evil, any power Satan has over them is removed by prayer and blessing so that they may inflict maximal damage.

The ritual is as fearsome as it is impressive. The exorcism of salt begins as follows:[11]

> *God's creature, salt, I cast out the demon from you by the living*
> ✠ *God, by the true* ✠ *God, by the holy* ✠ *God, by God who*
> *ordered you to be thrown into the water-spring by Eliseus to*
> *heal it of its barrenness. May you be a purified salt, a means of*
> *health for those who believe, a medicine for body and soul for*
> *all who make use of you. May all evil fancies of the foul fiend,*
> *his malice and cunning, be driven afar from the place where*
> *you are sprinkled. And let every unclean spirit be repulsed by*
> *Him who is coming to judge both the living and the dead and*
> *the world by fire.*

The blessing that follows transforms the salt into a weapon against evil.

> *Almighty everlasting God, we humbly appeal to Your mercy*
> *and goodness to graciously bless* ✠ *this creature, salt, which*
> *You have given for mankind's use. May all who use it find in*
> *it a remedy for body and mind. And may everything that it*
> *touches or sprinkles be freed from uncleanness and any influ-*
> *ence of the evil spirit; through Christ our Lord.*

The priest then exorcises the water:

> *God's creature, water, I cast out the demon from you in the*
> *name of God* ✠ *the Father almighty, in the name of Jesus*

✠ *Christ, His Son, our Lord, and in the power of the Holy*
✠ *Spirit. May you be a purified water, empowered to drive*
afar all power of the enemy, in fact, to root out and banish
the enemy himself, along with his fallen angels. We ask this
through the power of our Lord Jesus Christ, who is coming to
judge both the living and the dead and the world by fire.

The blessing follows:

O God, who for man's welfare established the most wonderful
mysteries in the substance of water, hearken to our prayer, and
pour forth Your blessing ✠ *on this element now being prepared*
with various purifying Rites. May this creature of Yours, when
used in Your mysteries and endowed with Your grace, serve to
cast out demons and to banish disease. May everything that
this water sprinkles in the homes and gatherings of the faithful
be delivered from all that is unclean and hurtful; let no breath
of contagion hover there, no taint of corruption; let all the wiles
of the lurking enemy come to nothing. By the sprinkling of
this water may everything opposed to the safety and peace of
the occupants of these homes be banished, so that in calling on
Your holy name they may know the well-being they desire, and
be protected from every peril; through Christ our Lord.

Holy water is used throughout exorcism, both at the Rite's
beginning and whenever the exorcist sees fit. It is instrumental
when a demon is obstinate, combative, or prevents the victim from
communicating with the exorcist.

Blessed salt is used in the same manner. At the beginning of an
exorcism, I try to place some on the victim's tongue. The demons

find it oppressive and attempt to spit it out. Anyone who has had too much salt on his tongue can attest that it is impossible to remove it simply by spitting it out. Its presence is a constant source of pain to demons throughout the exorcism.

Oil of Exorcism (i.e., Oil of Catechumens)

From her earliest days, the Church anointed those preparing to become Christians (catechumens) with the oil of exorcism, today commonly known as the oil of catechumens.[12] Most priests are only aware of this oil's use within the baptismal rite, but it can be used at any time for its exorcistic qualities. It is wonderfully effective. During an exorcism, I anoint the victim's hands, forehead, temples, back of the neck, and spine. The demons find these areas especially sensitive, and the oil injures them. I reapply it liberally during the exorcism.

A priest colleague told me a fascinating story about an infant's baptism. There were rumors that the man the family picked to be the godfather was involved in criminal activity and that he lied about practicing the Christian faith. Little did he know how much his lie would embarrass him.

During the baptismal ceremony, when the priest applied the oil of exorcism to the baby's chest, the man jumped some seven feet into the air backward, landing on top of the altar on his knees while belting out the thunderous howl of a wolf. Aside from the efficacy of the power of the oil, worth noting is the bond or "circuitry" that exists when people form relationships with one another. The anointing of the baby received *here* was felt by his godfather standing over *there*. When the man agreed to be godfather, he consented to be spiritually related to the baby. When the baby was anointed, that connection caused the oil's exorcistic effect to flow back to him, afflicting the demons inside him.

The Communion of Saints and their Relics

If even a saint's image is injurious to a demon, so much more so are his relics. His mortal body will one day be reunited with his soul in the final resurrection (Phil. 3:20–21) and thus remains a part of him.

Sacred relics are proof of the truth of one of Christ's great promises: His followers will do even greater works than He did (John 14:12). No one can doubt that throughout the Church's history, many miracles have occurred through the intercession of the saints. History is replete with such testimony. Even long after their deaths, the mere presence of their relics has occasioned countless miracles.

For over two decades, I have ministered with relics in an evangelization ministry known as Treasures of the Church. In that period, I have seen various illnesses and medical conditions—cancers, stroke effects, osteoporosis, necrosis, even lifelong paralysis, et cetera—disappear completely when the afflicted person has venerated a relic in faith. These miracles were instant, complete, and permanent.

I have received thousands of letters from people reporting how their faith was deepened by praying in the presence of sacred relics. However, the same holiness within relics that produces healing and increased faith also delivers an exorcistic effect.

The great Saint John Chrysostom († 407 AD) describes relics as subverting and dissolving "the snares . . . and all the devices of the Devil."[13] Saint Hilary of Poitiers († circa 368 AD) observes how demons "howl" when relics are in their presence.[14] Saint Jerome († 420 AD) declares that even the dust of the saints' bodies torment the demons and causes them to burn with "invisible flames."[15]

A most remarkable ancient account comes from Saint Ambrose, the bishop of Milan († 397 AD). Ambrose had built an enormous basilica, but he lacked relics to place beneath its altar—a practice observed since apostolic times. In a dream, he was shown the location of the graves of the city's first two martyrs—Saint Gervasius and Saint Protasius—who were murdered some two centuries prior.

Ambrose set out to uncover their bodies. Knowing only the graves' general location, he was unsure of the martyrs' precise burial places. Ambrose, however, made provision for this. Along with his excavation team, he brought along a possessed demoniac whose presence he was sure would provide a miraculous sign to disclose the relics' location. When the demoniac came near the grave, he was seized and thrown to the ground in a gesture indicating the saints were immediately present, a fact that excavation confirmed. The two martyrs were moved inside the basilica, and multiple demoniacs were liberated in their presence. Ambrose has left us a detailed account of the torments the relics inflicted.

> We have today heard [the demons] say, that no one can be saved unless he believes in the Father, the Son, and the Holy Spirit; that he is dead and buried who denies the Holy Spirit, and believes not the almighty power of the Trinity . . .The evil spirits said today, yesterday, and during the night, [to the relics] "We know that ye are martyrs . . . Ye are come to destroy us."[16]

Especially noteworthy is the claim that the demons spoke to the relics *as if they were speaking to the saints themselves*. In the exorcisms I have performed, I have always encountered this phenomenon. When I apply a relic to the demon, he will often turn to it and say, "I %&$#n hate you!" Sometimes, even before I take a relic out of the case, the demon will yell out, "I hate that one! Leave him in there!" I have never seen a demon regard a relic as mere "matter" but as the saint himself. Countless times I have heard them testify that sacred relics are formidable weapons that cause them injury.

Bells

Who does not take pleasure in hearing the melodious ringing of a church bell? Still, it may surprise some to see bells on an exorcist's weapons list. The Church learned long ago the power bells possess: they put to flight the powers of the air.

Exorcists (and their team members) often use bells during exorcisms. Not only does their ring injure demons, but it subverts their power and, for a time, renders them unable to defend themselves. This result should not be surprising. When the Church blesses a bell, it entreats God to make its ring produce this very effect: "Deign, we implore you [Almighty God], to pour out the dew of thy blessing ✠ on this bell . . . and let it ward off every disturbance of the evil spirit."[17]

Even if it has not been blessed according to the Church's formal ritual, if it has been used for sacred purposes—such as at Mass during Consecration of the Eucharist—a bell's ring is injurious to demons. The reason is ironic. A bell's ring praises God, which is the very purpose for which the devils (as angels) were created but refused to do. All praise renders God present, for Scripture tells us that God delights to manifest Himself when He is praised (Psalms 22, 42, and 43). Since bells fulfill the task demons have abandoned, they have superseded them in dignity, and because their activity renders God present, it is harmful to them.

If the Church takes small, handheld bells seriously enough to have an exorcism and blessing for them, it takes a principal bell that hangs in a bell tower and whose ring travels vast distances with great seriousness. Case in point, the Church has a blessing for a bell's metal even while still in a molten state. Once cast, a bishop subjects the bell to a long series of blessings and exorcisms so its ring may yield a supernatural effect. After a choir chants seven psalms, the bishop mixes salt with water while reciting prayers of exorcism.

These prayers are similar to those used in the rite of blessing holy water described earlier, but they include a petition that God transforms the bell into a weapon. After washing the bell inside and out with holy water, the bishop prays:

> *[Lord,] grant, we beseech Thee, that this vessel, prepared for Thy Holy Church, may be sanctified ✠ by the Holy Ghost, so that, through its touch, the faithful may be invited to a reward. And when its melody shall fall upon the ears of the people, may they receive an increase of faith; may all the snares of the enemy, the crash of hail-storms, hurricanes, the violence of tempests be driven far away; may the deadly thunder be weakened, may the winds become salubrious, and be kept in check; may the right hand of Thy strength overcome the powers of the air, so that hearing this bell they may tremble and flee before the standard of the holy cross of Thy Son depicted upon it, to Whom every knee bows of those that are in Heaven, on earth, and under the earth, and every tongue confesses that our Lord Jesus Christ, swallowing up death upon the gibbet of the cross, reigneth "in the glory of God the Father" (Philippians 2:10), with the same Father and the Holy Ghost, world without end. Amen.*[18]

The bishop then anoints the bell with the oil of the sick and with sacred chrism and names it after a saint whom he invokes as its patron. He then prays:

> *Do Thou pour out upon this bell a heavenly benediction ✠, so that at its sound, the fiery darts of the enemy, lightning strokes, hail-storms and the damage of tempests may be driven far away, and . . . may those whosoever assemble at its call*

be free from all the temptations of the enemy, and may they always follow the teachings of Catholic faith . . . Pour out upon this bell the dew of Thy Holy Spirit, so that at its sound the enemy of the good may always flee, the Christian people may be invited to faith, the hostile army may be struck with terror.[19]

For centuries, church bells have communicated with the greater community. A bell's ring summons believers to worship, joyfully proclaims that two spouses are united in marriage, somberly announces a person's death, and loyally reports the time of day. With each ring, however, the bell also peals an exorcism through the air. In some instances, a bell's ringing even serves as a counterpoint to the Church's liturgical prayer. For example, when a bell announces someone's death, its ring drives evil spirits away from the now separated soul. Later, at the burial, the Church completes its intercession by praying, "Hasten to meet him, Angels of the Lord! Receive his soul and present him to God the Most High. May Christ, who called you, take you to himself; may angels lead you to the bosom of Abraham."[20] While the bell's "voice" drives the wicked angels away, the Church's voice implores the holy angels to lead him to paradise.

That the consecration for a steeple bell includes the petition for its ring to dissipate storms and mitigate their effects reflects the Church's belief—one inherited from Judaism—that diabolical agency can manifest itself in severe weather. Fierce inscriptions were often written on bells declaring their power over such. For example, the major bell of the Erfurt Cathedral in Germany declares, *Fulgus arcens et demones malignos* ("I ward off lightning bolts and malignant demons"). A bell at a church in northeastern France asserts, *Ego sum qui dissipo tonitrua* ("It is I who dissipate the thunders").

And at Basel, Switzerland, another simply states, *Ad fugandos demones* ("For scaring away demons").[21]

The Liturgical Calendar

The liturgical calendar consists of the various liturgical seasons, holy days, and feasts that mark the year. If worship can be called the Church's breath, the liturgical calendar is the rhythm of her breathing.

The date selected for an exorcism is not insignificant. I find exorcisms are more effective when conducted on important liturgical days, such as those that honor the mysteries of Christ (Christmas Day, the Incarnation, Good Friday, Easter Sunday, the Ascension, et cetera) and those that revere God (Pentecost, Trinity Sunday, et cetera). Saints' feasts are also significant since the saints are not disinterested parties in our fight against evil; they lend their assistance through their intercession. A feast ordinarily celebrates the saint's entrance into Heaven, which is painful for the Devil because of its irony. Satan gave up his place in Heaven to destroy humans, but now a human occupies the very place he surrendered. Aside from paying a saint homage, every feast day declares Satan a loser.

Satan despises all saints, but there is one he loathes the most: Mary, the Mother of God. Mary is the only person who was fully obedient to God's will, and her obedience began the chain of events that enabled the Savior to win the world's salvation. Without Mary, there would be no Incarnation. Without the Incarnation, there would be no reconciliation with God. Without reconciliation with God, there would be no salvation. Without salvation, Heaven would be closed, and humans would remain the Devil's possession forever.

Several years ago, I assisted another exorcist during an exorcism that occurred on July sixteenth, the day Catholics venerate the Blessed Virgin Mary under her title as Our Lady of Mount Carmel. Mount Carmel is where the prophet Elijah challenged the 450 prophets of Ba'al. I had helped with this possession case for years, and it was one of the most difficult I have ever encountered. Although the victim received weekly exorcisms, her situation dragged on for years. She had three demons, mute spirits who were as stubborn and powerful as any I have ever encountered. They never uttered a word (cf. Matt. 9:32; Mark 9:17; Luke 11:14), and they kept their eyes perpetually closed. Their faces exhibited nothing but smugness and mocking defiance.

Years of exorcisms had driven out merely one demon from the victim—and the weakest demon, at that. Years later, it seemed like we were no closer to driving out the other two. However, on this day, the demon who manifested was Ba'al, whom we had battled countless times before in this poor woman.[22]

The account of Elijah's triumph over the prophets of Ba'al, recorded in 1 Kings 18, was read aloud during the session by one of the team members. In those verses, each side called on its deity to consume their sacrifice of a bull by producing a miraculous fire. Ba'al's prophets went first, calling on him for hours, to no avail— no fire appeared. It was then Elijah's turn who ordered his sacrifice to be drenched with water, and only after, did he pray. At his petition, fire fell from the sky, so intense it consumed the bull, the wood beneath it, the stones, the earth, and even the water that filled the trench around it. The witnesses proclaimed, "The LORD, he is God; The LORD, he is God" (1 Kings 18:39); then, seizing all 450 of Ba'al's prophets, they brought them to Elijah, who slaughtered them.

The exorcist provoked Ba'al, asking him what it felt like to be humiliated by Elijah on Mount Carmel, losing every one of his prophets. The demon barked out an ugly profanity. The priest and I looked at each other stunned. He spoke! He had never done so before.

We kept praying, asking Elijah to battle this ancient enemy once more. The ordinarily calm and cool Ba'al became more agitated and vocal with each invocation of Elijah. His pain increased until he was overwhelmed and howled in agony. Elijah did the wounding, as we exorcists were doing nothing. "Stop it! Stop! Leave me alone!" he shouted as he flailed his arms wildly. Ordinarily, this demon would not make the slightest physical movement but exhibited complete and unbothered defiance. The epitome of smugness and self-satisfaction, his stoicism and self-control were some of the eeriest qualities I have ever seen in a demon.

All demons are defiant. But Ba'al was doubly so. When we commanded him to answer a question, he ignored it. Only after a lengthy calling upon the Lord, the angels, or the saints would he comply. However, he did so only with bodily signs—through hand gestures—but never verbally. We knew he was capable of speech. All demons are. But nothing we did could ever force him to do so.

The fact that Ba'al showed physical distress was something we had never witnessed. Suddenly, he screamed, "Nooooo!" repeatedly. Shortly afterward, he belted out an enormous agony-laden scream that filled the chapel. Then he was gone.

On the Feast of Our Lady of Mount Carmel, the hero of Mount Carmel, Elijah the Prophet, emerged to exorcise his old nemesis.

There are many more tools exorcists may use, such as the praying of the Rosary, the chanting of sacred music, and the use of incense, but no single element is vital for an exorcism's successful outcome, including the Rite of Exorcism, which surprises some. Remember that no official Rite of Exorcism existed for the first fifteen centuries of the Church. Instead, exorcists simply prayed in faith and used whatever was available to them: the community's prayers, the words of Scripture, the intercession of the saints, et cetera.

In most of the exorcisms I have conducted, I did not use the Rite but chose instead to pray extemporaneously, supplementing my prayers with the use of relics, sacramentals, and holy images. Put simply, I pour out my faith in God on behalf of the victim. There are many ways in which the demon has me beat: his intellect is far superior to mine, his understanding of human nature—and of me in particular—far outweighs the knowledge I possess of him, my physical strength is no match for his, and he is endowed with patience and endurance to levels that I can never match. Nevertheless, there is one area in which I—and, presumably, every exorcist—has him completely outmatched. I possess more faith than he has. In the realm of divine faith, I have yet to hear a demon brag about his superiority.

Without a doubt, the Rite of Exorcism is a hammer that wounds demons effectively. As an official prayer of the Church, the Bride of Christ, it powerfully expresses her divine faith. If the exorcist himself lacks faith, though, the tool is ineffective. Far from being magical, the Rite of Exorcism funnels and joins the faith of both the Church and the exorcist to pound against the demon until he flees. Without that faith, the demon remains perfectly safe inside the victim he occupies.

SEVEN

THE OCCULT WORLD

THE CASE OF
THE OUIJA BOARD THAT WOULDN'T DIE

The Ouija board planchette[1] spelled out "SIGN" with a continuous and unhesitating motion. "What is that supposed to mean?" asked Matthew.

Gowan sneered. "It means you're dumb enough to believe you're communicating with a spirit."

"I swear this thing is moving by itself," Walt interjected. "None of us is moving it!"

"I've read about people getting messed up by Ouija boards," Anton blurted. "I know it's stupid to believe in them, but after seeing this one move, I admit I'm intrigued."

"If it says it can produce a sign, let's see if it does," Peter impatiently remarked.

Matthew, Tom, Walt, Gowan, Peter, and Anton were friends in their late teens and early twenties at the apartment of a seventh friend—Ed. He had offered his place for beer drinking while he was away. Tom found a Ouija board on his living room shelf and suggested they try it. After saying, "I invite whoever is out there to

159

communicate with us," Tom placed his finger on the planchette and, joined by the fingers of the others minus Gowan, began lightly pushing it around the board. After a few moments, the planchette moved with a life of its own, alternating between tracing out the shapes of a circle and a star.

While none had ever experimented with a Ouija board before, all but Gowan were intrigued. For him, believing in the spirit world—or even believing in God, for that matter—was absurd: the equivalent of believing in pixies and tooth fairies.

Tom asked out loud, "You moving this planchette . . .who are you?" The planchette stopped patterning and spelled: "Stevie. I am eight." "Stevie" identified himself as the spirit of a young boy who had died fifty-two years prior. The members of the group peppered him with different questions. "How did you die?" "Where did you grow up?" "Where are you now?" "What's it like being dead?" For each question, the planchette spelled an answer: "Car accident"; "Dunhill Road"; "In the room with you"; "Awful. I'm scared."

"Ask if he swings on monkey bars," mocked Gowan, convinced that his friends were moving the planchette themselves. In response, Stevie spelled, "I hate Gowan." Matthew asked Stevie whether he could do something to prove to Gowan he was real. "Yes," Stevie replied. "Sign." Ed, the apartment's owner, had a stolen STOP sign nailed to his wall. It hung directly behind the couch where Gowan was sitting. Within seconds, the metal sign fell and landed on Gowan's head with a thud. For several moments no one spoke. Gowan himself finally broke the silence with a laugh while still rubbing his head. "It was just a coincidence," he said confidently. "This stupid thing was held by a single nail."

By this point, no one other than Gowan thought what was happening was make-believe. If Gowan also believed it, he never let on but continued to vocalize skepticism about the Ouija board.

The group challenged Stevie to do something to Gowan that would make him believe. "Vomit," it spelled out. "Hah!" Gowan blurted. "There's no way in hell I'm gonna vomit."

Suddenly Gowan wasn't just vomiting; he was projectile vomiting. From his place on the couch, vomit projected from his mouth with such force that it hit the wall four feet in front of him at eye level. His friends scattered, trying to avoid being hit by splashes of gastric fluids.

After Gowan cleaned his vomit off the wall and floor, the group was back in conversation with Stevie. "What else can you do with Gowan?" one asked. "Sleep," the planchette spelled out. With a chuckle, Gowan said, "I'm wide awake." In under half a minute, Gowan was audibly snoring on the couch, fast asleep. The five others took turns attempting to wake him—one even slapping him hard on the face—with no success. Nothing could rouse him. Finally, someone asked Stevie whether he could make Gowan wake up. Almost instantly, Gowan awoke, rubbing his eyes and asking how long he had been sleeping. "Ten minutes," someone said. "It feels like ten hours," Gowan mumbled.

By now, it was apparent they were interacting with something powerful and dangerous. While each was afraid, no one wanted to be the first to admit it. At the same time, what the group saw was so intriguing that each wanted to see "just a little bit more."

At this point, even Gowan believed his friends were in true communication with a spirit named Stevie, and he too took his place around the board. They began asking Stevie the most obscure questions—"Who played shortstop for the 1932 Red Sox?" "What is the circumference of Neptune?" "What is 456,546 x 870,872?"— and the planchette spelled out the answer immediately. It took longer for them to type the question on the computer's internet browser to verify the answer than for the Ouija board to spell it out.

By now, Gowan was the most vocal with amazement. His face displayed the astonishment of someone who had just discovered another world. One of the others even remarked to Stevie, "Even Gowan believes in you now."

"I HATE HIM," the planchette responded.

"What else can you do to him?" another one asked. The planchette immediately spelled out, "KILL HIM." A chill ran through their veins as—with a start—they simultaneously pulled their fingers off the planchette. Matthew slapped it from the board to prevent the planchette from spelling anything else. But rather than simply landing on the floor, it shot off the table as if self-propelled, thumping one wall, then ricocheting across the room and slamming the opposite wall, where it struck a framed picture of Jesus. The image belonged to Ed's grandmother, who had willed it to him. The planchette struck with such force that the glass shattered.

"I'm throwing this damn thing away!" Matthew declared, placing the Ouija board back in its box. Followed by the others, he carried it down the hallway and dropped it down the garbage chute.

Relieved that the board was now a memory, the group went to the convenience store across the street to buy cigarettes and beer. Once their purchase was complete, they returned to Ed's and let themselves in the apartment. On top of the coffee table—as though it had never been discarded—was the Ouija board. The planchette, moving autonomously, spelled, "You die," over and over.

"We need to get rid of this thing," Peter said.

"We did," Tom replied. "A lot of good that did."

"The damn thing is Ed's anyway," Walt interjected. "Leave it where it is. I'm not touching it anymore." The suggestion sounded good to everyone. They all turned around and left.

The week that followed was the most unpleasant any of them had ever experienced.

Each had conflicts with family members and friends, bouts of "bad luck," and unnerving occurrences. Two were fired from their part-time jobs for no reason. Three of them lost all the data on their computer hard drives. One could not get his car to start, while another found all four tires flat each time he went to use it. All of them experienced flickering lights and randomly moving objects inside their homes.

Each of them also had someone close to him report seeing him lying dead in a coffin in the most vivid dream that person had ever had. Though different people had the dreams, the scene was always the same: his body was being prepared inside a mortician's lab; was lying in a church while his funeral was unfolding; or was rotting in a grave.

But the most disturbing aftereffect was that of a presence they sensed was always around them. It was more than just a feeling of being watched; some were physically attacked by it. For example, Anton felt the blankets pulled off him one night, and a hand forcefully pushed his chest into the bed. With most of his body buried in the mattress, he reached up and felt a thick, muscular arm he could not overpower. Struggling to breathe, Anton squirmed and managed to turn his body and wrest it from beneath the arm. When he turned on the lights, he was amazed to find no one else in the room, though his chest sported an appalling hand-shaped bruise, complete with the marks of outstretched fingers.

One morning, as Matthew was sitting on the edge of his bed putting on his socks, something blunt—like a baseball bat—whacked the back of his leg, sending him to the floor, wincing in pain. He was left with an enormous welt on his calf and walked with a limp for over a week.

Peter discovered a live cockroach inside his glass of water during dinner. He wondered how it could have gotten there as he had filled the glass straight from the tap. Getting a new glass from the dishwasher, Peter filled it with tap water. Later, when he went to drink from it, a live cockroach was swimming inside it.

None of them knew how to stop the torture. Neither did any dare to tell his family what was happening. Some feared being reprimanded for dabbling in the occult. Others feared being ridiculed for believing in superstition.

Peter's mother occasionally visited a monastery of Carmelite nuns whom she asked for prayers. As a child, he'd often gone with her, so he personally knew the prioress, Mother Maria. She had always impressed Peter with her friendliness, humility, and wisdom. He was confident that he could confide in her and she would know how to put an end to their haunting torments.

Taking Anton with him, Peter drove to the monastery, rang the doorbell, and asked for Mother Maria. After a short while, Mother Maria met them inside the parlor, and Peter told her everything.

"You opened the door to evil," she reproved. "That was foolish."

"I know," Peter replied. "I just want to undo it. What can we do?"

"Repent and go to confession," she said somberly. "Burn the Ouija board too. Then you should be fine."

Peter and Anton went to the local church and asked the priest for the Sacrament of Confession. With a newfound peace the Sacrament gave them, the two drove to Ed's apartment and collected the Ouija board, which was exactly where they last saw it, though now it was motionless. They went to the convenience store, purchased a can of butane lighter fluid, and drove to the edge of town, pulling into a cornfield.

The cornfield stood behind a stone fence, which would give them privacy from the passing cars. Between the wall and the cornfield was a dirt path, slightly wider than a tractor. On the path's edge, about two feet from the first stalks of corn, Peter and Anton piled sticks and twigs onto a bed of dried leaves. It was getting dark, so the two worked quickly, soaking the pyre with butane and then lighting it with a match.

As the fire devoured the kindling, the two broke the Ouija board into pieces and fed them into the flames. Because it was made from particleboard, the fire quickly consumed it. That is, except the piece containing the word NO, which would not burn. Building up the fire with more kindling did nothing. While the flames got higher and the fire got hotter, the piece sat in the middle of the fire and would not burn.

By this time, the sun had gone down, and it was dark. Suddenly, a truck pulled in off the road and turned toward them with its headlights shining. With hearts pounding and aware of how bizarre their doings looked, Peter and Anton began to think of a reasonable explanation for their trespassing and fire. The truck did not stop when it reached them but slowly passed them. Seeing the driver, who was looking straight at them, made the hair on the back of their necks stand. It was an old man, dressed in a checkered shirt and overalls. He had no face—no mouth, no nose, no eyes. His face consisted of skin over a flat, featureless skull. Frozen, they watched the truck drive past them and straight onto the cornfield, knocking down the tall stalks of corn in its way. Once the entire truck was in the cornfield, it simply vanished.

"Did you see that?" Anton blurted.

"How the hell could I miss it?" Peter answered. "Let's finish and get out of here."

By this time, the piece containing the word NO was smaller as the fire had begun to consume its edges. Anton kept squirting it with lighter fluid while Peter fed more sticks into the fire. Slowly, the piece became smaller and less legible. Finally, after ten minutes, with the butane can spent of its contents, the fire incinerated the last of it.

Neither Anton nor Peter experienced any more disturbances. After Tom and Matthew also went to confession, the tormenting stopped for them as well. In fact, the experience with the Ouija board was the onset of a spiritual conversion for all four. They began attending church and developed a prayerful life. They fell in love with Christ, dedicated their lives to serving Him, and eventually became leaders within their faith communities.

Unfortunately, the story did not have a happy ending for Walt and Gowan, who did not follow their friends down the path of repentance and conversion. Although they could see its positive effect on their friends, they refused to make God the center of their lives.

Walt was involved in a terrible car accident that left him permanently unable to work. Relationally, he went from woman to woman but was never able to find someone with whom he could share his life. Gowan was eventually arrested for possessing illegal content on his computer and served several years in jail. When released, he could only find work as a pizza delivery driver. While it's impossible to prove that Walt and Gowan's misfortunes were due to their encounter with the Ouija board, the contrast between their lives and that of the other four friends was so dramatic that it cannot be discounted as a possibility.

Looking back, the reason why the evil spirit had such easy access to Gowan during the Ouija board session (making him vomit, putting him into a deep sleep, et cetera) may have been because of the state of his soul. If it was weighed down by mortal sin, Gowan already belonged to the Devil. In which case, that would explain why the demon wanted him dead. A soul that dies in the state of mortal sin is damned. If this applied to Gowan, all the demon needed to gain him forever was for him to die.

There is a saying that one never stays the same after engaging a Ouija board. One either becomes better by giving his life to God and receiving His power and mercy, or one becomes worse. The lives of these six friends bear witness to the saying's truth.

THE OCCULT
One of the most common ways evil spirits attach themselves is through participation in the occult. The word "occult" comes from the Latin *occultus* ("that which is hidden or secret"), and it refers to the manipulation of powers hidden, or outside, the ordinary realm of nature.

The First Commandment states, "I am the Lord your God . . . You shall have no other gods before me" (Exod. 20:3). Participants in the occult sin against this commandment because their action commits at least one of the following offenses:

- Refusing to trust in God's goodness (e.g., that He will sufficiently provide for one's needs; that He will lead one to happiness, et cetera);
- Refusing to accept God's predetermined limits (e.g., the limits of one's natural human powers, the limits He has built into reality, et cetera).

These are precisely the sins the Devil committed at his fall. Thus, engaging in the occult mimics his primordial rebellion against God. *Occultism is the satanic desire to be God*; it denies God's identity as God and attempts to appropriate rights belonging to His divinity. It is why occultism is one of the easiest ways to acquire demons and why the demonic hold on occult participants is so difficult to break. To do violence to any of the Ten Commandments is gravely sinful, but to violate the First Commandment is the gravest sin since it is equivalent to renouncing God. Expelling demons who have entered through this sin requires that the victim repent of sin *and* submit to God's sovereignty.

With the de-Christianization of Western society, occultism is on the rise. Exorcists are called on to cast out more demons acquired through the occult than through any other means. The following is a list of some of the more common occult practices.

Ouija Boards

Among occult practices, perhaps no single activity has entangled more souls with demons than the use of the Ouija board. The famous 1971 William Peter Blatty novel-turned-movie, *The Exorcist*, was based on a true story. A chance encounter with a Ouija board was the cause of a fourteen-year-old boy's diabolical possession; in the story his character was changed to a girl. "Robbie," as he is known by pseudonym, was invited to participate in a Ouija board session by his aunt, a devotee of spiritualism who used it to communicate with the dead.

Part of the Ouija board's lure is its simplicity. Anyone may use it, either alone or with others, even in the comfort of one's own home. Manufacturers market it as a game, and it is readily available from toy stores or legions of online retailers. There is so little to a Ouija board that one can easily make his own. Its characters may be written on a sheet of paper, and something as simple as a ring can serve as a planchette. With little effort, one can produce a portal to the occult world.

Most Ouija board encounters begin with an "innocent" curiosity that leads to a decision to try it. A young woman once told me about her experience during high school while hosting a sleepover for her girlfriends. Her mother purchased a Ouija board from a department store for the occasion. Her mother's thinking was innocent enough. While she had heard stories about people becoming haunted by evil spirits after using the board, she took it for granted they were make-believe. She thought it would keep the girls nicely entertained for the evening, trading secondhand tales of Ouija board encounters while trying to make contact with a bogus "spirit world." Unfortunately, the evening's entertainment ended quickly.

Shortly after the girls began asking the board questions, the planchette spelled out, "Hello." They replied hello in return. At that moment, the family's three lounging dogs stood and growled as they gazed at the space above the board. Walking backward, the dogs lifted their gaze continually higher as though they were seeing something emerge from it. Each released a high-pitched whimper and bolted from the room. None of the dogs ever entered that living room again.

The dogs' reactions should have been enough to make the girls stop. Unfortunately, they were not. The girls asked the board foolish questions, the answers to which haunted them for years. These included queries about their past, such as "What happened on my twelfth birthday?" or "Where was my mother's maternal grandmother from?" The board always responded accurately. Two asked, "How will I die?"—"suicide" was the reply to one and "murder" to the other. For years, each suffered terribly about whether she would die as the Ouija board claimed. It worried one so much that she required two stays in a mental hospital before finishing high school.

Another asked, "When will I die?" The planchette reported back "18." From the day she turned eighteen, she experienced terrible anxiety about whether that day would be her last. She detested being alone, hated being inside a vehicle for fear it would be in an accident, and was terrified of the dark. Many days she was too anxious even to go to school. For a year, until she turned nineteen, fear of dying was the dominant motive behind many of her decisions.

While this case lacks the external phenomena of the case of the Ouija board discussed above—cockroaches manifesting in glasses of water, a piece of the board refusing to burn in a fire, et cetera— it is evident the girls were demonized. Their experience with the board left them with more than just psychological marks. The demon established a relationship that enabled him to manipulate and increase the girl's anxieties. While none of the girls became possessed per se, the demon's machinations left them bereft of peace.

Unfortunately, the girls' parents never brought them to a priest. Had they done so, the demon's hold could have been broken, Christ's victory could have been preached to them, their peace could have been restored, and they would not have needlessly suffered for years.

Séances, Mediums, and Necromancy

The Devil and his demons are parasitic. Incapable of pity, they will do anything to seize their prey. One of the most trying experiences someone can go through is the death of a loved one. If the death is sudden, the pain can be exponentially worse. It is natural for the deceased's loved ones to wonder about his eternal fate and whether he is at peace. Unfortunately, some allow this wonder to steer them toward necromancy—contacting the dead.

Scripture sternly warns against necromancy: "Do not turn to mediums or seek out spiritists, for you will be defiled by them. I am the LORD your God" (Lev. 19:31 NIV). It also spells out the consequences for doing so: "I will set my face against anyone who turns to mediums and spiritists to prostitute themselves by follow- ing them, and I will cut them off from their people" (Lev. 20:6 NIV).

God's use of the image of a prostitute to describe necromancy is telling. A prostitute receives money in exchange for the use of her body. One who seeks a medium pays for the service of contacting the dead. Yet, God calls the seeker—not the medium—a prostitute.

The seeker hands himself to unclean spirits who have their way with him. It is the spiritual equivalent of prostitution.

For many, the temptation to hear from a deceased loved one is enough to make them turn to necromancy. But one should beware: demons have observed you your whole life. Though they do not have direct access to your thoughts and cannot directly read your mind, they have had access to every observable event in your life, such as your conversations, behavior, and sins. And they observe these events with the capabilities and properties of angelic beings, as discussed in Chapter 1, which they can use to produce an illusion of the reality you take for granted.

For example, because he is incapable of forgetting anything, a demon can imitate the voice, appearance, gestures, personality, style, and even bodily scent of everyone you have ever known with perfection. He can make himself appear so much like your dead grandmother, for example, complete with references to your past interactions with her to make you believe that it is she who is speaking with you. One can never trust knowledge obtained through necromancy. Christ Himself calls the Devil "the father of lies" (John 8:44).

Fortune-telling, Soothsaying, Tarot Card Reading, Palm Reading, et Cetera

Many who call themselves fortune tellers, soothsayers, diviners, or readers are frauds who take a gullible person's money in exchange for false and invented information. On the other hand, a significant number are under the power of evil spirits who have vested them with demonic abilities.

No matter how much Christian faith someone possesses and how much good he accomplishes, any use of the occult is offensive to God and separates him from Divine favor:

*There shall not be found among you . . . any one who prac-
tices divination, a soothsayer, or an augur, or a sorcerer, or a
charmer, or a medium, or a wizard, or a necromancer. For
whoever does these things is an abomination to the LORD.
(Deuteronomy 18:10–12)*

To justify their occult practices, fortune tellers, soothsayers,
and the like identify themselves as prophets who serve God's people
by helping them navigate life's difficulties. However, the difference
between an occultist and a prophet cannot be starker. Prophets
accomplish God's will, and the abilities God grants them are a blessing, never cause harm, and are always consistent with His Word. His
prophets also do not charge a fee. None of this is true of occultists.

A woman once came to me in tears, admitting she had been
seeing a diviner for eighteen months. "I always knew it was wrong,
Father, but everything he said always came true, and he knew how
to bring about exactly what I wanted."

There were three things she had asked the diviner to accomplish. She wanted her son and daughter-in-law to conceive, sought a
promotion at work, and desired her sister to be cured of cancer. The
diviner prescribed different remedies for each. To produce a grandchild, the woman needed to mash a white powder he supplied into
her son and daughter-in-law's food and feed it to them clandestinely.
After doing so, her daughter-in-law conceived within a month. She
needed to burn a live cat in her backyard to receive a promotion at
work. She obtained a kitten and, without being caught for the illegal act, tied him inside a cloth bag and burned him in a makeshift
firepit. Afterward, she received the promotion, even though she
recognized that she was the least qualified among the candidates.
Finally, for her sister's healing, she had to place a leather necklace
with a medal hanging from it around her sister's neck. The medal

had the image of the sun on one side and the moon on the other. Within a month her sister was cancer-free.

"Everything was going fine, Father, but on my last visit, the man told me he wanted more money," she said. "I gave him over six thousand dollars, but he wanted five thousand more. I just couldn't afford it. He got furious."

Upon arriving home, the woman found the severed head of a rooster on her porch. In her kitchen, another one was floating inside her water cooler jug. Her cell phone rang. It was the diviner, threatening to undo everything and promising that, unless she paid, the next severed head would be her own. Though she had never given him her cell phone number, she somehow knew it.

Within two weeks, the woman lost her job, and her sister's cancer returned. Terror filled her that something dreadful would befall her unborn grandchild. Suddenly, her son texted that his wife was hemorrhaging badly and that he was taking her to the hospital. The woman quickly drove to the church and relayed everything to me. I led her through the Sacrament of Confession and renunciations of her occult choices. She also made a vow before God never to consult a diviner again. Meanwhile, though her daughter-in-law remained in the hospital for over a week, she was able to keep the baby, giving birth to a healthy boy six months later.

It is a human tendency to be anxious about the future and to desire to control it. Christ, however, gives us a remedy to overcome it: unfailing trust in God.

Reiki and Other Elements of the New Age Movement

Reiki offers what everyone desires—stress reduction, relaxation, and healing. Its technique is a "laying on of hands" by a practitioner who purports to tap into one's unseen ki (qi) or "life force energy." In so doing, he raises the client's ki, bringing healing and inhibiting stress and sickness. Reiki has taken America by storm. Spas, salons, and even Christian retreat centers offering Reiki have sprung up everywhere, catering to the voracious appetite of an ever-increasing client base, 80 percent of whom are upper-middle-class women. It has become fashionable and a status symbol to receive Reiki treatments.

Reiki contains no dogma, and there are no beliefs to which one must subscribe to receive Reiki or even to be one of its practitioners. Those who practice it claim it aids everyone, regardless of faith, belief structure, or personal spirituality. While Reiki is not a religion, it contains just enough spirituality to make some believe that in receiving it, they are connecting with the supernatural, though in a manner having none of the "sticky" elements of traditional religion, such as dogmas or moral rules. Furthermore, Reiki's practitioners claim it is compatible with any medical treatment. The International Center for Reiki Training describes it as a cure-all with seemingly magical qualities.

> *Reiki is a simple, natural and safe method of spiritual healing and self-improvement that everyone can use. It has been effective in helping virtually every known illness and malady and always creates a beneficial effect. It also works in conjunction with all other medical or therapeutic techniques to relieve side effects and promote recovery.*[2]

Reiki's slogan might as well be "All gain with no pain." At this point, one should be getting images of traveling snake oil peddlers, for the concept is the same: charlatans selling fraudulent wares. Of course, the marketing strategy is the same: *Can you afford to miss out on something so wonderful?* Unlike classic snake oil, however, which, though ineffective, was harmless, the same cannot be said for Reiki. The center describes training in Reiki as follows:

> *An amazingly simple technique to learn, the ability to use Reiki is not taught in the usual sense, but is transferred to the student during a Reiki class. This ability is passed on during an "attunement" given by a Reiki master and allows the student to tap into an unlimited supply of "life force energy" to improve one's health and enhance the quality of life.*[3]

That should set off alarm bells. Reiki is all about the transference of invisible power, which has no basis in science and which even its practitioners have not intellectually mastered through learning but have mystically received it through transference. Thus, those on the receiving end of Reiki, no matter how benevolent their practitioner may be, are dangerously opening themselves up to unknown spiritual entities.

In response to Reiki's growing popularity even among Christian retreat and spirituality centers, the United States Conference of Catholic Bishops' Committee on Doctrine has issued a document entitled, *Guidelines for Evaluating Reiki as an Alternative Therapy.* The document warns that:

> *To use Reiki one would have to accept at least in an implicit way central elements of the worldview that undergirds Reiki theory, elements that belong neither to Christian faith nor to natural science. Without justification either from Christian faith or natural science, however, a Catholic who puts his or her trust in Reiki would be operating in the realm of superstition, the no-man's-land that is neither faith nor science.*[4]

Reiki's skyrocketing popularity is partly due to its similarity and compatibility with New Age spirituality, which has grown explosively in the last few decades. The New Age movement originated from occult and metaphysical religious groups in the 1970s and 1980s that believed in a coming "new age" of human enlightenment and being. Like Reiki, the New Age movement is eclectic in its beliefs and does not have a set creed to which its members must subscribe. One of its central tenets is that human wellness originates from psychic energy. The energy may emanate from astrological events, contact with special objects (e.g., mountains, trees, crystals, et cetera), or by channeling invisible preternatural beings. Besides channeling, Reiki and New Age practitioners have sometimes integrated other forms of traditional occultism into their spiritual practice, such as tarot reading, numerology, astrology, yoga, mediumship, and the Ouija board.

While in the past, those who practiced New Age were usually eccentric and strange, today, practitioners represent all levels of society: teachers, healthcare workers, engineers, business executives, and perhaps even the friendly neighbors next door.[5]

The main principles behind the New Age movement can be summarized as follows:

- Traditional forms of religion with their rules, doctrines, and creeds are oppressive and stifling.
- Our being requires elevation, which occurs through the reception of paranormal/supernatural/psychic energy.
- The divine is inside us—it *is* us—and right and wrong can be discerned based on the energy something gives or takes from us or the "bad energy" it leaves behind.

These beliefs are incompatible with the Christian faith and are breeding grounds for demons.

Freemasonry

The Freemasons (aka the Masons) are among the world's oldest fraternal organizations, tracing their origins to the early eighteenth century. Multiple branches make up the fraternity, which has spread worldwide. Many who join the Masons do so for social and business networking purposes.

Though Masonic officials deny it, Freemasonry has long been accused of being a spiritual cult. The United Grand Lodge of England, the oldest Masonic Grand Lodge in the world, describes Freemasonry's relationship with religion:

> *All Freemasons are expected to have a religious belief, but Free-masonry does not seek to replace a Mason's religion or provide a substitute for it. It deals in a man's relationship with his fellow man not in a man's relationship with his God.*[6]

Freemasonry's membership requirements are simple: one must be an adult male of good moral character who believes in a supreme being. The organization makes no specification about the supreme being and affirms that members may belong to the religion of their choice.

At first glance, Freemasonry can appear to be just what it claims to be: a social fraternity. But there are contradictions between its claim that it is not a religion and the practices in which it engages.

For example, a Masonic lodge is a temple containing altars where

- prayers are recited
- a moral code is preached
- ceremonial vestments are worn
- the "Supreme Being" is worshipped
- feast days are celebrated

• elaborate burial rites are offered for its members

If the organization is not religious, why make it look so much like it is?

Among the most disturbing aspects of Freemasonry are its rituals and oaths of initiation, which are spiritually problematic. For the sake of simplicity, I will limit my discussion in this chapter to just the first oath, which every aspiring Mason must take upon entry to the first degree: Entered Apprentice.

According to Masonic manuals, to be initiated as an Entered Apprentice, a candidate strips himself of his clothing and jewelry—including his wedding ring—and vests himself in a blue pajama-type suit. When the ritual begins, he rolls up one pant leg and uncovers the left part of his shirt—exposing his heart—which is touched with the point of a sword. Blindfolded and with a rope tied in a noose around his neck, he is brought to the lodge's senior deacon, who asks, "Who comes here?" The junior deacon, who always responds on the candidate's behalf (the candidate is never permitted to answer for himself), replies, "[Candidate's name], who has long been in darkness, and now seeks to be brought to light, and to receive a part in the rights and benefits of this worshipful Lodge . . ."[7]

In allowing the junior deacon to say this on his behalf, a Christian candidate has de facto agreed that the light of Christ has been insufficient for him. He has called the Son of God—He who declared Himself to be "the Light of the World" (John 8:12)—a liar who has left him in darkness.

After permitting this blasphemy, the candidate recites an oath incompatible with Christian belief.

I . . . in the presence of Almighty God [some versions state "Great Architect of the Universe"] . . . do hereby and hereon

most solemnly and sincerely promise and swear, that I will
always hail [i.e., hide], ever conceal, and never reveal, any
of the arts, parts, or points of the hidden mysteries of Ancient
Free Masonry, which may have been, or hereafter shall be,
at this time, or any future period, communicated to me . . .
All this I most solemnly, sincerely promise and swear, with a
firm and steadfast resolution to perform the same, without any
mental reservation or secret evasion of mind whatever, bind-
ing myself under no less penalty than that of having my throat
cut across, my tongue torn out by its roots, and my body buried
in the rough sands of the sea, at low-water mark, where the
tide ebbs and flows twice in twenty-four hours, should I ever
knowingly violate this my Entered Apprentice obligation. So
help me God, and keep me steadfast in the due performance
of the same.[8]

The oath contains elements that are gravely incompatible with
basic Christian beliefs.

First, it is impossible that the "Almighty God," to whom the
oath is directed, is the Christian God, as such an oath could never
be made in His name. Christ exhorted his followers to abandon
elaborate oaths and to let their "yes" be yes, and their "no" be no,
declaring "anything more than this comes from evil" (Matt. 5:37).

Second, the oath is crafted in a manner as to appear that it supersedes all other covenants the Christian has undertaken, including
even his marriage vows. There is no occasion when the Church asks
a married Christian to remove his ring, which he wears as a sign of
the commitment he and his bride made before God. Neither does
the Church ask him to expose his heart to the point of a sword. If
one's own religion does not impose such radical symbolism, why
would a fraternity do so unless it sought to forge new bonds that

are even more primordial than the candidate's own religion? It is unconscionable that a Christian would place himself under an oath where his body is the penalty for something as trivial as belonging to a fraternal organization. A Christian's body is not his own: "Do you not know that your body is a temple of the Holy Spirit within you, which you have from God? You are not your own; you were bought with a price" (1 Cor. 6:19–21).

Third, the oath entails making the implicit claim that Freemasonry supersedes the Word of God. After reciting the oath, the candidate's blindfold is removed, and he finds himself kneeling before a Masonic altar, upon which a Bible has been placed, which he kisses to ratify the oath he has just made. However, in a gesture that can only be interpreted as a symbolic declaration that Freemasonry supersedes the Word of God, the emblem of Freemasonry—a square and compass—has been placed on top of the Bible. In fact, within the Masonic ritual, the Bible is described as merely a piece of "furniture."[9]

Fourth, sleight of hand is within the oath's symbolism and words. Masonry declares that its oaths possess only symbolic meaning and should not be taken literally. But this only intensifies the accusation that Masonry is itself a religion, distinct from and incompatible with Christianity. Symbols mean different things to different people, and there are at least three entities involved in a Masonic oath: the one making the oath, the Masonic officials overseeing it, and the "Almighty God" who receives it (who it has already been shown cannot be the Christian God).

Masonic officials assert the oath is not literal, but the commitment is not made to them. It is sworn to the "Almighty God," who is the only one to decide how to accept the proclamation made to him. It is free to accept it in any way it desires. So why not literally?

It is impossible to overstate the spiritual dangers to which the one taking the Masonic oath subjects himself. The oath's deceptive symbolism leaves him vulnerable to demonic transference. Numerous times during exorcisms, I have encountered demons who possess deceptive names. For example, I have encountered demons whose names were "Jesus," "the True Jesus," and "Lord." If the exorcist commands a particular demon to leave "in the Name of Jesus," which is what an exorcist always does because of the power of Christ's name, and there happens to be a second demon inside the victim who answers to the name "Jesus," then the exorcist's command will effect no change. If the exorcist did not specify the Divine Jesus—the Jesus who is the Son of God and Savior of the World—then the demons are free to interpret the command favorably. The demon commanded to leave may refuse to do so, leaving the exorcist at a loss as to the reason. Or worse, he may appear to depart but merely hides, continuing to work against both the victim and the exorcist. The exorcist spins his wheels, expending his time and energy, with no liberation for the victim. Just as demons can use a deceptive play on names and words in an exorcism, they can also do so in a Masonic oath.

Fifth, aside from the signs, symbols, and play on words, Masonic rituals and oaths are designed to forge *covenant relationships*. As an exorcist, I have encountered many people who have complained of repetitive dysfunctions, particularly in family relationships and career matters, because of the Masonic membership of their fathers and grandfathers. These include constant family conflict, an inability to complete one's education or to thrive in one's chosen career because of endless "bad luck," and repetitive patterns manifested through multiple generations (e.g., all husbands leave their wives, children die young while still in childhood, et cetera).

A case I had involved a fourteen-year-old boy who began having fits of rage against his father. The boy ignited with anger when his father merely walked into the room; multiple times, he attacked him. His reactions were out of character, as he and his father had always been close. When asked the reason for his rage against his father, he could never articulate one. The family had him medically examined, and doctors could find nothing wrong. His parents suspected the problem might be spiritual. They requested help from the diocese and that is when I got involved.

After interviewing him, I found nothing morally or spiritually wrong. Nevertheless, I began prayers of deliverance over him, taking authority over any attached evil spirits. Because his ethnic background included Scottish and English ancestry, I led the boy through renunciations of Masonic vows that might be present in the family line. As I did so, he manifested demonically, clenching his fists and showing signs of distress. After completing the renunciations, I prayed over him again, breaking any Masonic attachments and covenants connected to him. He never exhibited violent behavior toward his father ever again.

In another case, a middle-aged woman complained of frightening and debilitating nightmares she suffered for years. The dreams followed a similar pattern. She found herself inside a Masonic lodge where she was being offered to a hideous creature with a goat's head. She also experienced other phenomena. When she was home alone, she always felt something was watching her and, occasionally, even felt it touch her: a tap on the head or a caress on the leg. The phenomena were accompanied by an inner awareness that "it" was waiting for when it could lay claim to her. Her father, both grandfathers, and three of her great-grandfathers were Masons. Like in the previous example, after she renounced the Masonic vows made by these ancestors, all her symptoms ceased.

The teaching of the Catholic Church about Masonry is unambiguous.

> *The Church's negative judgment in regard to Masonic associ-*
> *ation[s] remains unchanged since their principles have always*
> *been considered irreconcilable with the doctrine of the Church*
> *and therefore membership in them remains forbidden. The*
> *faithful who enroll in Masonic associations are in a state of*
> *grave sin and may not receive Holy Communion.*[10]

For those who assert that the intention of an oath-taker determines the extent of the oath, it's important to remember that reciting an oath is agreeing to that oath. Words have meaning, and when one enters a contract, one does not get to define the terms of the contract apart from the other party. If the oath has spiritual implications, as Masonic oaths do, those implications are part of the deal, and they will affect our family members and us.

Astrology and Horoscopes

Astrology and horoscopes are also incompatible with the Christian faith. Like all occult practices, they offend God because they doubt His goodness and usurp His sovereignty.

Most horoscopes and astrological readings are the fictional work of a writer. When comparing them across publications, they often contradict each other or their predictions have no connection with one another. If it were possible to predict the future based on the position of stars and planets, then there would at least be more consistency since nothing can be more objective than the position of these massive solar bodies. If astrology were indeed a science, then a horoscope prediction would be scientific. It is not.

Many people who read horoscopes claim to do so purely for entertainment and regard the content as make-believe. However, consulting a horoscope puts that person in a relationship with its message, and the Devil understands how to manipulate that relationship for his purposes. Satan can make reality appear to unfold like a horoscope's text so that it seems what it stated was correct and accurate.

The occult is as accessible as the horoscope section of any website, magazine, or newspaper people read for relaxation, as innocent-looking as a board game purchased at the toy store, as trendy as the spa visit that offers energy-therapy alongside skin and nail treatments, and as innocuous as a club for building business contacts. It is never far away and is already well integrated into the lives of many, even without their knowing it. "For this people's heart has grown dull, and their ears are heavy of hearing, and their eyes they have closed" (Matt. 13:15). Occult practices are incompatible with Christianity, and it's foolish to underestimate their power.

EIGHT

WITCHCRAFT AND SATANISM

THE CASE OF
THE WITCH GIRLFRIEND

A s soon as Trent set foot on the Incarnate Word Bible College grounds, he began to experience peace—a deep peace—a peace unlike he had ever felt before. His accident and what preceded it were such awful experiences that they would forever remain ingrained in his memory. Eight days after arriving at the college, he didn't care if he ever left.

Since his arrival, Trent had prayed the Rosary countless times. He also spent many hours of silence before the Blessed Sacrament and went to Mass daily. For someone who had rarely practiced any faith since the eighth grade—over twenty years ago—the spiritual change in him was dramatic.

Trent was grateful for the Bible school's hospitality, the meals, and a guest room in the men's dormitory. There was someone within earshot of him if he needed anything. Most of all, Trent was the recipient of daily prayer ministry, increasingly freeing him of the nightmare of the last six months of his life. Through the school's students and faculty, Trent experienced God's love and the kindness of His faithful disciples as he had never experienced before.

Incarnate Word Catholic Bible College was a start-up school in only its sixth year of operation. Like all nonaccredited colleges, money was tight, and it was never far from financial insolvency. It rented the grounds of a vacant monastery and kept itself afloat by cutting costs wherever possible. In addition to paying tuition, students had chores assigned, such as cleaning the buildings and cooking for the thirty-nine registered students. Aside from being a financial necessity, the student body's cooperation brought about closeness and a sense of community that forged close bonds among everyone. Each student felt like he was part of something akin to what it was like in the early Church.

Trent's eighth day at the college meant it was now the sixth day he had not shown up for work. He had not even called the freight company to explain why he was absent. Certain he no longer had a job, he didn't care. He was not well enough to begin working this soon after the accident and was not in the proper spiritual space to be out on his own. *I can always get another trucking job,* he thought. *I'm where I need to be right now.*

A little over a week before, Trent had been driving a pickup on Stanwood Road when he hit a horse. The damage was tremendous; his truck was totaled. Its front end had collapsed and pushed the engine into the cab; any farther, it would have crushed his legs. His legs were pinned so tightly between the deformed dashboard and his seat that, until he could wiggle them loose, he had no circulation in his feet. The passenger seat had been ejected and was now in the ditch on the side of the road. The front axle was bent into a V and lay twenty-five feet away from the vehicle. The stallion he'd hit was now scattered bits of flesh and bone strewn inside the truck's cab and on the road behind it.

That Trent had even survived, let alone walked away with only a badly bruised chest—from colliding with the airbag—and a few cuts on his right arm where the horse's passing body drove glass into him, was astonishing. Someone looking at the wreckage would never believe the driver had survived.

The accident occurred just past one o'clock in the afternoon. Stanwood Road is a little-traveled road that divides long tracks of farmland in eastern Idaho. Trent discovered it years ago when he and a friend went elk hunting. Traveling the winding road was slower than the highway, but its views of the mountains were as scenic as any and made for a beautiful drive.

What usually added to the pleasure of driving on that road—the lack of other vehicles—almost made things turn tragic. After colliding with the stallion, Trent had waited trapped inside his truck, his legs immobilized, for someone to come along and help him. The area was so rural that there was no cell phone reception even if he could find his phone. After wiggling, twisting, and painfully pulling on his legs, he managed to get them out, though only by slipping off his shoes. The driver's door had also crumpled in the impact and wouldn't open, so Trent had to crawl out the window to get himself out.

The sound of the crash still rang in his ears. Trent began to limp southward down the road, looking for any sign of civilization. After walking almost a mile, he saw the sign for the Bible college, and he turned up the lane hoping to get access to a telephone to call for help. It did not take long for Trent to get noticed. Covered in the stallion's blood, with drying bits of the animal's flesh clinging to his face and shirt, he was a gruesome sight. A female student, walking from her dorm to the refectory, was so startled when she saw him that she screamed, causing a crowd to gather.

When John Brooks, the school's headmaster, came over, Trent explained what had happened. John led Trent inside to report the accident to the police. The operator dispatched a unit immediately, but it would be over thirty minutes before it arrived in the rural area. In the meantime, John offered Trent the shower in his quarters to wash himself of the blood, for which Trent was grateful.

When the police arrived, they took Trent's account of the accident, completed their report, and offered to drive him to a hospital to be examined, which Trent politely turned down. He felt so much peace in the short time he had been at the school he did not want to leave. Being treated at the hospital for just a few scratches was not worth it. John offered to let him stay at the college as long as he needed, and Trent could not think of anything he wanted more.

The Christian goodness that Trent saw around him left him speechless. These people did not know him, yet they treated him like a brother. One student promised to offer a holy hour for him in the chapel, while several more promised to pray the Rosary for him. Another one lent him a laptop to email family and let them know where he was.

While students and faculty dined that evening, John arranged for him and Trent to eat in his private dining room. Trent told him the extended version of how he'd got there after they sat down. As a long-haul truck driver, Trent crisscrossed the country, and, like all truckers, he had his favorite stops along his route, which he visited when he shut down for the night. The previous six months, Trent often had the same drive: Houston, Memphis, Wichita, and Seattle. He had discovered a restaurant about twenty miles outside Seattle where he liked to eat. While the food was good, what he found extraordinary was the waitress Evelyn. Exceptionally friendly, she engaged him in conversation throughout the evening. With each of Trent's subsequent visits, she waited on him, and the conversation continued from where it left off the previous visit.

Trent loved Evelyn's personality and found her both physically attractive and pleasingly feminine. By his fourth visit, Evelyn was overtly flirtatious and, halfway through his meal, said, "Okay, if you're not going to ask me out, I guess it's up to me. Would you like to have dinner with me tomorrow night?"

Both startled and flattered by her assertiveness, Trent smiled and replied, "I would love to have dinner with you. Where would you like to go?"

"My place," she said. "I'll have everything ready by six thirty," she added, handing Trent a piece of paper with her address, winking as she did so. "See you tomorrow," she said.

"Evelyn possessed an amazing charm and had everything I ever wanted," Trent admitted to John. "Her voice, manner, and walk were mesmerizing. She was the kind of person that made you forget about everything else."

While he loved the open road, Trent was well aware of his loneliness, and at thirty-four years old, his plans to get married and have children were passing him by. When Trent arrived at the address Evelyn provided, he could smell the marvelous dinner. She spotted him even before he rang the doorbell. "Right on time," she said, greeting him with a tight hug. It had been so long since he had experienced any human affection that he could have remained in that hug forever.

"Make yourself at home," she said as she finally let go of him. "I've got one more thing on the stove, and dinner will be ready."

Evelyn's home was an old stone farmhouse that had been absorbed into the growing town around it. It was recently renovated, the cost of which would have been a fortune. It turned out beautifully. The stone fireplace, the log walls, and the leaded windows created one of the most inviting rooms Trent had ever seen. He wondered how Evelyn could afford it on a waitress' earnings.

"You live alone?" he asked.

"Of course," she responded from the kitchen. "I bought the house five years ago and renovated it. Let me get you a drink," she said.

The house's decor was simple though elegant, with mirrors and art that fit the room perfectly.

"Here you are," she said, handing him a beer. Trent looked down at the beer she was giving him. In her hand was a bottle of La Fin du Monde, a beer brewed in a tiny brewery in Quebec, Canada. "Where did you get this?" he asked. "This is my favorite."

"I thought you might like it," she replied wryly. "I'm in the restaurant business. I have friends who can get me things." Of all the drinks she could bring him, he never expected a bottle of La Fin du Monde. He was introduced to it by an old trucker when he was in a bar in Montreal. "It's brewed in Chambly, about twenty miles from where you're sitting," the old man said, with a heavy Quebecois accent. It was a Belgian-style beer that Trent thought tasted like heaven. "Be careful how much," the trucker warned him. "Nine percent alcohol it has. Love it, but not too much," he said, laughing in his thick accent. Trent always looked forward to hauling into Quebec to have that beer. "Of all the drinks she could serve me, how did she ever think of this one?" he wondered in amazement.

Evelyn made a wonderful chicken and rice dish for dinner, with green beans, salad, and fresh-baked bread. He relished every bite. Throughout dinner, Evelyn told him about herself and how she had spent eight years of her childhood living in Europe, where she learned three languages. "My father was stationed in Europe from when I was six until I was fourteen. We still own a house in Germany," she said. "I go back every couple of years."

Though Trent was older than Evelyn by three years, she had seen much more of the world than he had. Had she not continually looked at him with indulgent eyes, he might have even felt intimidated by her.

After dinner, Evelyn suggested they move into the solarium at the back of the house. "We can see the sunset from there," she said. "Oh, and because it is already so late, you better just plan to stay the night," she added casually.

It was only seven thirty in the evening, but Evelyn had just clarified her desires. *I like that*, Trent thought to himself, amused at how coolly Evelyn found a way to get the awkward issue of sex out of the way while it was still early in the evening. "I wouldn't want to spend the night anywhere else," he replied.

Together they watched a beautiful sunset, had a few more drinks, and talked well into the evening, caressing each other on the couch. Trent felt better than he had in years. At this hour of the night, he would either be drinking by himself in a bar or inside his rig while watching a movie. Either way, it would be a night alone. It felt so good to have companionship, especially with someone who made it so apparent that she liked him. *Don't mess this up*, he told himself.

They had intercourse several times that night with twenty-minute breaks in between. Trent had never been with a woman this sensual.

They slept late into the morning. Upon waking, Evelyn reached over and began what Trent recognized as the caressing with which she signaled she wanted sex again. *A nymphomaniac*, he thought to himself. *I must be dreaming.*

After breakfast, Evelyn suggested Trent should just move in. When she said it, Trent had been thinking how wonderful it would be to live like this every day. Moving in would be simple, as everything he owned was in his rig. He had spent a fortune to buy the truck to live in it: it came complete with a bed and bathroom in the cab, just behind the seats. He still used his mother's house in Texas as his mailing address, but he planned to drive as much as possible to own a ranch one day. But, as he thought about it, he was not set on owning a ranch. Though he was from the South and always thought he would settle there, if he had Evelyn, he would be happy anywhere, including cold and wet Washington State. Trent was already taking it for granted that Evelyn would be part of his future.

By the late morning, Trent would have to be back on the road to make his next delivery on time, a haul to Memphis. Before he walked out the door, Evelyn grabbed him and began undressing him again. "One more time," she said. "I won't see you until you roll back in town next week."

Once in his rig on the highway, Trent relived the last two days. They were the happiest he ever remembered. Evelyn was beautiful, loving, financially stable, and crazy about him. Finding a woman like this was the dream he'd always had. Her thought continually occupied his mind, and he wore a constant smile.

Trent was amazed at how intuitive Evelyn was. Though he did not remember telling her, she somehow knew he would be back in Washington next week. Usually, it would be weeks before he cycled back through Washington. However, a dispatch operator at the freight line inadvertently switched the destinations of two trailers, and each went to the other's location. Trent was asked to make a route change to deliver one of them. Instead of driving from Seattle to Wichita, like he usually did, Trent would be making a pickup in Chicago, dropping it off in Denver, then taking the Denver load and hauling it to Tacoma, Washington. He would then have three days off he could spend with Evelyn in Seattle.

When Trent delivered his haul to Tacoma, he headed straight for Evelyn's, where the two agreed to meet. An envelope taped to her door marked, "Key for you. Keep it." Letting himself in, he called out to Evelyn, who answered from upstairs. As he walked into her bedroom, he found her waiting for him. "I thought you'd never come," she said.

Trent was in Seattle for three days. During that time, he and Evelyn had intercourse multiple times per day. When he got into his rig to depart, Evelyn walked out of her house with a suitcase in hand. "What's that for?" he asked.

"I'm coming with you," she replied.

"You're doing what?" he asked. "Evelyn, I'll be driving almost three weeks straight."

"I know," she replied. "I took three weeks off work. I want to come with you. It'll be so romantic. Besides, this way, I get to be with you on your birthday."

Trent couldn't believe it. As he set out on the road, he did so with a companion, an experience he had never had before. Having Evelyn meant he had someone to ride with, eat with, share the shopping with, and, best of all, someone with whom to spend the downtime. And she would also be with him on his birthday, which, again, somehow Evelyn intuitively knew.

Evelyn asked Trent to pull off the road three times in the first four hours so they could be intimate. Though Trent enjoyed the encounters, the stops required him to drive longer to keep his schedule. Anticipating there might be an issue with getting enough sleep at night, Trent told Evelyn that however frisky they were, he needed a seven-hour undisturbed hiatus through the night or driving safety would be compromised. She agreed. But when night came, he had to keep reminding her.

If Evelyn was ever bored or tired on their journey, she never showed it. Occasionally, she slept, listened to music, or just looked out the window and enjoyed the view of America. The only edginess she ever showed was when Trent interacted with another female on their journeys, such as with a waitress or a cashier. Evelyn never wanted Trent to speak with them but insisted on doing so, making her interactions with them brief and curt. If a pretty woman walked by when they were at a rest stop, Evelyn moved into "distract" mode, steering Trent's attention away so that he would not notice her. Her jealousy was the only defect Trent could find in her.

When they were back in Seattle, Trent had a little over thirty-six hours before he had to depart again. Since Evelyn's house was now also his house, he bought a used pickup truck to have something to drive besides Evelyn's car when he was home. She ensured Trent bought a full-size truck with seats that reclined to a completely flat position. He knew exactly why she wanted that feature.

By his fifth visit to Seattle, Trent was not as enthusiastic about the physical intimacy with Evelyn as he once was. It was not because he did not like the sex. It was because there was too much. Evelyn wanted it so much that his body could not recover fast enough between sessions, and Evelyn's appetite was insatiable. Other things couples typically did—such as going to the movies and going for long walks—Evelyn never considered; she did not stray far from the bedroom.

Trent brought up his concern as gently as he could. "Don't you like it when we make love?" Evelyn asked, obviously taken aback.

"Of course, I do," Trent replied. "But we're doing it so much my body is having a hard time keeping up."

"But, honey, sex is pure love," she retorted. "It's the total giving of oneself to the other. It's total closeness. Don't you love me?"

"Of course, I love you," Trent replied. "But love doesn't have to always be about sex."

"Why don't you like sex?" Evelyn asked, looking genuinely confused.

"I do like it," Trent insisted. "It's just that it is not everything. There are other ways to show love."

Agitated, Evelyn got up and walked out of the room. Trent waited a moment before going after her. In his wildest dreams, he never thought he would be telling his girlfriend they were having too much sex.

Trent found Evelyn in the kitchen making dinner. "I'm sorry for being so insensitive," he said. Evelyn put down the carrot she was peeling and rushed to embrace him. She took his hand, led him up the stairs back into the bedroom, and began undressing.

Two months later, Trent was on the road and did something he had never done before: he stopped to refuel and grab a bite in Hays, Kansas. Hays was deliberately off his route, but he wanted to test a theory. After refueling, Trent entered a grocery store to buy drinks and food. While walking in the produce aisle, he stopped and asked a saleslady where the nuts were. After she told him, Trent asked her where the brown sugar was. Then he asked her where the light bulbs, the cat food, and the sesame oil were. Finally, he thanked her, but before walking away, he asked, "I used to come here years ago. Does Jerry still work in the meat department?" Jerry did not exist but was someone he fabricated to prolong the conversation. "I have no idea who Jerry is," she replied.

"Short guy, with a stocky build," Trent added casually. "Wears glasses and speaks with a bit of a stutter."

"Sorry, but I have no idea who you're talking about," she replied. "But I have only been working here two years. The manager has been here for over fifteen. If you ask him, I'm sure he can tell you."

Next, Trent went to the deli counter and ordered a sandwich, making lots of small talk with the lady preparing his order. After commenting on the weather and asking how her day was, he asked her to recommend a cheese for his sandwich. The store had seven different kinds of cheese, and Trent asked her about them in painstaking detail. She went down the list then recommended the dilled cheddar. "Everybody loves it," she said. He thanked her, selected the dilled cheddar for his sandwich, paid for it, and left.

Trent next went into the steakhouse next door but left his cell phone—which he had powered off hours ago—inside the rig. Inside the restaurant, he sat at a table away from the view of any window. Before he gave the waitress his order, he engaged her in small talk about the weather, the specials, and what she recommended from the menu. It was four o'clock in the afternoon, and the restaurant had just opened. He was the day's first patron and, so far, the only one. He placed his order. As the waitress was preparing his drink, the restaurant's telephone rang. The waitress answered it. After a moment, she came back to him and asked, as he expected, "Are you Trent? The telephone is for you."

Trent knew it was Evelyn. He was alone in a restaurant he had never been to before, in a town where he had never stopped. And no one could see him in the restaurant. Yet, somehow Evelyn knew precisely where he was and with whom he spoke. "Hello, Evelyn," he said.

"Why is your phone turned off?" she asked tersely.

"It was low on battery, and I figured I didn't need it on while having dinner," Trent replied.

"Why did you leave it in the rig?" she demanded. "What if I needed to reach you?"

It's as if Evelyn had a magic eye monitoring him at each moment. Somehow, she always knew details about his life.

"Honey, I just wanted to have a quiet dinner," he replied. "It's been a hard day, and I just wanted some 'me time,'" he added, trying to sound exhausted.

"What were you talking about with those women?" she barked.

Trent feigned ignorance and replied, "What women?"

"The two women in the supermarket and this waitress," Evelyn snorted. "You spoke to each one for a long time."

There it is, thought Trent. *Evelyn always knows my exact where-abouts and precisely what I am doing at every moment. She knows. No one is telling her. And yet she knows.*

In the last week, Evelyn had called Trent twice, asking him why he was so chatty with the waitresses. He wasn't sure whether anything in his life was private and outside her gaze. A chill ran up his spine.

The next time they spoke was two days later. By this time, Evelyn was over her sour mood. Trent was to drop off his delivery at the Seattle warehouse and return to Evelyn's afterward. "I'll see you soon," he told her. "I'll be ready," she replied. But Trent was not looking forward to seeing Evelyn. Their relationship was atypical and odd. He could already anticipate what his stay with her would entail: sex and nothing else. He didn't feel like he was Evelyn's boyfriend so much as the man she used to satisfy her sexual appetite, which knew no limit.

When Trent arrived at Evelyn's, she was sitting undressed on the couch. She embraced him and gave him a long kiss. "I missed you," she said as she led him by the hand to the bedroom.

What followed next was something Trent will never forget. They engaged in a single act of intercourse that lasted hours. Though he was tired and wanted it to end after twenty minutes, he was somehow unable to stop. After one hour, he was utterly exhausted, and his body was in pain, but for some reason unknown to him, he found it easier to continue.

The fact that his body could sustain physical arousal for that length of time was baffling to him. Yet, if he tried to force his body to stop, at Evelyn's urging, an inner robotic compulsion forced him to continue, even though the pain he was experiencing was now excruciating. Though Trent had control of his mind, he had only partial control of his body, and Evelyn refused to let him stop. Finally, after five hours, Evelyn reached a point of satisfaction and allowed the encounter to cease. Trent fell onto the bed and lost consciousness.

When Trent awoke the following day, he was in agony. He was swollen and in excruciating pain. The act of relieving himself in the restroom was unbearable. The swelling barely allowed the urine to pass.

Hearing him moving in the bathroom, Evelyn called from downstairs, "Good morning, honey. I've got breakfast ready."

As Trent walked down the stairs, Evelyn was waiting with a picnic basket in one hand and a blanket in the other.

"After how beautiful last night was," she said, "I thought we could have breakfast in the park today."

Beautiful? Trent said to himself. *Last night was a nightmare. I felt like I was controlled and raped from the inside out, by something inside me.* He had no idea how to respond to her.

"Let's go before everything gets cold," she said.

Trent wanted to have breakfast at the park as much as he wanted his teeth pulled. Somehow, however, he was unable to express that he did not want to go. When Evelyn started moving toward the door and exiting the house, he found it all but irresistible to follow. It required a tiny fraction of the energy to walk behind her than it did to resist and remain still. Were it not that the impulse to obey was coming not from her but from inside him, he would have said that he felt like a dog dragged on a leash.

At the park, Evelyn spread the blanket on the grass, opened the basket, and started setting its contents. "Sit down and have some oatmeal," she said. Trent's body robotically obeyed when she said, "Sit down." She handed him a bowl of oatmeal, and he used every-thing he could to resist taking it. Though his body accepted the bowl, with all his force, Trent pressed his hand into his thigh, refusing to let it move, not only because he found oatmeal disgusting, but by now, he knew that he was in grave danger and needed to escape. In a way Trent could not understand, Evelyn was turning him into her slave.

"Take the oatmeal," Evelyn said, the smile disappearing from her face. "Afterward, we'll go home and make beautiful love again, just like last night," she added, her smile returning.

"I don't . . . want . . . a relationship . . . with you any longer," Trent stammered. "I'm leaving," he added. With that assertion, he felt as if something heavy that had been on his shoulders slid off him. He felt both lighter and more in control. "You and I are over, Evelyn," he blurted assertively, with a newfound strength.

Evelyn's face turned into one of the most menacing countenances he had ever seen. Suddenly, he couldn't breathe. His lungs were unable to draw air. Evelyn, was staring at him with the most intense mien he had ever seen. It felt to Trent as if two hands were around his throat choking him. Evelyn was not touching him, but she was somehow strangling him.

Just then, a Frisbee landed between them. Two men had been throwing it at a distance when a bad toss sent it landing on their picnic blanket. Its unexpected appearance broke Evelyn's concentration, and her stranglehold abated. In a flash, Trent shot up and ran as fast as he could toward his pickup truck, repeatedly saying, "Dear God, help me. Dear God, help me." Reaching his vehicle, he jumped inside, turned on the ignition, and pressed the gas so hard that the tires squealed as the vehicle shot into motion.

Trent kept driving until he got to southern Idaho. Then, the strangest thing occurred. While driving on Stanwood Road, a horse galloped at full speed toward him. To avoid hitting it, Trent veered left into the lane of oncoming traffic. But the horse changed lanes and was again on a collision course with the truck. Trent swerved back into the right lane. The horse reciprocated. By this time, a collision was unavoidable.

————————

John had been sitting silently, listening to every word Trent said. When Trent finished, John sat pensively. The college was a product of four individuals—John was one of them—whose spiritual journeys all passed through the Charismatic Renewal, a spiritual movement focusing on an intentional relationship with the Holy Spirit and the gifts He dispenses to the Church. Charismatic spirituality was very much at the heart of the college. Every Friday night, it hosted a gathering where people would praise and worship God in song, and those who desired it could receive prayer ministry. People came from all over the region—as far away as fifty miles—to be part of it. Many were physically healed at the meetings, and the Holy Spirit often manifested with prophecy and deliverance upon those who needed it.

"Trent," John said, "you have been through a lot. You need the Lord's power. We have a prayer group that meets soon. Many of the students and staff attend it, as do many people at large who drive in. It's open to everyone. Why don't you come and allow us to pray over you?"

"I would love that," Trent replied. "I've not been very religious, but I believe in God, and I know only He can help me right now."

"Praise God," replied John. "It will be impossible to get a priest here at this hour to hear your confession, but one always comes on Saturdays; he will be here tomorrow. Nevertheless, for the prayer to have any positive effect, you must repent of your sins. Your relationship with Evelyn was sinful—the two of you engaged in sexual intercourse, and you were unmarried. Do you repent of that?"

"I do," Trent replied.

John continued, "Do you repent of ignoring God, for not culti-vating a relationship with Him, for not making Him the center of your life?"

"I do," said Trent.

Finally, John said, "Do you repent of ignoring God's law, of not practicing your faith, of not observing your Sunday obligation to attend Holy Mass, and for all the other sins you have committed? And are you ready to give your life completely to God?"

"Absolutely," replied Trent. "Yes."

"Praise God!" John exclaimed. "You have rejected a life of sin and have placed yourself at the feet of the Lord. Tomorrow you will confess your sins and receive His forgiveness through the priest's absolution. For now, however, you are ready to receive the Holy Spirit's power."

The prayer gathering met in the chapel. A group of students who were musicians played worship music. John served as the gath-ering's facilitator and, introducing Trent, discreetly asked everyone to intercede for him so that he would be free of all ties "to an evil he had recently encountered." The music ministry led the group in a worship song, after which everyone invoked the power of the Holy Spirit upon Trent. The room became abuzz with a symphony of prayers, asking God to manifest His power in Trent and free him from the grip of evil.

As the prayers began, Trent started rocking from left to right, his sway increasing more and more. Suddenly, his eyes rolled into the back of his head, and he fell backward onto the floor, his body shaking and convulsing. After a few seconds, he screamed, and his head began shaking from side to side at a rapid pace. No one was fazed. Most were veterans of intercessory prayer long enough to have seen demonic manifestations before, that is, the clash between the Enemy and the Holy Spirit. They are the visible expression of the Devil having to give up the grip on his victim. In response, the gathering turned its prayers up another notch. They stormed heaven on Trent's behalf for almost an hour.

All Trent remembered was John introducing him. The next thing he knew, he was lying flat on his back, with people around him, praying. Over two hours had passed since the meeting started. Trent felt a beautiful peace that he had never experienced.

For the next several days, the people at the college continued to pray for Trent each evening. Each time there was some disturbing manifestation. It became less and less each day, however.

Trent stayed at the college another four months, soaking in the Lord's presence and discovering his identity in Him. He was grateful for the Christian community he found there, which taught him to live for God alone, a way of life Trent found irresistible once he tasted it.

I encountered Trent when he was in his second month at the college. By then, he was mostly free of the wounds from his time with Evelyn. Nevertheless, two symptoms endured, which caused him to seek me out. The first was that he had frequent disturbing dreams involving Evelyn torturing him. The second was a constant, enduring pain in his genitals, the same pain he experienced after spending his last night with Evelyn. He had visited numerous doctors and taken various antibiotics to no effect. Though his body looked normal, the pain never left.

I asked him whether Evelyn gave him anything he still had in his possession. He mentioned he still had a chain around his neck, and his truck had a visor clip she gave him. I told him possessing those things meant he remained connected to her. If he wanted to be free, he had to discard them. He agreed to do so. Next, I said a prayer of exorcism over him. He did not manifest during it but stated that he felt heat in his private area as it was happening. I blessed him and sent him on his way.

Trent was free and untroubled from that moment onward. He eventually met a wonderful Christian woman, settled with her, and started a beautiful family.

As it turns out, Evelyn owned the restaurant where she worked. That is why she could take time off whenever she desired. Evelyn is what some exorcists might call a "black widow" or a "Jezebel": a witch who lures unsuspecting men under the guise of a relationship but then turns into a predator who harms them. Her restaurant ensured a steady supply of truckers who were just "passing through" and knew nothing of her past relationships. Trent was only one of her victims. She had destroyed the lives of several truckers before him.

SATANISM

Satanism presents itself as the opposite of Christianity. In the Christian understanding of reality, God is sovereign. Through His Son's Passion, Death, and Resurrection, He has won the victory over Satan and his kingdom of darkness, ransoming His creation, which had been under the yoke of sin, sickness, and death, since Adam and Eve. In its theological understanding of reality, Satanism differs very little from Christianity. What is different are the labels of good and evil. Satanists view the Devil as their benefactor and God as their enemy. They regard the Devil's rebellion against God as the proper response to his Creator's limitations. As bizarre and perverted as it sounds, Satanists believe the Devil will one day defeat God and that he will show favor to those who have shown him devotion. They do Satan's bidding to curry his favor.

Satanism loosely exists in two forms: unorganized and organized.

Unorganized Satanism

This form of Satanism has no standardized belief system or formal structure and those who practice it identify themselves as Satanists for various reasons. At one pole are those wholly devoted to Satan. They desire to make him the center of their lives. At the other pole are atheists who have no belief in the supernatural. They use the label "Satanist" to mean rebellious and independent, two qualities inherent in the notion of Satan. And there is, of course, every form of expression between these two poles.

Unorganized Satanism is typically practiced by a single individual or, at best, by a loose circle of devotees, and there can be a notable lack of uniformity among them. Nevertheless, such persons can commit acts of terrible evil.

In the early years of my priestly ministry, I was stationed in Houston, Texas, a city with many prisons within a two-hour drive, which I regularly visited. I met more than a few inmates who claimed they were practicing Satanists before being incarcerated. One inmate serving a sentence for a triple murder admitted he never intended to kill anyone though he fantasized about murdering within the satanic ceremonies he practiced. One day, shortly after he emerged from the "trance" that he had induced himself during a satanic ritual, he found himself in the process of being handcuffed by police. He was inside the home of a family he did not know, and on the floor around him, the bodies of the home's three residents lay slain.

"It had to be me that killed them, Father," he said. "There was no one else around. But I didn't know them and never intended to kill them. I don't know how I ended up in their house."

Exorcists are often asked whether the Devil can kill people. Thankfully, God does not permit him to do so, at least not directly. However, should the Devil possess someone, he can use his host to do everything a human is physically capable of and lend him the preternatural assistance to do even more besides. The example of the murders this inmate committed is an illustration of that. What is also notable about this case is the killer's own experience.

When the Devil possesses, two spirits—the host's and the demon's—inhabit one body. There's a merging or "crossing over" of the two spirits: the demon experiences reality through his host's body (e.g., the demon will feel a touch on the host's arm as if it were his own), and the host often shares in the mind and experience of the demon. In the inmate's case, just after committing the murder, he saw a police cruiser pull into the driveway through the front window as he emerged from his trance. It was the middle of a bright and sunny Texas day, and there were no clouds in the sky. But even years later, as the inmate spoke with me, he was mystified by the fact that his arrest had occurred during the day as he distinctly remembered seeing the police car pulling in during the blackness of night. What he perceived was a reality as the Devil experiences it. For the Devil, everything is shrouded in darkness.

Organized Satanism

Organized or "cultic" Satanism is systematic and hierarchical. It exhibits a cult's typical characteristics: extreme loyalty to other cult members, complete obedience to the cult's hierarchy, total adherence to the cult's doctrines, degrading and self-immolating rituals, abuse, and violence.

Satanic cults do not advertise themselves and take great care to remain secret. They rarely accept new outside members, preferring to produce them from within the cult. Satanic cults attain new members via a supply of female members known as "breeders," whose task is to bear offspring for the cult. Their pregnancies often result from elaborate and violent raping ceremonies where sexual acts are part of satanic rituals.

The children born into a satanic cult enable one of its most heinous practices—blood sacrifice—where a victim's life is offered to Satan through ritualistic murder. Because cults have a regenerating supply of unregistered births, and because Satanism has a propensity for sexual perversion, some satanic cults engage in the production of pornography. Because breeder children are isolated from society, no one will ever recognize them if their images appear in print or online pornography.

When such children are too old to be used for this purpose, they are sacrificed in a satanic ceremony. Therefore, while one occasionally hears about law enforcement uncovering large caches of child pornography or a distribution network of the same, *one never hears about the rescue of the children used in such productions*. By the time law enforcement is involved, the victims have been sacrificed and are no longer alive.

I have had multiple possession cases that involved cultic Satanism. The victims born to the cult's breeders managed to escape. They carried unfathomable wounds. None were permitted to have the benefit of a childhood. Each was repeatedly raped, beaten, and tortured to assure their conformity to the cult and indoctrination with its aberrant beliefs. Two were also victims of mind control administered to further this end. Mind control is the use of psychological techniques to fracture a person's identity (thoughts, ideas, attitudes, values, and beliefs) to control it.

Members of both organized and cultic Satanism offer a so-called Black Mass, a blasphemous and obscene parody of the Catholic Mass. Presided over by a satanic "priest" wearing vestments similar to those of a Catholic priest, such a ceremony incorporates—though in an inverted meaning—the typical elements found in the traditional Christian liturgy: an altar, candles, vessels, and a consecrated Eucharistic Host, which has been stolen or smuggled from a Catholic Church. The satanic priest will mockingly desecrate the Host by placing it inside a woman's genitals or covering it with bodily excretions.

WITCHES, WITCHCRAFT, WICCA, AND PAGANISM

A witch practices witchcraft, a magical (i.e., paranormal) appropriation of occult powers through spells and the invocation of spirits. Historically, the term "witch" applied to females only, with their male counterparts being called "warlocks." In modern times, however, the term is used interchangeably among both genders. Some witches prefer to be called "Wiccans," who practice Wicca as opposed to witchcraft, because of the negative connotation that the terms "witch" and "witchcraft" possess.

Along with Satanism, witchcraft forms the second most identifiable occult grouping in the world. While some lump the two together under the generic label of "Satanists" or "devil worshippers," they have dramatically different spiritualities that are, in fact, incompatible. Satanism is patriarchal in character, while witchcraft is matriarchal. Though Satanists use women in their rituals and sexual practices, they are loathed and seen as disgusting. They are never regarded as equals. On the other hand, witches see the female as nature's summit of power, beauty, and perfection. Men are often seen as objects to control through sorcery and spells.

In contrast to traditional Satanism, which acknowledges the existences of God and Satan, a typical witch *might* believe in God, in a "Supreme Being," or in "the gods." But almost none believe in the Devil, at least not as Christianity traditionally conceives him. Most witches regard witchcraft as the "old religion," one that predates Christianity, Judaism, and all other monotheistic religions. As far as witches are concerned, non-pagan religions are "novelties" for which they have little respect. To state this differently, although

Satanism is a direct reaction to Christianity, witchcraft is not, and it does not have the same theological categories as Satanism. Although witches believe in "spirits" (both good and bad), they typically do not consider them to be personal beings (angels and demons) as a Christian (or even a Satanist) would define them. To many witches, these spirits are just impersonal forces of nature that can be manipulated through occult ministrations.

Though most who identify as witches do not regard Christianity as a means to perfection, they have great respect for Christianity as an enemy and are well aware of Christ and His Church's power. Father Michael, a parish priest with whom I am a good friend, has a self-proclaimed witch living across the street from his church rectory. Both he and the woman own cats that play outside together. One day, on the Feast of Saint Francis, the patron saint of animals, he blessed his cat, and since it was with the witch's cat, he blessed hers too. Later that week, the woman knocked tersely on his door, demanding whether he had harmed her cat. "Of course not," he replied. "Why would you ask such a thing?"

"Because it has refused to enter my home for the last three days," she said snidely.

Because of the power Christianity wields, witches view the Church as their enemy. Due to witches, holy water tanks in parish churches were historically locked, a practice that has recently fallen out of use but served a critical purpose. Witches are known to "swap" holy water with cursed water, contaminate the tank by dropping in a dead animal, or defile the holy water by placing their menstrual blood in it. The tragic effect: as Catholics bless themselves with holy water upon entering a church or fill their bottles to bring it home, they may be unwittingly subjecting themselves to the witches' cursed matter.

The effectiveness of just this simple strategy should give one pause. In doing these actions, witches attempt to prevent the efficacy of holy water, a sacramental whose purpose is to drive away evil. Imagine how effective evil could be if witches were free to remove that weapon by draining the holy water tank. Or, far worse, by replacing this weapon with their own, which the unwitting Christian then applies to himself. Witches can achieve this when they have access to the inside of holy water tanks.

Historically, witches hate saints' relics and steal them for use in their ceremonies, where they mock, desecrate, and destroy them. In this regard, witchcraft is similar to Satanism, wherein witches desecrate relics and the Eucharist in horrific rituals. While witchcraft and Satanism may differ in their rituals' ceremonial form and appearance, they are remarkably similar in content. Both involve blood and human sacrifice—especially of children—who are immolated upon altars. The Satanist does so to please Satan; a witch may do so to "gain the child's energy" or as a good given "in trade" to a spirit.

One of the most common practices used in witchcraft is sex magick,[1] the use of the orgasm to cast spells or to effect some other kind of desired reality. It is based on the notion that sexual energy is one of the universe's most powerful forces—powerful enough to create or destroy—that can be directed to specific purposes.

According to practitioners, a witch produces sex magick by mentally focusing on an outcome she desires to create. Having that outcome fixed in her mind, she will engage in sexual activity, at the height of which she will send the "energy" generated by her orgasm to produce the desired effect.

In Trent and Evelyn's case, it is all but certain Evelyn was using sexual intercourse to create sex magick, the effect of which was to achieve Trent's submissive control. While Evelyn may have been unaware she was employing demonic spirits—believing she was merely manipulating the occult, the impersonal forces of nature that witchcraft made available to her—the power behind her actions did not come from nature but demons. Demons produce the effect behind all occult practices.

————————

Witchcraft and Satanism are all around us. Because both tend toward radical individualism, their adherents rarely make their presence known in society, content to practice their lifestyle anonymously. Their anonymity often makes people unprepared for the evil they face when encountering them, to their harm.

NINE

CURSES

THE CASE OF
THE MOTHER'S CURSE

Years ago, I vacationed in Portugal during the summer. I traveled to various towns and villages to see their religious festivals, in addition to visiting family (my paternal and maternal ancestry is Portuguese).

Portuguese cities and towns celebrate their patron saints with a summer outdoor festival when the weather is nice. Festivities include a procession, music, marching bands, food, and elaborate displays of fireworks.

I saw the same, odd-looking man at each festival I visited. It was his job to transport the pyrotechnics, arrange them in a set, and discharge them. These are immensely powerful fireworks. Besides producing colorful patterns of light, their blasts are far louder than shotgun blasts. One could call them bombs. Handling such fireworks always carries a risk to one's safety.

The man wore a long, buttoned trench coat that came down just below his knees. His shins were bare, making it evident that he wore no pants beneath his coat. He seemed to be in his sixties and was an odd sight indeed. I guessed that the man chose not to wear pants to avoid their catching fire during the pyrotechnic lighting.

One sweltering and extraordinarily humid day, I attended a festival where I saw the now-familiar man at work arranging the fireworks for the evening show. Again, he was sporting the same long and heavy trench coat. The heat of the day was oppressive, and it made me uncomfortable just to look at him.

A cousin of mine was speaking to the man. In observing their conversation's casual manner, it was apparent they were friends, and I later asked my cousin about him. I was not expecting his response.

"The man's name is Francisco. Nice guy," my cousin replied. Anticipating I had questions about his appearance, he continued, "Francisco has no genitals, and he is missing much of his urinary system. His urine does not collect in his bladder but drips out of him as it forms. That's why he doesn't wear pants. That's also why he only works outdoors. His bladder is constantly draining itself in drips."

The story went from bad to worse. "My parents knew his mother. She got pregnant as a teen, out of wedlock. The pregnancy was rough. Because she had morning sickness every day and she was vomiting so often, her parents suspected she was pregnant. Ashamed to admit it, she denied it until she began to show. Though she denied it again when her parents asked her, she eventually was too large to deny it. Her father confronted her, but she roared, 'I am not pregnant! If I am pregnant, may the baby inside me be neither male nor female!'"

He continued, "When she later went into labor and gave birth, the tragedy became known. Francisco was born without genitalia. He was also missing much of what is needed for emptying the bladder. There was no way to tell whether the newborn was a male or female. It was only after the doctors performed testing that they could confirm the baby was a boy.'"

Francisco suffered his entire life because of his deformity. He lived as a recluse and never married, making a living doing odd jobs he could do outdoors. He could not afford adult diapers.

SPOKEN CURSES

The word "curse" is often used to connote crude words in speech—i.e., cussing. While cussing and cursing can often mean the same thing in everyday speech, properly speaking, they are not the same. A curse is speech or action calling for harm to befall someone or something. In contrast to a blessing, which empowers, strengthens, and gives life, a curse drains, weakens, and kills.

There are many reasons why someone would curse: to get revenge; to destroy a marriage (or some other relationship); to establish an unholy relationship; to cause financial hardship; to bring disturbance and unhappiness to someone; to cause another's sickness or death; et cetera.

Blessings and curses exist because of the way God has constructed reality. God created a moral universe, a universe where it is possible to choose good or evil. Adam's choosing of the latter—or, stated differently, his rebellion against God—destroyed the primordial blessing of paradise under which he was living. It also became the occasion for history's first curses, which God pronounced Himself: He cursed the serpent (Genesis 3:14), Eve (3:16), the earth (3:17), and finally, Adam (3:17–19).

A curse is simply an invocation of justice, or the righteous calling forth of punishment for evil. For this reason, God's cursing is good and holy. However, God never curses for the sake of punishment alone; He never desires to just "get back" at the transgressor with mere justice. God's curses are medicinal, and they become the means for a blessing. Eve's curse, for example, was a condemnation to experience intense labor pains. Still, her supreme glory consists in motherhood through which she will become the mother of all the living (Gen. 3:20). The Savior—who will undo the evil committed by her and Adam—will be born from one of her daughters. Adam's curse was being condemned to labor, but labor becomes the means of his salvation and that of his progeny (Col. 3:23–24). The Savior will one day labor to bring salvation to the human family. Although God's curses are bitter when they are received, it is the bitterness of medicine, one that produces health and blessing.

Thus, there is such a thing as holy cursing. Holy cursing intends to bring about the will of God. Even Saint Paul curses when he says, "But even if we, or an angel from heaven, should preach to you a gospel contrary to that which we preached to you, let him be accursed" (Gal. 1:8).

I regularly invoke such curses. When I drive past a prominent place of evil—a pornography shop, an adult strip club, or an abortion clinic, for example—I trace the sign of the Cross in its direction and invoke a "holy curse":

> *May you be struck invisible.*
> *May the curse of Almighty God be upon you.*
> *May you wither and die as the cursed fig tree. (Cf. Mark 11:21)*

To be clear, I direct my curse toward the *evil work* that occurs within the respective facility (the lust marketed in the porn shops and strip clubs; the murder of babies in the abortion mills, et cetera). My curse is *never* toward the sinners who perform the work. For them, I pray for conversion and ask God to turn them away from the evil they have embraced.

In opposition, evil cursing desires to wound sinfully or to selfishly manipulate a person. Such cursing can inflict terrible damage. The curse uttered by Francisco's mother is an example. Francisco paid dearly for his mother's words.

The effectiveness of a curse is due to three principles:

1. Words have power.

A word created the universe. By Adam's word, the animals of creation were named, and God Himself abided by what Adam called them

(Gen. 2:19). The Church pronounces the words of baptism while pouring water, and the pagan recipient becomes a new creation in God (Rom. 6:4). A man and woman pronounce their vows at their wedding, and they become one flesh (Gen. 2:24). Other examples abound.

In the case of Francisco, his mother's words led to the altering of physical reality. She may never have intended to mutilate her baby, yet her words affected him in utero when she spoke. This is not because she could manipulate mysterious and unseen forces in nature merely by speaking, but because her words gave the legal right to demons who can.

2. Every evil curse is a mystical conjoining to Satan.

When someone curses another, he imitates Satan, whose rebellion was a curse against God and everything God loves. This imitation opens him to a connection with Satan wherein demons can enter the curse and produce what it invokes. Demons are the fuel that power curses.

Francisco's mother refused the truth. She refused to own up to the fact that she had sexual intercourse outside of marriage, that she was pregnant as a result, and that the baby inside her was a living being, a person God created in His image. In choosing a reality different from what God's providence and design had permitted, she made an act of rebellion akin to Satan's. Tragically, Satan pounced on it.

3. Humans are mystically connected.

Humans are interconnected. Having the same two original parents, all humans have a common bond. Our shared human DNA is evidence of this bond on a physical level, and the common inheritance of Original Sin is evidence on a spiritual level.

In Francisco's case, though his mother committed the evil, Francisco endured its consequences. Even after his mother repented,

Francisco suffered the curse's effects his whole life. The fact that it was *his* mother who invoked it was the reason for its severity and effectiveness. She not only shared Francisco's bloodline but as his mother, she possessed spiritual authority. If a stranger had stated similar words, they would likely not have affected Francisco. But because it was *his* mother—speaking words so emphatically and with such contempt—it was the open door that evil required to produce a tragic result. Her words gave evil permission to damage her baby.

To believe in curses is neither irrational nor simplistic. All human societies seem to have curses within their understanding of reality. Rather than being isolated to particular cultures or peoples, belief in curses is a human phenomenon.

The best way to tell if one is cursed is to look for destructive patterns. Curses reveal themselves through repetition. While everyone has a string of bad luck here and there, if the "bad luck" occurs with a regularity that defies probability and rational expectation, then a curse might be the cause.

Common symptoms of curses include:

- Frequent nightmares and disturbed sleep.
- Sudden and persistent health problems.
- Financial difficulties or legal troubles.
- Relational difficulties.
- Loss of energy (emotional, physical, mental, and spiritual).
- General "bad luck."
- Random aches and pains.
- Scattered mind, confusion, and disorientation.
- Uncharacteristic forgetfulness.
- Mechanical failures and frequent breaking down of physical objects.

PHYSICAL CURSES

A physical curse is a curse attached to an object through some ritual. The cursed item is placed in its intended victim's possession, and its evil is released. Such curses are sometimes called object-bound curses, malefices, fortunas, effigies, or just plain hexes or spells.

Physical curses have the power to unleash a great evil. I knew a family who experienced significant financial hardship after their appliances and electronic devices suddenly broke down. The refrigerator, the freezer, the family computer, the stove, the clothes dryer, and the furnace all stopped working. When replaced, within a week, their replacements broke down as well. One month into the ordeal, a strange woman knocked at the family's door, brazenly claiming to have caused the chaos through a curse. Two family members recognized her, recalling her as a random passerby who requested to use their bathroom some two months earlier. Out of kindness to a stranger in need, they allowed her into their home.

The woman demanded three thousand dollars to remove the curse, but the family had little money. They bought used appliances, but buying used meant the devices had no warranty. They had spent so much on appliances that, even if they wanted to pay the ransom, they could not. When the family told that to the woman, she replied, "Then it will continue."

The family did not know what to do to alleviate their situation. Then something occurred. One of the daughters found a strange object inside the bathroom closet. Partially tucked inside a gap in the wall—not visible unless one looked beneath the bottom shelf toward the back wall—was a rolled sheet of plain paper, inside of which was a pin with an imitation pearl at the end. She showed it to her family members and, when no one claimed its ownership, she threw it away. When the trash was hauled away three days later, all appliances began working immediately. Putting the clues together, they realized—in a way they could not understand—that the pin had caused the chaos. They also realized it must have been the woman who planted it since it was found in the bathroom she had used.

Physical curses cannot only cause destruction and chaos. They can manipulate someone into making a choice he would not ordinarily make. Patrick, a relative of a friend, was given an assortment of homemade candies by a female coworker who desired a relationship. She regularly flirted with him, even though more than once he replied that he had no interest. One day, as Patrick was finishing his shift, the woman handed him a bag of candy, saying, "I made these just for you. They're the best candies you've ever had." He placed them on the passenger seat and forgot all about them by the time he got home. He found them the following day as he was heading to work. Ready to enjoy one, he picked up the bag and looked inside. All the candies had turned to hair.

It is impossible to say what would have happened had Patrick consumed a candy. Clearly, it would not have been good. Why did they specifically turn to hair? I have no idea. Physical curses can manifest a wide range of characteristics. But their transformation—the loss of their deceptive appeal—was a sign that at least part of the curse behind them was no longer operative. Thankfully, they had only had a few hours in which to work. Had it been for a more extended period, Patrick might have eaten one of them and fallen victim to it.

Some curses are more effective than others. This is often due to the *level of sacrifice* put into them. Most curses require something of value to be offered at the time of their generation such as:

- Time: some cursing rituals require a great deal of time to accomplish.
- Money: paid to a sorcerer to create the curse; offered payment to a deity for the curse's success, et cetera.

- Comfort: some curses are fueled by self-injury or extreme mortification on the part of the one cursing to "feed" the evil behind it.
- Blood sacrifice: the life of at least one person or animal offered to animate the curse.

Obviously curses are not cheap. They cost something to the person invoking them.

When being prayed over for the breaking of a curse, the victim— who may have been unaware he was cursed—may suddenly vomit a strange object. These can include feathers, hair, nails, stones and even sticks. It is a mystery how the object got inside the person in the first place, but the power behind some curses is broken only when the victim expels it.

BREAKING A CURSE

The best way to defend against a curse is to avoid coming under its power in the first place. Being a committed disciple of the Lord and pursuing His holiness is the best way to ensure this. When one walks with the Lord, one possesses His blessing, shares in His authority, and operates under His protection, as Saint Paul attests, "If God is for us, who can be against us?" (Rom. 8:31 NIV).

Paul had good reason to preach Christian courage. No evil or misfortune that ever came against him could overpower him. When a snake bit him on the beach in Malta, for example, he shook it off into the fire while it was still biting him and carried on with what he was doing as if nothing had happened, to the bystanders' amazement (Acts 28:5). Because of Paul's confidence and nonchalance, the Maltese thought him to be a god.

Later, after Paul was asked what to do with meat sacrificed to idols—meaning it had been offered to demons (1 Cor. 10:20)—he said to eat it without worry. He was so full of Jesus that the dangers he encountered, whether physical or spiritual, did not worry him in the least. God's protection gave him so much confidence that nothing else gave him concern or anxiety, not even cursed meat.

The confidence exhibited by Saint Paul stands in marked contrast to the anxiety that modern-day people exhibit. As I write this, typing the question, "How to break a curse?" into an internet search engine yields a barrage of articles authored by witches and occult practitioners offering remedies for undoing curses that—ironically—*have been done by other witches and practitioners of the occult.* Far from being liberating, the abandonment of Christianity and the reversion to paganism has merely subjected people once again to spiritual slavery—the same slavery the world was under before the coming of Christ. In fact, the internet search yields almost no Christian results, even after I scrolled through multiple pages of returns. Neo-pagan spirituality seems to subject one to endless predatory curses. By their lack of concern, Christians are—evidently—protected from curses in a way pagans are not.

If ever a Christian finds himself under a curse's debilitating power, his first concern ought to be to *close any doors* by which evil has a claim on him. Remember, evil is subject to the rules of sovereignty. The victim of a curse should immediately get rid of all sin of which he is guilty. The following are the five most common failures.

1. Failure to repent.
To be free of the power of evil, one needs to be free of evil-doing. Repent of sin, especially mortal sin, and stop committing further sin to allow God's grace to do its work. Even if one's sin is not the direct cause of one's being cursed, sin closes us off from God's grace, which in turn makes us vulnerable to the evil that comes against us.

Breaking a curse's power comes entirely from grace, and grace cannot dwell in one who chooses sin over God. Sins that seem to make one especially vulnerable to curses, and demonic activity in general, are sexual sins and sins that involve the occult.

2. Failure to worship God in the manner He desires.

If God is not the center of our lives, then we are not living as His disciples. Discipleship means a commitment to daily prayer (i.e., faithfully dedicating time to prayer; not just time we have "left over"), studying the Word of God, performing works of charity, and participating in Mass on Sunday and Holy Days of obligation. If we are not worshipping the God of Heaven in this manner, we are worshipping some other god.

3. Failure to receive the Sacraments.

Jesus Christ gave the seven sacraments to heal the world. To refuse the Sacraments is to reject Jesus Christ. Period. Among the Sacraments, the Sacrament of Confession is crucial, as it restores us to the purity of our Baptism, the Sacrament that made us Christians and made us sharers in the Divine nature. Failing to confess a specific mortal sin, not because we forgot having committed it, but out of shame for having done so, or out of pride because one regards admitting having done it as being "beneath oneself," closes one off to sacramental grace.[1]

4. Failure to remove what is useless and destructive.

If there are people in our lives that bring us down by distracting us from holiness and leading us into sin, or by transferring their dysfunctional or destructive tendencies onto us, then we may need to end our relationship with them. Such applies even to long-term friends and acquaintances. If someone is a stumbling block to our pursuit of Heaven, it is better not to have that person in our life. The same applies to any particular thing, such as a possession or even one's job.

5. Failure to forgive.
Forgiveness is one of the great commandments of Jesus, who Himself is the very mercy and forgiveness of God. As such, we are obliged to forgive from the heart those who have hurt and wounded us. In fact, we commit ourselves to forgive others each time we pray the Our Father: "forgive us our trespasses *as we forgive those who have trespassed against us.*" God's recompense for those who forgive is glory (Pro. 19:11).

If none of these five failures apply, yet a person still suffers from a curse's effect, then one must engage in direct combat against the curse through one of the following acts:

1. Pray and ask the Lord to lift the curse.
Do not assume the Lord will remove a curse from you without *your active participation.* Though God wants to see you liberated, more so than you do, He has too much respect for your free will to violate it. For God to have the freedom to act against your curse, you need to permit Him to do so, and this requires you to use words. Do not assume you have already allowed Him!

2. Forgive whoever has cursed you (whether you know who it is or not) and pray for him.
The Lord Himself says, "But I say to you, Love your enemies and pray for those who persecute you" (Matthew 5:44). These words must be the basis of our attitude to one who has cursed us. Daily prayer and sacrifice for the person or persons responsible for the curse conforms us to Christ and drains the curse of its power.

3. Look for what could be a cursed object.

Attempt to locate a cursed object in your vehicle, among your belongings, in your home, or even on your person (e.g., does the chain around your neck have a new object on it—e.g., a new medal—that you never put there?). If you find anything that does not belong to you or has been significantly marred, disfigured, or modified by someone, even someone unknown to you, discard it. Be cautious when receiving a gift, especially a previously owned object (e.g., an antique). If a curse's effects began after receiving that object, discard or destroy it and see whether that brings the curse to an end.

Locating a cursed object can be extraordinarily difficult as the one who cursed it will always intend that it not be found. Should one locate it, douse it with holy water, burn it, or otherwise destroy it. Anything that remains should be discarded. It must no longer be on one's property. Destruction ensures that it afflicts no one else.

4. Rebuke the curse and pray against it.

Offer daily prayers, penitential sacrifices, and fasting for the breaking of the curse.

5. Ask holy persons, especially the Saints in Heaven, for their prayers and intercession.

Saint James tells us, "The prayer of a righteous man has great power in its effects" (James 5:16).

6. Seek out a Catholic priest and ask for his assistance in breaking the curse.

Not all priests are equally experienced in this area. Some may have never encountered curses and may merely offer one a blessing. This is insufficient. A curse's effect is the work of a demon. Locate a priest who is willing to exorcise it, along with your home, vehicle, business, or wherever you sense that the curse is operative. If this does not resolve the problem, contact your local Catholic diocese and request the services of the exorcist.

There is a distinction between a curse and its effects. Even if a curse is broken or expires on its own (some are by their nature temporary), what it caused may be permanent and irreversible. What happened to Francisco, the man born without genitalia, is one example. His mother's curse led to a lifelong physical deformity, one he had to live with the rest of his life.

———

The notion that curses are real offends the sensibilities of many Christians, many of whom believe they are superstition.

Nevertheless, as the opposite of blessings, curses are just as real, and they can produce significant harm. Especially severe are those curses produced by someone in special authority: parents toward their children; spouses toward one another; employees toward their employers; et cetera. The closer the relationship, the more damaging and destructive a curse can be.

The material world can play a part in the delivery of curses. Just as physical objects can be blessed, they can be cursed and serve as a conduit for evil.

The best way to protect oneself against curses is to be in the grace of God by living as His friend. If we walk with the Lord, we possess His protection, and our enemies are limited in their ability to hurt us. Indeed, Saint Paul declares, "If God is for us, who is against us?" (Rom. 8:31).

TEN

GHOSTS AND HAUNTINGS

THE CASE OF
THE REAPPEARING HEART ATTACK VICTIM

A good friend of mine married a woman who is employed as a nurse at St. Mary's General Hospital in Kitchener, Ontario. She told me a story about a man who died of cardiac arrest in room 104 shortly after being admitted to the emergency room sometime in the early 1990s. After his death, the dead man repeatedly appeared to the hospital staff.

One such occasion involved a recently hired nurse who had just begun her afternoon shift. She went into 104 to retrieve medical supplies. Though once a fully functional medical room, it was being used to store medical supplies. Only occasionally, if all other facilities in the ER were full, was it employed as an overflow medical room.

Upon entering, she was shocked to discover a man lying on a stretcher unattended.

"Why didn't anyone tell me we are holding someone in room 104?" she demanded at the nurses' station. "How long has he been there?"

"What are you talking about?" the head nurse replied.

"There's a cardiac patient in 104. When did someone last check on him?"

Stopping what she was doing, the head nurse turned her face until she looked directly at the junior nurse. "There's no one assigned to that room," she declared.

"There is. And he looks terrible."

"I think you've just seen our ghost," the head nurse declared. "He is a man who died of cardiac arrest in room 104 about eight years ago. His ghost occasionally appears—"

"I didn't see a ghost," the young nurse interrupted, offended at the suggestion she could not differentiate the real from the unreal. "I saw a real person."

"Let's check it out together."

When the two nurses entered Room 104, they found no one. Neither was there a stretcher or any evidence a patient had ever been there. The room held only the usual shelves of medical supplies.

"But I saw him!" the young nurse insisted, dumbfounded.

"No doubt you did," her colleague replied. "I've seen him myself. Sometimes this room's call button rings, and we find no one here when we respond."

GHOSTS

Ghosts are real. They are not just the subject of scary movies or fictional books. While the Catholic Church has no defined teaching on ghosts, highly respected Catholic theologians have held that spirits who wander the earth—and are occasionally permitted to be seen—are souls of deceased humans experiencing their Purgatory.[1] In other words, they are souls who have received their judgment and been found worthy of salvation but are nevertheless undergoing the purification required to enter Heaven. Why must souls be purified?

Because one cannot stand before God without being in a state of perfection. In the words of Saint John Paul II:

> [T]he encounter with God requires absolute purity. Every trace of attachment to evil must be eliminated, every imperfection of the soul corrected. Purification must be complete, and indeed this is precisely what is meant by the Church's teaching on Purgatory. The term does not indicate a place, but a condition of existence. Those who, after death, exist in a state of purification, are already in the love of Christ who removes from them the remnants of imperfection.[2]

A more apt way to speak of such spirits might be *distressed souls*, since they are experiencing the distress of purgation.[3]

The New Testament references a post-death state of purification before a soul's entrance to Heaven when Jesus declares every sin can be forgiven, except blasphemy against the Holy Spirit, "either in this age or in the age to come" (Matt. 12:32). While Our Lord assures His followers that God forgives sins *in this life*, the phrase "in the age to come" implies a kind of forgiveness obtained in a future, post-death age. The Book of Revelation also alludes to temporary pain in the afterlife where God "will wipe away every tear from their eyes, and death shall be no more, neither shall there be mourning nor crying nor pain any more, for the former things have passed away" (Rev. 21:4). The verses immediately preceding this passage declare that these tears are *not* shed in this life but the afterlife when Christ has *already* instituted a "new heaven and a new earth" (Rev. 21:1). Catholic theology has consistently interpreted the source of those tears as the fire of purification that Saint Paul says the saved will endure (1 Cor. 3:11–15). This very fire appears to be what Saint Paul has in mind when he prays that his friend Onesiphorus be raised to eternal life "on that Day," implying that the *already deceased* man may not yet be there (2 Tim. 1:16–18).

It is extraordinarily rare for a person to see a distressed soul, and if that happens it is because God, in His mercy, has permitted it so that the soul may receive prayers that will hasten its purgation.

When I found out about the dead man's periodic appearances at the hospital, I was still in the seminary. While I could not offer Mass for him, I arranged for a priest to do so. It has now been over eighteen years since that Mass, and none of the hospital staff have seen him since. A Mass for his soul's repose appears to be all he needed.

It is noteworthy that this distressed soul never spoke. God rarely permits dead souls to speak. On those occasions when He does, it is only to ask for prayers. But once done, God seldom allows it to say anything else. It will not comment on the weather, ask how you are doing, or share the kind of music it prefers, and it will never reveal "tantalizing" information, such as secret and occult knowledge.

Demons may fool people by disguising themselves as "friendly" or "benevolent" ghosts who offer unique and privileged information unavailable through any other means. *There are no such things as friendly ghosts!* There are only ghosts in need, that is, distressed souls who require prayers or demons who pretend to be ghosts.

Occasionally, a distressed soul requires more than just prayers. I know a case where a deceased man appeared to his family repeatedly. They prayed for him and arranged for Masses, but he kept appearing. Finally, he spoke to his eldest daughter, revealing an act of theft he committed during his life. A boulder marked the edge of his property from that of his neighbor, and he had dishonestly moved it to increase his property's size. The dead man could not rest. The neighbor's stolen land had to be restored. After the boulder was restored to its rightful place, the dead man never appeared again.

Ghosts and Demons: Diagnosing the Cause of a "Haunting"

Exorcists often deal with dwellings that exhibit "haunted house" or "poltergeist" phenomena: figures appearing out of nowhere, disembodied voices heard speaking in adjacent rooms or halls, unsettling and disturbing sounds (rattles, bangs, moans, crying, et cetera), and general mischievous phenomena.

An exorcist must diagnose whether the phenomena are caused by a distressed soul or a demon. A proper diagnosis is crucial, as either entity can produce them, and prayers addressing one type of entity will not affect the other.

The key to distinguishing demons from ghosts is to observe whether there has been a change *in the persons experiencing the phenomena*. Experiencing a ghost is unnerving for most people. But while it may leave one *scared*, an encounter with a demon leaves one *terrified*.

A distressed soul *never terrifies*, as that would hinder the very purpose for which God permits the distressed soul to be seen: securing prayerful assistance

Why does God permit a ghost's manifestation to frighten at all? Why not remove everything scary from the experience? Just because something is unpleasant does not mean it is bad. The pain experienced in breaking a leg is undoubtedly unpleasant. It serves to signal a severe problem—a broken bone—which is a good and helpful thing. Besides, if the manifestation of a distressed soul did not mildly "shock" and "disturb" us, we might not take his presence seriously enough to do what it asks: offer prayers and supplications on his behalf to end his purgation or Purgatory.

Having assessed the level of fright within those experiencing the haunting phenomena, the exorcist responds with the appropriate type of prayer: either prayers of supplication or exorcism. Should his discernment be incorrect, and the cause of the phenomena is the other type of entity, switching to that corresponding mode of prayer is easy, and his only loss is that of time. Nevertheless, since most exorcists have great demands on their time, any savings is beneficial.

Ghost Hunters

One of the worst things someone can do when encountering a distressed soul is to call in a paranormal investigator or "ghost hunter," as they only aggravate the problem. Though they claim to be helpful, their approach is to communicate with the unknown entity. Should the entity be a demon, this is egregiously dangerous, as conversing with it solidifies its rights to be there. More so, a paranormal investigator or ghost hunter lacks the Church's authority, so there is no compelling reason for the entity—demon or ghost— to obey his commands. Ghost hunters always leave a situation in a worse state. Because they typically charge money for their "services," they will also leave one poorer.

Paranormal investigators and ghost hunters are charlatans who practice pseudoscientific deception and are often looking for content to use for a book, television show, or internet video. Years ago, the producers of a popular ghost-hunting TV series requested that I perform an exorcism on one of their show's ghost hunters, who had fallen victim to a possession. It was not surprising that he had become demonized. On the show, he often declared to the "source" of the haunting, "I come in peace. I want to be your friend." Having such a conversation with a demon solidifies its bond with the speaker and grants the demon rights to him.

This particular ghost hunter was hospitalized, struck with a series of mysterious and inexplicable illnesses (he was in a coma-tose-like state, and when he spoke, a different personality spoke through him). Not only were the medical staff unable to diagnose his illness, but every treatment they gave him was ineffective. What is more, strange phenomena occurred around him continuously. For example, a steady but sourceless stream of water dripped from the ceiling on top of him, no matter which room he occupied in the hospital. While I believe the producers were genuinely concerned for their colleague, they were adamant about recording the exorcism performed on him for use in their show. I refused to contribute to the false education of their viewership and declined involvement.

Damned Souls

Encountering "damned souls" has easily been the most unexpected discovery I have made as an exorcist. When I say *damned*, I mean just that: souls who have died and been judged by God, and who have been found unworthy of Him, meriting condemnation to hell for all eternity.

Like a demon, a damned soul can inhabit a victim, speak through him, animate his body, and behave in a manner indistinguishable from a demon. He is also capable of exhibiting great fury and violence.

Many exorcists encounter damned souls without realizing it, usually during an extraordinarily difficult exorcism. The entity they encounter (what they believe to be a demon) will be unusually strong, and exorcism prayers do not affect him. They do not pain or torment the damned soul, drain him of energy, nor cause him even the slightest annoyance.

The Church's prayers of exorcism were composed to combat fallen angels, not damned human souls, so the prayers will seem to be ineffective. Bewildered, an exorcist may think that the problem lies within himself:

- "My faith is not strong enough."

- "There is something morally wrong with the state of my soul" (even though he has prepared himself properly).
- "I am an incompetent exorcist."

A colleague of mine—a seasoned exorcist who has faced more damned souls than anyone else I know—has remarked that some damned souls are more sadistic and violent than even demons.

How can this be? Damned souls seem to manifest when higher-ranking demons possess. They appear to be attached to the demons as if each is attached to a specific demon for eternity. From my experience within exorcisms, it appears as though the demon becomes that soul's "guardian demon," a perverted counterpart to a Guardian Angel. On earth, that soul received the protection and assistance of a Guardian Angel, but in his damnation, it is forced to guard, protect, and do the evil bidding of its guardian demon in eternity. Demons ensure compliance by afflicting their entourage with horrific tortures. Damned souls seek to avoid this by pursuing their guardian demon's interests and protecting him from an exorcist. (If such is not the very definition of hell, then I do not know what is!)

In my experience, only one thing seems to cut off the power of a damned soul in an exorcism: speaking to him of God's mercy. Damned souls are in a state of horrific misery. They have only unending pain, misery, and shame to look forward to for all eternity. When I encounter such a soul, I speak of God's mercy and invite him to ask the Lord for it. A typical dialogue might sound like this.

ME: You know you're not happy. God created you for happiness. Turn to Him even now and receive it. Ask Him to forgive your sins.

DAMNED SOUL: I am happy, you son of a *%#$R priest! You're
the unhappy one.

ME: You know that's not true. Your existence is one endless
torture. You were not created for torture. God created you
for Himself, for your joy, and His.

DAMNED SOUL: That's all a &@^$#% lie. You don't even
believe that.

ME: It's not a lie. And I do believe it. Ask Jesus now for mercy,
and He will give it to you. Just say, "Jesus . . . Mercy." That
will be enough. He will save you from all your misery.

DAMNED SOUL: He has no mercy for me.

ME: That's not true. Just say, "Jesus, mercy."

Then suddenly, he is gone. In his place, his guardian demon
takes over the possession, as if to ensure that hell endures no losses.
The dialogues I have with damned souls rarely reach this point.
Usually, the mere mention of mercy is enough to make the guardian demon manifest.

Why would an exorcist offer mercy to a damned soul since it is
Christian dogma that a soul is judged by God immediately upon
death and is *irrevocably* either saved or damned? In other words,
why would an exorcist offer a damned soul a cessation to his suffering when there is no possibility for such a cessation?[4] I have no theological answer for this question, but as an exorcist, I have a practical
one: *because it works at making the damned soul go away.* Whether
he leaves of his own accord (because hearing about Christ's mercy
is too painful) or whether it is his demonic guardian that removes
him, I cannot say. Personally, having dialogued with damned souls
numerous times and witnessing the "switch" whereby their guardian demon suddenly replaces them, I am inclined to believe it is the

latter. I believe the guardian snatches them away. Ultimately, that is what hell is: one's desire for goodness is never fulfilled.

Ghosts Who Manifest During Exorcism

One last topic worth mentioning is the manifestation of ghosts—distressed souls—during an exorcism. A personality who does not exhibit the characteristics of a demon or a damned soul—anger, violence, belligerence, and other qualities that demons and damned souls exhibit—can occasionally manifest. A ghost will show meekness, humility, sorrow, suffering, and even trepidation. When asked to identify itself, it does so reluctantly, not out of defiance, but because of these very dispositions.

The following is a dialogue from one such encounter. While every conversation with a distressed soul is unique, this one is typical of how an exchange between an exorcist and a distressed soul might sound.

> EXORCIST: [*upon discovery of a new personality that does not respond to prayers of exorcism*] In the name of Jesus, tell me whether you are a demon or a human?
>
> DISTRESSED SOUL: [*after much coaxing and commanding, faintly said*] Human.
>
> EXORCIST: How did the Lord Jesus judge you?
>
> DISTRESSED SOUL: [*after a long silence*] I was saved. The Lord in His goodness saved me.
>
> EXORCIST: Tell me your name.
>
> DISTRESSED SOUL: My name is unimportant.
>
> Exorcist: How long ago did you die?
>
> DISTRESSED SOUL: A long time ago.
>
> EXORCIST: Twenty years?
>
> DISTRESSED SOUL: More like twenty generations.

EXORCIST: Is there anyone left from your family to pray for you?

DISTRESSED SOUL: No.

EXORCIST: May I pray for you?

DISTRESSED SOUL: [*expressing both astonishment and gratitude*] You would do that?

EXORCIST: Absolutely. I will offer Masses, the prayers of my Breviary, and rosaries. Tell me your name.

DISTRESSED SOUL: It doesn't matter what my name is.

EXORCIST: How can I pray for you if you don't tell me your name?

DISTRESSED SOUL: [*after a pause*] My name is Robert.

EXORCIST: Where did you die?

DISTRESSED SOUL: [*after a pause*] Limoges [a city in central France].

EXORCIST: How did you die?

DISTRESSED SOUL: [*after a pause*] I was sick for a long time. I realized I died when I appeared before the Lord for judgment.

EXORCIST: Where are you now?

DISTRESSED SOUL: [*with a look of incomprehension, like such a question is unanswerable*] I don't know.

EXORCIST: What do you do?

DISTRESSED SOUL: I wander.

EXORCIST: Are there others like you?

DISTRESSED SOUL: A great many.

EXORCIST: Tell them I will pray for them as well.

DISTRESSED SOUL: [*smiling and starting to weep*] Oh, thank you! Thank you!

EXORCIST: [*holding out his crucifix*] This is the crucifix I use in exorcisms. Hold it while I say a prayer for you right now and for the others.

DISTRESSED SOUL: [*Animating the victim's body, receives the crucifix and kisses it. He weeps while the prayer is said.*]

EXORCIST: Almighty Father, I bring You Robert and all wandering souls and ask for Your mercy upon them. Comfort them and hasten their purgation. Let them receive many suffrages and penances through the living so they may soon dwell with You and Your saints in Heaven. Amen. [*At the "Amen," the distressed soul immediately departs.*]

Nearly every encounter I have with a distressed soul within an exorcism contains the following elements:

1. The soul exhibits a profound meekness that could easily be mistaken for fear: his words, tone, and gestures all communicate, "I am unimportant."
2. He makes a request for prayer (or gratefully accepts it when it is offered, should he be unable to request it himself) such that by the end of the encounter, it is evident this is why he manifested.
3. An acknowledgment that his suffering is just and that God is the perfect good.
4. He exhibits piety and reverence toward the Christian faith and holy things.

It is the nature of demons and damned souls to be deceptive, but they would never humble themselves to display even one of them.

Two questions may be asked at this point: Is there a connection between *the distressed soul* and *the person undergoing exorcism*? Why did the distressed soul manifest during an exorcism?

Regarding the first question, only rarely have I found any connection between the distressed soul and the victim or the exorcist. In one case, three distressed souls manifested in the victim in succession, each of whom was his relative. In this case, however, each distressed soul was directly connected to a generational curse that caused the possession.

Regarding the second question, when asked why they came at *this* particular moment, distressed souls often do not know the answer; or they may respond with an answer such as, "I saw light and followed it." In other words, the exorcist's prayers and God's response produce a grace visible to these souls, and they are drawn to it to obtain help.

Once a distressed soul has departed, I have never seen him return. I suspect that each visit is a concession by God, made after a significant amount of a soul's purgation is complete, the purpose being to obtain the prayers that will complete it. This is, however, only my supposition. I continue to pray for the repose of each soul that has ever manifested to me. In this way, the soul cannot lose.

———

Far from being merely the subject of scary movies or fictional books, ghosts are real, and belief in them is ubiquitous in human cultures. There is no inconsistency between the Christian faith and belief in ghosts as long as the Christian understands ghosts to be souls who are being "delivered from their sin" (2 Mac. 12:45). Once cleansed, they will enter Heaven and embrace Him Who is the object of all their longing, the All-Holy God, before Whom no one can stand having the slightest imperfection.

The manifestation of distressed souls, which occurs even within exorcisms, reminds us that fraternal bonds do not cease with death but transcend it. As brethren in need, distressed souls merit our mercy and prayer.

ELEVEN

SEX AND SEXUALITY: PORTALS TO THE SOUL

THE CASE OF
THE NEVER-ENDING LABOR DAY WEEKEND

Christopher was a mess. His balance was shaky, his face was ashen, and his hands trembled. He walked into my office slowly, as if he had no energy to spare, looking as if a slight breeze would knock him over.

Though Christopher was not in the least religious, his friends had encouraged him to see a priest as he had tried everything else to improve his situation. For the last three months, he suffered from a debilitating depression that prevented him from engaging in every-day activities. In his mid-twenties, Christopher had built up a thriving graphic design business, was enrolled part time in a fine arts graduate program and had managed to accomplish all this without incurring debt.

But one day all came to a screeching halt. "I don't know what happened," Christopher said. "Everything was going well, and then I entered hell. I started to feel scared, really scared, all the time. I locked myself in my room, never wanting to come out. Gradually, I stopped answering the phone, even when I knew it was a friend calling or the delivery person bringing the food I had just ordered. I cry all the time, for no reason."

Christopher had seen various physicians and a psychologist for his condition. None, however, were able to diagnose the cause of his depression. Aside from undereating—a by-product the physicians attributed to his depression—none could find anything wrong with him. But even after three weeks of forcing himself to eat, a strategy suggested by more than one doctor as worth trying, his depressive state remained unchanged.

Since the illness began, Christopher had lost forty-five pounds, had lost his business, and had abandoned his graduate program. Unable to work, he had missed all his contract deadlines, and most of his clients had long stopped calling. Missing payments resulted in phone service cancellation.

Christopher wasn't even sure how to articulate what he was experiencing. Over and over, all he could say was, "I've entered into hell." He had received the results of a battery of psychological and medical tests, which he shared with me. I asked a physician and a psychologist who assist me in this ministry to help interpret them. Nothing indicated a diagnosable medical condition.

"When did you start feeling this way?" I asked him.

"Three months ago," he answered.

"Are you able to pinpoint a specific day?"

Thinking about it for a moment, he replied, "The Tuesday after Labor Day."

"That was the first day you felt like this?"

"Yes."

"What did you do on Labor Day?"

"I was at a beach house vacationing."

"Who were you with?"

"A friend."

"Male or female?"

"Female."

"Was she your girlfriend?"

"No."

"Did you have sex?"

Clearing his throat, Christopher replied, "Yes."

"How long had you known her before you spent the weekend with her?"

"Just a day. I met her that Friday. We agreed to spend the long weekend at a beach house I rented." He explained that he met her through a dating app, and the only thing he knew about her was that her name was Lisa.

I summarized the scenario: "You knew this woman for less than a day, had sex with her all weekend, the Tuesday after Labor Day, this depression started, and you were in perfect health before that. But the doctors have been unable to diagnose a medical problem?"

"Yes," he answered.

"Then, Christopher," I said, "I suspect you experienced a demonic transference through Lisa. She probably gave you demons."

Christopher's face took on a look of confusion and mistrust. He had no relationship with God and no religious formation. Although he appeared to be a decent and hardworking individual, he was acquainted only with the world's ways and morality. He related his belief that demons are the stuff of horror movies, having about as much existence as leprechauns or tooth fairies. The notion that they can transfer from one person to another—as if they were the spiritual equivalent of a biological disease—seemed ridiculous.

Catholic teaching around sexuality may be perceived as strict by some. Such teaching is not prudish or naive, or, least of all, trendy. It is positive and beneficial and timeless. I tried to explain to Christopher in terms he'd understand. "Christopher, God didn't create sex merely for the pleasure of the participants. He created it to be holy. Through sex, we assist Him in creating, as sexual intercourse is how God brings about new life. It produces a union so strong that it endures long after the sexual act is complete."

I went on to tell him how the only moral and safe way to engage in intercourse is with one's spouse as Saint Paul explains, "Do you not know that he who unites himself with a prostitute is one with her, as one body? For it is said, 'The two will become one flesh'" (1 Cor. 6:16). Sexual intercourse entails bonding with one's partner at such a deep level that he or she gains rights to your body, and vice versa, because you and your partner have become one at the deepest level of your being. Among other things, this entails that whatever is spiritually within your partner has complete access to you and becomes part of you. And whoever else has bonded to that partner—i.e., past sexual partners—also becomes bonded with you. Also, if a sexual partner has demons, they also become part of you and remain as long as the spiritual union between you and your partner exists.

"We need to renounce the bond you made with Lisa and then ask Jesus to sever it," I said.

Christopher's face was blank. After a few moments of silence, he said, "There is no bond. The sex with Lisa is over. I've had other sexual partners in the past, and this never happened."

In the thinking of the world, Christopher's objection was reasonable. I had to find a way to explain it to him that made sense.

"Think of it like this, Christopher," I began. "Imagine you decide to leave the windows and doors of your house wide open while you're away on vacation. Upon your return, you find everything is as you left it, and you begin to form a belief that there is no problem with leaving your home unsecured anytime you are away from it. It isn't intelligent, but you can begin to believe that, nonetheless. Then, each time you go away and return and find your home undisturbed, your confidence increases. However, one day, you return and find that a family of raccoons is now living in your home and regard it as their own. And they don't appreciate the fact that you think it belongs to you and don't want them there. Now, go ahead and try and get the creatures out of your house. Have you ever tried to corner a threatened raccoon?"

Christopher sat silently for several moments, looking wearied and exhausted. "This sounds far-fetched, Father," he said with an exhale. "I'm sorry for wasting your time. There's something medically wrong with me. The doctors just haven't found it yet." He got up and left.

I did not hear from Christopher for another six months. He later called requesting another appointment. When he arrived, he looked much worse than before. He was thinner, and his eyes were so sunken that they appeared blackened from a fight. By now, he had suffered for nine months with his debilitation.

"I'll do anything you want me to do," Christopher pleaded. "I just want this to end before it kills me."

"Okay. Let's begin," I said. I asked, "Do you believe in God, Christopher?"

"Honestly, no. But if God can make this go away, I sure will," he replied.

His answer was perfect: he was honest about his lack of belief but was open to being proven wrong. "Then let's give God that chance," I answered with a smile as I began sprinkling him with holy water. "This is holy water. It has received a blessing to drive away evil." I put on a stole, placed my hand on his shoulder, and began to pray:

Lord, I give You thanks. I thank You for creating Christopher. I thank You for gifting him to the world and enriching it with his presence. I thank You for bringing him into my life. I ask You to send Your Holy Spirit upon him to heal and recreate him according to Your image and likeness. Let Your Holy Spirit envelop him completely and penetrate his whole being. Let Your Spirit flow through his flesh, blood, bones, and organs. Let Him penetrate his mind and flow through his memory, imagination, intellect, and will. Heal everything out of order, and restore Christopher to health, made new by Your power and love. Show him You are real.

By this point, tears were flowing down Christopher's cheeks, and he was sobbing out loud. It was obvious God was doing something. I said to him, "Christopher, repeat after me. In the name of Jesus . . ."

After a few moments, after regaining composure, he answered, "In the name of Jesus."

I then pronounced the following renunciations, pausing after each sentence so that he could repeat it.

I renounce the sexual relationship I had with Lisa.
And all other sexual relationships I have ever had.
I sever myself from all my previous sexual partners, especially from Lisa.
I give her back everything I took from her.
And I take back what I surrendered to her.
I ask You to bless her, heal her, and bring her into Your heart.
I forgive her for any and every evil she may have willed against me.

After hesitating, he repeated, "I forgive her for any and every evil she may have willed against me."

Finally, I said, "I ask You in Your goodness to bring to order what Lisa and I have disordered."

"I ask You in Your goodness to bring to order what she and I have disordered," he repeated.

Employing exorcistic language, I continued, "I ask You to sever from me and every demonic attachment, every evil spirit, and everything that is not of You."

"I ask You to sever from me and every demonic attachment, every evil spirit, and everything that is not of You," he repeated.

"I want no part of them, I only want You and the life that You offer, and I choose Jesus today to be my personal Lord and Savior."

Repeating, and with greater force, he declared, "I want no part of them, I only want You and the life that You offer, and I choose Jesus today to be my personal Lord and Savior."

"Amen," I said.

"Amen," he repeated.

Turning to Christopher, I pointed to an image of Jesus on my office wall and said to him, "Now I'm going pray for you. Just look at that image as I do so and ask Jesus to come into your heart and remove everything that is not of Him."

As he focused on the image, I began: "Lord, in Your goodness, I ask You to show mercy to this child of Yours, Christopher. Reveal the infinite love You have for him by freeing him from the morbid illness he suffers that is choking the life out of him. Restore him to health so he may serve You in happiness and joy for the rest of his life. I beg You to show him Your goodness. Amen."

Turning now toward the demon or demons attached to Christopher, I said: "In the Name of Jesus, I bind you every evil spirit, every unclean demon, together with all your labors and machinations. Upon my word, I command you to depart from Christopher and go immediately to the place the Lord Jesus Christ, Son of God, and Savior of the World, commands you. You are never to return to Christopher again. You must leave wholly and completely, leaving behind no residue, you may not contaminate anyone or anything else as you depart, and you must not retaliate in any way. I command you to leave, in the mighty name of Jesus . . . *now!*"

Christopher's body began to tremble even as he continued to look at the image of Jesus. I took a deep breath and slowly blew it on him.[1] By the time I finished, he was perfectly still.

I continued to pray silently over him for another three to four minutes, and he was again filled with emotion. Afterward, I sat back down in my chair.

Christopher's face did not look as pale as before and looked peaceful. God's healing grace was evident. I asked him, "As I was praying over you, did you see anything, hear anything, or feel anything?"

"Yes," he replied. "When you thanked God for making me, I felt heat coming from your hand and going inside me. It was very hot. I have never felt heat like that. As I started the renunciations, I saw Lisa's face. She was angry and looked evil. I never saw her like that before. Then she disappeared."

"What do you feel now?" I asked.

"I feel peace," he said.

"Praise God!" I responded.

The demons and the debilitating depression left Christopher that afternoon. That day was the first of a new life in God. He enrolled in religious instruction and was baptized into the Catholic Church the following Easter. He is involved in his parish and speaks to youth groups on the importance of sexual purity.

THE DEMONIC SIDE OF SEXUAL SIN

The sexual appetite is one of nature's most potent drives. Males belonging to horn-bearing species will battle each other for days for the right to brief mating with a female. Bears, lions, and primates engage in extreme violence for the same reason. While salmon males do not battle each other per se, both males and females fight raging currents as they swim up rivers to spawn. In many insect species, females kill and consume the male partner during or after copulation—and sometimes even before. Nature has ensured species survival by the unrelenting drive to reproduce, often at mortal risk to its participants.

Humans will give up food, money, and even power for sex. But while animals act according to the instincts God created, humans are prone to go beyond what mere reproduction requires. We often desire more than just sex with an attractive partner: we cultivate perverted appetites with no comparative parallel in the animal kingdom.

From the beginning, God intended sex to be holy—an extension of His creative power—and laid principles to order and govern it.

BIBLICAL PRINCIPLES FOR SEX

- The Biblical creation account reveals that man and woman are creation's pinnacles (Gen. 1:31), bearing God's image and likeness in different, though complementary ways (Gen. 1:27).
- God created the woman out of the man's own body (Gen. 2:22), and both are reunited in marriage. It is why "a man leaves his father and his mother and cleaves to his wife, and they become one flesh" (Gen. 2:24). When the Pharisee questions Jesus about divorce, Jesus cites this text, declaring that in marriage, the spouses are no longer two but one in a permanent bond (Matt. 19:6).
- God created sex before sin, and while sin wounded human sexual nature, the dignity accorded to sex before the Fall remains unchanged. "Let marriage be held in honor

among all, and let the marriage bed be undefiled; for God will judge the immoral and adulterous" (Heb. 13:4).

- Scripture condemns adultery and other sexual immorality (e.g., 1 Cor. 6:12–20). Even willful lustful thoughts severely violate God's plan for human sexuality (Matt. 5:28).
- Homosexual behavior is a grave aberration of God's plan (Rom. 1:24–27; 1 Cor. 6:9).
- Since our bodies are members of Christ's body (1 Cor. 6:15), what we do with them matters. He who joins himself to a sexual partner becomes one in body with that partner and opens his spirit to the same (1 Cor. 6:16). Among other things, this means that through sex, one subjects himself to inheriting any demons his partner may possess. But even if one's partner has no demons, using one's sexuality apart from God's design opens the door to the demonic. There is no "safe sex" apart from sex according to God's creative plan.

The sexual revolution, far from bringing greater happiness, has increased human suffering. The explosion of sexual perversion— abortion, contraception, adult and child pornography, human sex trafficking, prostitution, homosexuality, and sexual addictions (masturbation, pornography use, et cetera)—all testify to this. One can see in them a fulfillment of Saint Paul's teaching that God will avenge indulgence in lust (1 Thess. 4:6). Saint Augustine of Hippo wrote, "The punishment for a disordered soul is its own disorder."[2] Nowhere is this more evident than in the lives of the sexually immoral.

Theresa, a young lady in her mid-twenties, came to me looking for relief. Recurring, demon-themed nightmares plagued her. Objects moving by themselves within her home were common. What she called "devil touches," sensual caresses of her genital area by an invisible being, afflicted her day and night. While the first two symptoms are common, "run-of-the-mill" demonic manifestations, the last one is uncommon and rare. Theresa admitted that she did not find the sexual touching unpleasant, but it occurred at random times, even when she was waiting on clients at the bank where she worked.

Since the phenomenon was sexual, I asked Theresa to share her sexual history. She had been sexually active since the age of sixteen. For those nine years, she'd had three partners. Curiously, however, the manifestation had only started after she was hired at the bank two years prior. By this time, Theresa was twenty-three years old and was cohabitating with her boyfriend of four years. The two had an eight-month-old daughter.

To make matters stranger, while Theresa had always been heterosexual, her sexual appetite had grown to include same-sex relations. It began with a coworker at the bank. The two of them went to a bar after their shift one day, and after a couple of drinks, Theresa found herself kissing the woman, who reciprocated. Within thirty minutes, they were in Theresa's apartment engaged in sexual activity.

The same pattern began to repeat itself with other female coworkers. Theresa invited them out, and after spending as little as ten minutes together, each felt an overpowering lust. Before long, they would be at Theresa's or, if her partner might be home, at the other woman's home—or in one of their vehicles, if that was all that was available.

Theresa was a petite woman with a personality that matched her small stature. Her character was unassuming, almost meek. She answered every question I asked her—embarrassing as they were—simply and straightforwardly. Because it is difficult for people to speak about their sexual history, they often gloss over relevant details or omit them altogether. It often curtails the exorcist's ability to help. I appreciated Theresa's candor.

Theresa described how, within five months, she had developed a sexual relationship with eight of the twelve women who worked at her branch. She stated she had such confidence in her ability to seduce her female coworkers that she challenged herself to lure a new one every month. None of the women had ever experienced same-sex attraction before meeting Theresa. When targeted by her, however, each woman not only found herself with a new appetite but also powerless against Theresa's advances. None had refused her, even those who had always been faithful to their husbands.

"None of the women ever refused your advances?" I asked.

"Never. I call one when I want it, and she complies," Theresa responded.

"But surely they occasionally refuse if for no other reason than your schedules do not align, and they are not free when you are?"

"At times, some have said they can't, but I never accept refusal. I decide when and where we have sex. I decide what kind of sex we have. They're not in charge." Leaning back into her chair and narrowing her eyes, she added, "It doesn't matter what they want. I'm in charge. I decide."

The arrogance that emerged in Theresa's tone and demeanor was startling. Once the conversation switched to her female partners, her meek and unassuming personality vanished, and she spoke about them callously, as though they were her personal property.

"Are you suggesting the women drop everything when you call and do your bidding, just because you asked?"

"I don't ask," Theresa responded. "I tell them what I want, and what I say goes. I called one once while she was preparing for her kid's birthday party. But I wanted sex, so I told her that was her priority."

"And she complied?"

"You better believe she complied."

"How did she get out of being at the birthday?"

"She missed part of it."

"How did she manage that? What did she say to her family to excuse herself?"

"Who cares?"

Theresa spoke like a coldhearted abuser. Her words sounded more like that of a human trafficker than a lover. It was absurd that women whose only connection to one another is that they work at the same bank should all powerlessly succumb to her seductions, especially when none of them had had a same-sex attraction before meeting her. "Don't you think there is something abnormal in what you are describing?" I asked. "In less than a year, you have developed a sexual relationship with eight out of twelve of your female coworkers. Do you not find that odd?"

Theresa paused for a few moments. "Hmm, I never thought about it that way," she responded, her look of arrogance and superiority diminishing. "I guess that is odd."

I continued. "Do you also not find your manner toward these women peculiar? You speak about them as if they are yours to control."

"But I *am* in control," she exclaimed, pointing at herself. "I'm in charge, and what I say goes."

"Theresa, you realize you're a sexual predator, don't you? You have somehow gained control over these women, and they have become your sex slaves."

Her face lost all expression. After a moment, she said, "I never thought about it like that."

"Theresa, eight coworkers are in your control, you can demand sex from them at any moment, and each feels compelled to comply, with none feeling free to refuse. Does that not strike you as strange?"

"Yeah, I guess that is strange," she answered. A look of anxiety began to form on her face.

"Have you ever had this power over anyone before, before meeting these women?"

"No," she replied. "I never had sex with a woman before. Only with my boyfriend."

"Theresa, I think a demon is the cause of the sexual touching you've been experiencing. I also think the same demon has made you a sexual predator. One of your previous sexual encounters was perhaps the entry point. But the demon's hold is so strong that you are blind to the fact that you are abusing and torturing other human beings and relishing in doing it. In addition to owning your sexual appetite, he manipulates your intellect by clouding your awareness of the most obvious facts, such as that you have become a sadistic narcissist and a sexual predator."

Theresa needed deliverance prayer. I would not administer it until she changed employment. Daily interaction with her co-workers would undermine the efforts to liberate her. Their presence would be a constant temptation, rousing her sexual appetite, compromising her will, and thus making the work of liberation more difficult than it needed to be. It is never prudent to pit strength against strength when facing a demon.

Fortunately, Theresa was serious in her desire to seek liberation, and within six weeks, following her request, her bank transferred her to another branch. As soon as she was settled into a new job and had destroyed her former co-workers' contact information, we began her deliverance.

Demons respond in a variety of ways when prayers are invoked against them. Theresa's demon had a formidable strategy: he prevented her from engaging in renunciations by stimulating her sex organs. At times, Theresa became so lost in the manipulation that she was induced to orgasm.

I prayed and forcefully commanded the demon to stop, yet my prayers achieved nothing. The demon was in charge. The problem was not that he disobeyed me. The problem was that I had no jurisdiction over him. His activity on Theresa was so pleasurable for her that she welcomed it. She permitted the demon to remain where he was, preventing any authority on my part from casting him out.

Theresa needed to want the demon's expulsion *more* than she enjoyed his stimulation. To drive a wedge between her and the demon, I appealed to her motherhood. I reminded her that her daughter's mother was a sadistic sexual predator.

"Is the slavery you are inflicting on your helpless victims the moral and spiritual inheritance you want to leave your little girl?" I asked. "What will your daughter think when she discovers her mother has a demon through whom she ensnares sex slaves? Do you think it is healthy for her to live under the same roof as the demon inside you?"

The challenge to moral uprightness and maternal integrity gave Theresa the strength to detest the demon. With that strength, Theresa made the necessary declarations that her liberation required: "I renounce the spirit of sexual predation . . . the spirit of lesbianism . . . the spirit of lust . . ."

Just before the demon left her, a large crow landed on the sill outside my window and began loudly pecking at the glass. Besides being a distraction—because it was odd and creepy—I have no idea what its purpose was. In the end, it made no difference. With a scream, the demon departed. Although Theresa was tempted to revert to a life of sexual predation for some months afterward, she resisted by remaining focused on protecting her daughter.

Theresa's case illustrates the kind of transference of spirits that immoral sexual activity can cause. God intends sex to permanently strengthen marriage by joining the partners together in a one-flesh bond. When sex is misused, demons can become integrated into that bond.

INTIMATE BONDS

A couple approaching middle age once came to see me asking for a blessing so they could conceive. After fifteen years of marriage, Zack and Nella were still without a child, and Nella anguished over it. I prayed with them and gave them the desired blessing. Then Zack provided a key detail: they had not conceived because Nella would not engage in intercourse. Nella did not answer when I asked why. After a long silence, Zack spoke up: "We have intercourse once or twice a year, at best," he said. "She refuses any more than that."

"I'm confused, Nella," I admitted. "You want a baby but don't want to make a baby?"

"Sex is a hang-up for me, Father," she said. "I only had one boyfriend before Zack. We were sexually active, and I enjoyed it. I stopped enjoying it after him."

"Why?"

"I have no idea. I parted on good terms with Peter. It just didn't work out. I deeply love Zack, but I can't seem to bring myself to enjoy sex anymore."

"Can you think of a reason why? Was there something unique or different about sex with Peter that you cannot experience with Zack?"

"Not at all, Father," she responded. "It's just a mystery to me."

"Did Peter abuse you in any way? Or did you have some bad experience with him?"

"Peter was always good to me. I liked him, and I thought we would marry one day. That is until we broke up, and I met Zack." Saying this sentence, she affectionately leaned on Zack, who was next to her, and placed her hand in his. "I liked the physical intimacy I had with Peter. In fact, I always told myself when I was with Peter that even if we never married, I would always be available for Peter and that he could always have me."

"You said what?" I interjected. "You told yourself that he could always have you?"

"Yes," she replied. "I know it's stupid. But that's how much I thought I liked Peter."

"You made an inner vow," I said. "You sealed your physical intimacy with a legal bond."

"What does that mean?"

"That means you still belong to Peter. You may be rejecting Zack because you are still spiritually tied to Peter."

"Father, I don't love Peter anymore. He is married to a friend, and occasionally I see him at parties and such. I don't desire him anymore, and he is the kind of guy that would never hurt a fly. I could not see him doing any 'black magic' or 'sorcery' stuff to hurt me."

"Peter does not have to be operative in this at all. You made a vow—a covenant—and doing that has implications. I suspect there is a demon guarding and protecting that vow."

I led Nella through a series of renunciations, rejecting the acts of fornication she committed with Peter and the sinful vow she made in her heart toward him. I then led her through a series of attachment prayers—the opposite of renunciations—whereby she gave the rights that she gave Peter to her husband, Zack. At the end of these, Nella reported that she heard a loud internal growl and felt a tightness suddenly "give way" inside her abdomen.

Zack and Nella called me the next day, sharing that Zack rested his hand on Nella's abdomen as they got into bed that night. Usually, when this occurred, Nella's hand instinctively swept it away. This time, however, she didn't do that. Zack brought her attention to that fact, and Nella was as surprised as he was. In her words, it felt "perfectly comfortable." They had marital relations that night. From that point on, Nella engaged in relations with ease and facility. Her frigidity was gone.

One final example illustrating how demons use sexual acts to bond themselves is that of a ten-year-old boy named Francis. A sixteen-year-old male neighbor his parents hired to babysit him sexually abused him, forcing Francis to give him oral sex. After the second occurrence, Francis reported it to his parents. There followed a long and painful police investigation and criminal trial. After the abuser was convicted, the family decided to give themselves a fresh start by relocating across the country.

His parents enrolled him in a local summer camp to distract Francis from the abuse he experienced and the trauma of leaving his friends behind. Though their decision was well-intentioned, for Francis it was fateful. Unknown to his parents, one of the camp counselors was a pedophile, and of the two hundred children enrolled at the camp, Francis was the one he targeted to abuse.

While one could assert that the pedophile's targeting Francis was a complete coincidence, there are details to Francis' story that challenge that assertion. Francis was adopted from Russia at the age of three. The only information the state adoption agency provided was the following:

1. His mother was a prostitute.
2. He was conceived in a rape where his mother was severely and permanently injured.
3. He was sexually abused by a male relative who was raising him.

There is too much of a pattern of sexual abuse in Francis' life to believe the incidents involving his babysitter and the summer camp counselor were coincidental. Through sex, two people form a bond even if one is an abuser. Until broken, the bond that forms is real and lasting. And should demons be attached to one's partner, the bond serves as a conduit through which they can transfer to a host. In Francis' case, the demons attached to him linked him to new and fresh abusers.

I wish I had a happy ending to report about Francis. His parents were not Christians and wanted a quick fix to the problem. When ministry to their son took too long for their liking, they stopped bringing him. Despite agreeing that Francis' problem was demonic, they failed to grasp the path to his healing. His parents chose not to pursue Francis' reception of Christian catechesis and formation. And deliverance ministry was never possible. They wanted their son's problem to go away without embracing its solution—Jesus Christ, the conqueror of the kingdom of evil.

Eventually, the family moved to another part of the country. Francis remains in my prayers.

THE DEMONIC ELEMENT OF PORNOGRAPHY

The bond between sexual partners is one reason pornography is so addictive. Aside from the addictive nature of porn on a natural level, the spiritual element is a significant factor in making pornography a habitual dependence.

The Lord teaches that he who looks lustfully at someone has already committed adultery (Matt. 5:28). More than just incurring sin, such a look establishes a one-flesh bond. Concretely, one who looks lustfully at those depicted in pornographic images becomes bonded to them. By logical extension, however, *he also becomes bonded with anyone who is also bonded to those images*. Thus, to use pornography is to connect oneself at a one-flesh level to a web of myriads of persons.

Furthermore, within that web, demons travel about freely. Thus, we can understand why it is so difficult to curb porn addiction: porn users are spiritually grafted to a web of hellish dysfunction spiritually ministered by demons.

BREAKING FREE FROM BONDAGE TO SEXUAL SIN

No one can eliminate the influence of sexual demons—or any demons—without grace. And grace must be pursued and cultivated. Once obtained, it must be treasured, protected, and guarded against being sullied.

The greatest source of grace comes from the Sacraments. Through them, God bestows His very life and turns us into Himself.

A daily encounter with the Lord in prayer is also essential for obtaining the grace necessary to sever immoral sexual bonds and impurity from our lives. Anyone desiring to be free of the spiritual residue from a morally corrupted sexual relationship should spend at least a quarter hour in prayer each day. The more time one spends in prayer, the more the Lord can work on us, grafting us onto Himself and pruning from us what is useless.

Praying with images can be especially helpful, especially during sexual temptation. Traditionally called *visio divina* (divine looking), holy images—images depicting Our Lord, the Blessed Virgin Mary, a saint, or a biblical scene—drive out tempting images that compete for our attention. In Catholic tradition, holy images, especially icons, are visible prayers. Simply to gaze at such an image is prayer.

As with any deliverance, renouncing our moral mistakes is essential to achieving liberation. As discussed throughout this book, renunciations are the "legal annulment" of agreements—which we can make without even realizing it—whereby evil takes advantage of us.

The sexual appetite is so powerful that people will sacrifice virtually anything to gratify it. The abortion industry is the product of the modern desire for sex without responsibility. Babies are being slaughtered to pay the cost of erotic freedom.

Sexual activity has spiritual implications. God intended the sexual act to bring about a lifelong, one-flesh bond with one's marriage partner. Those who embrace sexual promiscuity do so to the detriment of themselves and the entire human community.

Finally, because of the generational potential of sin, our immediate family members and all who follow us stand only to benefit from our purity and freedom in Christ.

CONCLUSION

The Devil's fury is the cause of immense misery. From the beginning, he has coveted man's happiness and will stop at nothing to possess it. Unbounded in intellect, steeled in will, and cunning in disposition, the Devil prowls about the world "like a roaring lion, seeking someone to devour" (1 Pet. 5:8). He devoured our first parents, Adam and Eve, and continues to do so wherever sin, sickness, and death are found in those created in God's "image and likeness" (Gen. 1:26–27).

Were it not for Jesus Christ, who undid this destructive pattern, the Devil's devouring would continue without end, consuming each human person and relegating him to an eternity of unending misery. Saint John Henry Newman so aptly stated that when Jesus Christ, the Second Adam, entered the world, the Devil's fury had not only met its match, it encountered its defeat.

> *O loving wisdom of our God!*
> *When all was sin and shame,*
> *A second Adam to the fight*
> *And to the rescue came.*[1]

In reality, the outcome of the fight between Christ and the Devil was never in doubt, even though the Incarnate God endured temptations, betrayal, rejection, torturous crucifixion, and death. The serpent's intellect proved weak before the Creator, his strength docile, and his cunning amateurish.

It takes someone with the brilliance of Newman to articulate with such simplicity the sheer incompatibility of the two ancient opponents.

Wonderful providence indeed, which is so silent, yet so efficacious, so constant, so unerring! This is what baffles the power of Satan. He cannot discern the hand of God in what goes on; and though he would fain meet it and encounter it, in his mad and blasphemous rebellion against heaven, he cannot find it. Crafty and penetrating as he is, yet his thousand eyes and his many instruments avail him nothing against the majestic serene silence, the holy imperturbable calm which reigns through the providences of God. Crafty and experienced as he is, he appears like a child or a fool, like one made sport of, whose daily bread is but failure and mockery, before the deep and secret wisdom of the Divine counsels. He makes a guess here, or does a bold act there, but all in the dark. He knew not of Gabriel's coming, and the miraculous conception of the Virgin, or what was meant by that Holy Thing which was to be born being called the Son of God. He tried to kill Him, and he made martyrs of the innocent children; he tempted the Lord of all with hunger and with ambitious prospects; he sifted the Apostles, and got none but one, who already bore his own name, and had been already given over as a devil. He rose against his God in his full strength, in the hour and power of darkness, and then he seemed to conquer; but with his utmost effort, and as his greatest achievement, he did no more than 'whatsoever Thy hand and Thy counsel determined before to be done' (Acts 5:28). He brought into the world the very salvation which he feared and hated. He accomplished the Atonement of that world whose misery He was plotting. Wonderfully silent, yet resistless course of God's providence! "Verily, Thou art a God that hidest Thyself, O God of Israel, the Saviour;" and if even devils, sagacious as they are, spirits by nature and experienced in evil, cannot detect His hand, while He works, how can we hope to see it except by that way which the devils cannot take, by a loving faith? how can we see it except afterwards as a reward to our faith, beholding the cloud of glory in the distance, which when present was too rare and impalpable for mortal sense?[2]

If the struggle against evil is a constant part of the human condition, then so is the solution—Jesus Christ, the Second Adam and Savior of the World—even if each generation must rediscover Him.

I pray that this book has aided the reader in that rediscovery. Though its subject matter is unsettling by its nature, my intent is to share the Good News of Christ's victory, educate others on avoiding the entrapments of the Adversary, and give confidence in the Bride of Christ—the Church—who delights both in announcing Christ's victory and dispensing the spoils.

BIBLIOGRAPHY

Ambrose of Milan, St. *Epistola XXII*: in "The Letters of St. Ambrose." *A Select Library of the Nicene and Post-Nicene Fathers of the Christian Church, Second Series: St. Ambrose: Select Works and Letters.* Vol. 10. Edited by P. Schaff & H. Wace. Translated by H. de Romestin, E. de Romestin, & H. T. F. Duckworth. New York: Christian Literature Company, 1896.

Amorth, Gabriel. *An Exorcist Tells His Story.* San Francisco: Ignatius Press, 1999.

Aquinas, St. Thomas. *Summa Theologiae*, 2nd rev. ed., Translated by the Fathers of the English Dominican Province. New York: Benziger Brothers, 1947–1948.

Augustine, St. *Confessions.* Translated by Henry Chadwick. New York: Oxford University Press, 2008.

Catechism of the Catholic Church, 2nd ed. Washington, DC: United States Catholic Conference, 2000.

Chrysostom, St. John. "In Martyres Aegyptios." In *The Faith of Catholics: Confirmed by Scripture and Attested by the Fathers of the First Five Centuries of the Church*, 2nd ed. Vol. 3. Edited by J. Waterworth and T. J. New York; Cincinnati: Fr. Pustet, 1885.

Code of Canon Law: Latin-English Edition, 3rd ed. Washington, DC: Canon Law Society of America, 2020.

Congregation for the Doctrine of Faith. *Declaration on Masonic Associations*. Vatican City. November 26, 1983, retrieved from http://www.vatican.va/roman_curia/congregations/cfaith/documents/rc_con_cfaith_doc_19831126_declaration-masonic_en.html.

American Psychiatric Association. *Diagnostic and Statistical Manual of Mental Disorders*, 5th ed. Washington, DC: American Psychiatric Association, 2013.

American Psychiatric Association. *Diagnostic and Statistical Manual of Mental Disorders, Text Revision*, 5th ed. Washington, DC: American Psychiatric Association, 2022.

Duncan, Malcolm C. *Duncan's Masonic Ritual and Monitor or Guide to the Three Symbolic Degrees of the Ancient York Rite*, 3rd ed. New York: Dick & Fitzgerald, 1866.

Exorcisms and Related Supplications, English Translation According to the Typical Edition, International Commission on English in the Liturgy: Washington, DC, 2017.

"Halloween Viewed Favorably by Most Americans." Public Policy Polling, press release, October 30, 2012. Retrieved from https://web.archive.org/web/20170520192335/http://www.publicpolicy-polling.com:80/pdf/2011/HalloweenRelease+Results.pdf.

"Hallucinations." *Alzheimer's Association*. (n.d.). Retrieved July 18, 2022, from http://www.alz.org/help-support/caregiving/stages-behaviors/hallucinations

Hilary of Poitiers, St. "Contra Constantinum Imperatorem," in *The Faith of Catholics: Confirmed by Scripture and Attested by the Fathers of the First Five Centuries of the Church*. Vol. 3. Edited by J. J. Waterworth & T. J. Capel. New York; Cincinnati: Fr. Pustet & Co., 1885.

Hippolytus of Rome, *The Apostolic Tradition of Hippolytus*. Translated by Burton Scott Easton, Ann Arbor, MI: Cambridge University Press, 1964.

Ignatius of Loyola, *The Spiritual Exercises of St. Ignatius of Loyola Translated from the Autograph*. Translated by Father Elder Mullan, S. J. New York: P. J. Kenedy & Sons, 1914.

Jerome, St. "Against Vigilantius," in *St. Jerome: Letters and Select Works*. Vol. 6. Edited by P. Schaff and H. Wace, W. H. Fremantle, G. Lewis. Translated by W. G. Martley. New York: Christian Literature Company, 1893.

Lee, Philip, et al. "Acute Psychosis Precipitated by Urinary Tract Infection in a Patient with Gliosis of the Basal Ganglia." *American Journal of Medical Case Reports* 7, no. 12 (2019): 329–333. doi:10.12691/ajmcr-7-12-7

Lynch, James Sylvester Mary. *Rite of the Blessing of a Bell, or of Several Bells According to the Roman Pontifical with Additions to the Rubrics*. New York: The Cathedral Library Association, 1912.

Melton, J. Gordon. *New Age Movement*. Encyclopædia Britannica, retrieved 27 July 2020 from www.britannica.com/topic/New-Age-movement

National Conference of Catholic Bishops. *Order of Christian Funerals*, New York: Catholic Book Publishing, 1989, pp. 126–127.

Newman, John Henry. "The Dream of Gerontius," *Verses on Various Occasions*: London: Burns, Oates, 1868.

Newman, John Henry. *Selection Adapted to the Seasons of the Ecclesiastical Year from the Parochial & Plain Sermons of John Henry Newman*, London: Longmans, Green, 1920.

"'Nones' on the Rise." Pew Research Center. Washington, D.C., retrieved July 18, 2022, from www.pewforum.org/2012/10/09/nones-on-the-rise/

Pope John Paul II. "General Audience of Wednesday 4 August 1999." Vatican City, retrieved July 18, 2022, from https://www.vatican.

va/content/john-paul-ii/en/audiences/1999/documents/hf_jp-ii_aud_04081999.html.

The Revised Standard Version of the Bible: Catholic Edition. Washington, DC: Division of Christian Education of the National Council of the Churches of Christ in the United States of America, 1966.

Roberts, A., Donaldson, J., & Coxe, A. C., eds. *Ante-Nicene Fathers: Fathers of the Third Century: Hippolytus, Cyprian, Novatian, Appendix.* Buffalo, NY: Christian Literature Company, 1886.

The Roman Ritual. Vol. 2. Translated by Rev. Philip T. Weller, Boonville, NY: Preserving Christian Publications, 2008.

The Roman Ritual, Complete Edition. Translated by Rev. Philip T. Weller, Milwaukee: The Bruce Publishing Company, 1964.

United States Conference of Catholic Bishops (Committee on Doctrine). *Guidelines for Evaluating Reiki as an Alternative Therapy*, March 25, 2009. Retrieved 18 July 2022, from https://www.usccb.org/about/doctrine/publications/upload/evaluation-guide-lines-finaltext-2009-03.pdf

"What Is Freemasonry's Relationship with Religion?" United Grand Lodge of England, (n.d.), retrieved July 25, 2020, from www.ugle.org.uk/about-freemasonry/frequently-asked-questions.

"What Is Reiki?" The International Center for Reiki Training, retrieved July 18, 2022, from https://www.reiki.org/faqs/what-reiki

White, Andrew Dickson. *A History of the Warfare of Science with Theology in Christendom*, Vol. 1, D. New York: Appleton and Company, 1896.

Woods, Richard J., O.P. "The Possession Problem," in *Chicago Studies*. Edited by George J. Dyer, Vol. 12, no. 1, 1973, pp. 91–107.

NOTES

INTRODUCTION

1   A. Roberts, Donaldson, and A. C. Coxe, eds, *Fathers of the Third Century: Hippolytus, Cyprian, Novatian, Appendix*, vol. 5 (Christian Literature Company, 1886), p. 417.

2   Quoted in Richard J. Woods, O.P., "The Possession Problem," in *Chicago Studies*, ed. George J. Dyer, 12, no. 1 (1973): pp. 99–100.

3   American Psychiatric Association, *Diagnostic and Statistical Manual of Mental Disorders: Text Revision*, 5th ed., 2022, p. 332. In the previous edition of the *DSM*—the *DSM-5*, published in 2013—the second sentence reads, "For example . . . an individual may be 'taken over' by a demon or deity, resulting in profound impairment, and demanding that the individual or a relative be punished."

4   Ibid., p. 331.

5   Dr. Paul R. McHugh, former psychiatrist-in-chief for Johns Hopkins Hospital and its current Distinguished Service Professor of Psychiatry called transgenderism a "mental disorder," noting that those who undergo sex-reassignment surgery are twenty times more likely to commit suicide than the comparable nontransgender population. See Paul, McHugh, "Transgender Surgery Isn't the Solution." *Wall Street Journal* (May 13, 2016), accessed online at http://www.wsj.com/articles/paul-mchugh-transgender-surgery-isnt-the -solution-1402615120?reflink=desktopwebshare_permalink.

CHAPTER ONE: THE REALITY OF THE DEVIL

1   Gabriele Amorth, *An Exorcist Tells His Story* (San Francisco: Ignatius Press, 1999), p. 168.

CHAPTER TWO: WHAT IS DEMONIC ACTIVITY?

1   See *Catechism of the Catholic Church*, 2nd ed. Washington, DC: United States Catholic Conference, 2000, pgs. 1989-92.

2 An essential principle to live by is the fifth rule from St. Ignatius of Loyola's (1491 – 1556) famous Rules for the Discernment of Spirits: *"Since in desolation evil attempts to make a bad choice appear good and sound, during a period of spiritual desolation one should never make a major decision, but patiently wait and abide by the decision and course one was on prior to the desolation's beginning."* (Ignatius of Loyola, *The Spiritual Exercises of St. Ignatius of Loyola Translated from the Autograph.* Trans. Father Elder Mullan, S.J. New York: P.J. Kenedy & Sons, 1914. p. 35.)

3 *The Roman Ritual* is the official book of the rites and ceremonies that are performed by a Catholic priest.

4 Without reconciliation, all efforts to clean the place will be futile. The priest is not a sorcerer or worker of magic. His actions are only efficacious to the extent that the victim is in communion with God.

5 I do not mean "incarnation" in the sense that the Son of God became man, i.e., when He took on a nature that was not His own, but in the sense that a Christian is made a member of the Body of Christ, an image so often used by Saint Paul in his Epistles (Rom. 12:5; 1 Cor. 12:12–27; Eph. 3:6, 4:15–16, and 5:23; Col.1:18 and 1:24).

CHAPTER THREE: WHAT IS EXORCISM?

1 US Conference of Catholic Bishops, *Exorcisms and Related Supplications: English Translation According to the Typical Edition* (International Commission on English in the Liturgy: Washington, DC, 2017), p. 33.

2 It is not the case that Jeremy's teeth actually grew to two inches and then later shrunk back to normal. Demons lack the power to produce such changes. They are, however, master illusionists and can make teeth *appear* longer and fiercer.

3 Protestants often criticize the Catholic practice of praying to the saints. This criticism, however, comes from a misunderstanding of what it means "to pray." As any dictionary can confirm, "to pray" means "to ask." It does not mean "to worship." Both Catholics and Protestants agree that worship is due to God alone. Shakespeare used the word "prithee" throughout his plays, a contraction of the phrase "I pray thee." It is equivalent to saying, "I ask you." In Act 3, Scene 4 of Macbeth, for example, Macbeth "prays" to Lady Macbeth when he asks her to look at the ghost which has suddenly appeared: "Prithee, see there! Behold!"

To Catholics, praying to the saints is holy. Within his Epistles, Paul often asks those to whom he is writing to pray for him (e.g., 2 Thess. 3:1–2; Phil. 1:19; Rom. 15:30). He did not view their prayers as superfluous, nor did he regard it sufficient merely to pray for himself. The logical question is, why should this intercession of one Christian for another stop at death? All Christians believe that, for those who die in God's friendship, death is birth into Heaven's glory. Catholics, however, regard it as absurd that those experiencing Heaven possess less power and ability than they possessed on earth. How could they lack in Heaven—when they are in God's very glory—a power they enjoyed on earth?

4 *Exorcisms and Related Supplications,* §14.

5 For the sake of protecting the exorcist's craft and the tools he uses, I will reveal no others. Since they are helpful only if a victim is unaware of them, it would be inappropriate to publish them.

6 Manifestations a victim can exhibit that aid in diagnosing the presence of demons:

- Referring to oneself in the plural, such as "We" and "Our" (as in Mark 1:23–24; and 5:9).
- Violence (as in Acts 19:16).
- Screaming (as in Mark 5:5).
- Muteness (as in Luke 11:14).
- Unnatural bodily movements (as in Mark 9:20).
- Bodily contortions (as in Mark 9:18).
- Self-injury (as in Mark 5:5).
- Attempting suicide (as in Mark 9:22).
- Speaking in a different voice.
- Sounding and moving like an animal.
- Exhibiting paranormal abilities.
- Insulting and using obscene language.
- Bodily wounds suddenly appearing and disappearing.
- Sudden and intense nausea.
- Vomiting strange objects.
- Spontaneously falling asleep.

CHAPTER FOUR: DOORWAYS: HOW DEMONS ENTER A PERSON

1 Confession is the act of reconciling with God and His Church. Following Christ's exhortation to the Apostles, His first priests, in John 20:23, the Catholic Church has always taught that only an apostolically ordained priest can dispense God's forgiveness.

2 The contents of a person's confession is absolutely confidential and a priest is never free to divulge what a penitent reveals *for any reason whatsoever.* The Catholic Church calls this confidentiality the Seal of Confession. To be clear, what I have said about Linda and Charlie is no violation of the seal, a I have not divulged the identity of either person. "Linda" and "Charlie" are aliases of persons whose identities remain secret.

3 To be clear, his baptism is not destroyed; but its effects cease to be operative. Baptism marks the soul with a permanent and indelible mark. A mortal sin, however, renders it ineffective.

4 *Catechism of the Catholic Church,* 2nd ed. (Washington, DC: United States Catholic Conference, 2000), no. 1855.

5   Other examples abound. The carelessness of Noah's son Ham led to the cursing
     of the entire nation of Canaan (Gen. 9:25). The final plague meted out by
     God in Egypt consisted of mass death inflicted on every Egyptian's firstborn
     for the sin that Pharaoh had done (Exod. 11:1–12:36). The story of David's
     adultery with Bathsheba is perhaps the most detailed scriptural example of a
     generational curse. David tried to cover his sin by murdering Uriah, which
     brought immense misfortune upon David and his descendants (2 Sam. 10:7–
     14). A further instance involving David occurred when Satan incited him
     to take Israel's census (1 Chron. 21:1). For this choice, God forced David to
     choose a punishment to inflict on the nation. The least harmful to him seemed
     pestilence, and seventy thousand were struck dead (1 Chron. 21:14).

6   Simple exorcism—also called a minor exorcism—is prayer meant to free
     someone who is demonically harassed. It is also called to deliverance prayer. In
     contrast, major or solemn exorcism is the Catholic Church's official prayer to
     liberate those whose demonic influence has reached possession.

7   A most curious yet fascinating and fortunate aspect of his case is that each
     time a part of the curse was broken, his siblings' situation also improved (e.g.,
     they experienced stability in their marriages, gained better employment, saw
     improvement in their health, et cetera).

CHAPTER FIVE: AN EXORCISM SESSION

1   Saint Thomas Aquinas, *Summa Theologiae*, 2nd, rev. ed., trans. *Fathers of the
     English Dominican Province*, (New York: Benziger Brothers, 1947–1948), I–II,
     Q. 85, Art. 3, respondeo.

CHAPTER SIX: HEAVENLY BACKUP

1   In 2024, 4,000 *lire* would be worth approximately $11,500.

2   Giovanni Alberti, *Alessandro Serenelli: Storia di un uomo salvato dal perdono*,
     Santuario Madonna delle Grazie e S. Maria Goretti, 2004, p. 309.

3   Ibid, p. 310.

4   While exorcists may use both Rites, the older Rite is by far the one most widely
     used. In this book, I will provide passage reference for both Rites, where
     applicable. For the former, see *The Roman Ritual*, Vol. 2, trans. Rev. Philip T.
     Weller, Boonville, New York: Preserving Christian Publications, 2008. For the
     latter, see the already cited, *Exorcisms and Related Supplications*.

5   The rules are included in the Rite of Exorcism. See *The Roman Ritual*, vol. 2, p.
     169; *Exorcisms and Related Supplications*, no. 13.

6   Pope Pius XII, Encyclical Letter *Mediator Dei,* paragraph 69. Quoted in the
     Catechism of the Catholic Church, 2nd ed. Washington, DC: United States
     Catholic Conference, 2000, no. 1548.

7   Canon 1172 of the *Code of Canon Law* (promulgated in 1983). There is no
     corresponding canon in the *Code of the Canons of the Oriental Churches*
     (promulgated in 1990).

8   I have taken this sample prayer and those that follow from the 1614 Rite because that is what most exorcists use. There are two English translations of this Rite, both by Father Philip T. Weller: the original 1952 translation which is written in more formal English, and a more idiomatic translation (where, for example, "Thee" and "Thou" have been changed to "You" and "Your") published in 1964. For ease of reading, I am using the latter translation for these prayers. *The Roman Ritual, Complete Edition*, trans. Rev. Philip T. Weller (Milwaukee: The Bruce Publishing Company, 1964), pp. 650–651.

9   Ibid., pp. 651–652.

10 Some may wonder whether I had blessed the stole before using it since it is customary for a priest to do so. I had not. Everything happened so quickly that I did not even think of it until after the meeting.

11 Cf. *The Roman Ritual, Complete Edition*, pp. 395–397.

12 In his treatise, *The Apostolic Tradition*, Saint Hippolytus of Rome has left us a description of this ancient practice: Then the presbyter, taking hold of each of those about to be baptized, shall command him to renounce, saying: I renounce thee, Satan, and all thy servants and all thy works. And when he has renounced all these, the presbyter shall anoint him with the oil of exorcism, saying: Let all spirits depart far from thee. The Diocesan Bishop blesses the Oil of Exorcism once a year during the Chrism Mass (which is celebrated during Holy Week). (Hippolytus of Rome, *The Apostolic Tradition of Hippolytus*, trans. Burton Scott Easton, Ann Arbor, MI: Cambridge University Press, 1964, pp. 45–46.)

13 Saint John Chrysostom. *In Martyres Aegyptios*: in J. Berington and J. Kirk (1885). *The Faith of Catholics: Confirmed by Scripture and Attested by the Fathers of the First Five Centuries of the Church*, vol. 3, 2nd ed. J. Waterworth and T. J. Capel, eds. (New York; Cincinnati: Fr. Pustet & Co), pp. 275–76.

14 Saint Hilary of Poitiers. Ibid., p. 256.

15 Saint Jerome. (1893). "Against Vigilantius." in P. Schaff & H. Wace (Eds.), W. H. Fremantle, G. Lewis, and W. G. Martley (Trans.), *St. Jerome: Letters and Select Works* (vol. 6, p. 421). New York: Christian Literature Company.

16 Saint Ambrose of Milan. *Epistola XXII*: in "The Letters of St. Ambrose." *A Select Library of the Nicene and Post-Nicene Fathers of the Christian Church, Second Series: St. Ambrose: Select Works and Letters*. vol. 10. P. Schaff & H. Wace (eds.), H. de Romestin, E. de Romestin, and H. T. F. Duckworth (trans). New York: Christian Literature Company, 1896. pp. 439–440.

17 *The Roman Ritual*, vol. 3, p. 365.

18 Lynch, James Sylvester Mary, *Rite of the Blessing of a Bell, or of Several Bells According to the Roman Pontifical with Additions to the Rubrics* (New York: The Cathedral Library Association, 1912), pp. 22–23.

19 Ibid., pp. 25–27.

20 National Conference of Catholic Bishops, *Order of Christian Funerals* (New Jersey: Catholic Book Publishing Corp., 1989), pp. 126–127.

21 For these descriptions and others see White, Andrew Dickson, *A History of the Warfare of Science with Theology in Christendom*, vol. 1 (New York: D. Appleton and Company, 1896), p. 345.

22 We knew his name to be Ba'al because of another previously exorcised demon. Before casting it out, when he was exhausted from the exorcism, we compelled him to disclose the names of the other two possessors. We knew the names he gave were correct because each demon came forth when summoned by it.

CHAPTER SEVEN: THE OCCULT WORLD

1 A planchette is a small plastic slider that spells out messages as it glides across the Ouija board.

2 "What Is Reiki?" The International Center for Reiki Training, *Reiki.org*, https://www.reiki.org/faqs/what-reiki, (accessed 18 July 2022).

3 Ibid.

4 United States Conference of Catholic Bishops (Committee on Doctrine), *Guidelines for Evaluating Reiki as an Alternative Therapy*, Paragraph 11. Located at http://usccb.org/about/doctrine/publications/upload/evaluation-guidelines -finaltext-2009-03.pdf

5 According to J. Gordon Melton, PhD, Distinguished Professor of American Religious History at the Institute for Studies of Religion, at Baylor University,
 The movement . . . spoke to the sick and psychologically wounded, especially those who had been unable to find help through traditional medicine and psychotherapy. Aligning themselves with the Holistic Health movement—which advocated alternative and natural healing practices such as massage, natural food diets, chiropractic, and acupuncture—believers in the New Age promoted spiritual healing. They also sought the integration of older divinatory practices (astrology, tarot, and *I Ching*) with standard psychological counseling. (Melton, J. Gordon. *New Age Movement*, Encyclopædia Britannica, published on April 07, 2016, www.britannica.com/topic/New-Age-movement, accessed July 18, 2022.)

6 "What is Freemasonry's Relationship with Religion?" United Grand Lodge of England, www.ugle.org.uk, www.ugle.org.uk/about-freemasonry/frequently -asked-questions, accessed July 25, 2020.

7 Malcolm Duncan, *Malcolm C. Duncan's Masonic Ritual and Monitor or Guide to the Three Symbolic Degrees of the Ancient York Rite*, 3rd ed (New York: Dick & Fitzgerald, 1866).

8 Ibid., pp. 34–35.

9 Ibid., p. 51.

10 Congregation for the Doctrine of Faith, *Declaration on Masonic Associations*, November 26, 1983. Retrieved from http://www.vatican.va/roman_curia /congregations/cfaith/documents/rc_con_cfaith_doc_19831126_declaration -masonic_en.html.

CHAPTER EIGHT: WITCHCRAFT AND SATANISM

1   Witches often spell the magic practiced by witchcraft as "magick" to
    distinguish it from the sleight-of-hand magic practiced on a stage, e.g., that
    performed by Harry Houdini.

CHAPTER NINE: CURSES

1   As long as we desire to make a complete confession, even forgotten sins are
    forgiven in the Sacrament.

CHAPTER TEN: GHOSTS AND HAUNTINGS

1   Not only did Saint Thomas Aquinas, for example, believe that the souls of those
    in Purgatory can appear to us as "ghosts" (*Summa Theologiae* Suppl., 69, 3), he
    was twice visited by them. Around the time of his canonization in 1323, the
    Dominican friar Bernardo Gui wrote a biography of Thomas. In it, Gui reports
    that Thomas was visited by the soul of Romanus, the Master of Theology. The
    latter succeeded him at the University of Paris. Romanus disclosed that his soul
    had spent fifteen days in Purgatory but was now in Heaven. The second ghost
    was that of Thomas' deceased sister, who revealed she was in Purgatory and
    needed prayers and Masses. Thomas dutifully granted her request. Later, she
    appeared again to inform him that she was now in glory.

2   Pope John Paul II, "General Audience of Wednesday 4 August 1999," http://
    w2.vatican.va/content/john-paul-ii/en/audiences/1999/documents/hf_jp-ii_aud
    _04081999.html. Accessed July 18, 2022.

3   While it is outside the scope of this chapter to give an exhaustive account of the
    Catholic doctrine of Purgatory, some theological explanation will help make
    sense of the empirical facts presented in this chapter.

    Christian revelation stands on the shoulders of, and is best interpreted
    through, Jewish tradition. The Jewish people offer atonement on behalf of
    the dead. In the Kaddish, for example, they pray for the forgiveness and
    justification of the deceased, that the soul may pass through the in-between
    state after death, traverse the "Heavenly Court," and arrive at God's bosom,
    righteous and deserving of eternal life. A son of the deceased prays the Kaddish
    each day for eleven months and then on each death anniversary. The El Malei
    Rachamim is a similar prayer asking God to forgive the sins of someone who
    has recently died. It is recited during the burial and at memorial services held
    throughout the year.

    Jewish prayer for the dead is described in 2 Maccabees 12:38–45, where
    Judas Maccabeus orders prayer and sacrifice to be offered for his dead soldiers.
    They all died with talismans depicting idols in their possession, which God
    forbids.

    "Then, under the tunic of every one of the dead, they found sacred
    tokens of the idols of Jamnia, which the law forbids the Jews to
    wear. And it became clear to all that this was why these men

had fallen. So . . . they turned to prayer, beseeching that the sin committed might be wholly blotted out. And the noble Judas . . . took up a collection . . . and sent it to Jerusalem to provide for a sin offering. In doing this he acted very well and honorably, taking account of the resurrection. For if he were not expecting that those who had fallen would rise again, it would have been superfluous and foolish to pray for the dead. But if he was looking to the splendid reward that is laid up for those who fall asleep in godliness, it was a holy and pious thought. Therefore, he made atonement for the dead, that they might be delivered from their sin." (2 Maccabees 12:40-45)

Protestant Christians do not regard 2 Maccabees as divine revelation and do not include it within their Bibles. At best, they will relegate it to a section they call the Apocrypha. It is, however, included in the Septuagint, the Greek translation of the Old Testament compiled during the third and second centuries BC, and this fact carries no minor significance. The Septuagint is the version of the Jewish Scriptures (now called the Old Testament) used by Christ and His Apostles in their ministry. Two-thirds of the New Testament's quoting of the Old Testament is taken from the Septuagint, and nowhere does the New Testament warn against the writings that Protestants now call the Apocrypha. On the contrary, the New Testament cites Apocryphal texts, such as in Hebrews 11:35, which is a reiteration of 2 Maccabees 7.

4 *Each man receives his eternal retribution in his immortal soul at the very moment of his death, in a particular judgment that refers his life to Christ: either entrance into the blessedness of heaven through a purification or immediately, or immediate and everlasting damnation.* (Catechism of the Catholic Church, no. 1022) For Scripture's description of the torments of hell as eternal, see, for example, Revelation 14:11; 19:3; 20:10. Further evidence can be seen in the fact that the Church, which Scripture calls "the pillar and bulwark of the truth" (1 Tim. 3:15), has never prayed for the souls of the damned.

CHAPTER ELEVEN: SEX AND SEXUALITY: PORTALS TO THE SOUL

1 For the meaning and purpose of this action—called exsufflation—see Chapter 5.

2 Saint Augustine, *Confessions*, trans. Henry Chadwick (New York: Oxford University Press, 2008), p. 15.

CONCLUSION

1 John Henry Newman, "The Dream of Gerontius," *Verses on Various Occasions* (London: Burns, Oates, 1868), p. 333.

2 John Henry Newman, *Selection Adapted to the Seasons of the Ecclesiastical Year from the Parochial & Plain Sermons of John Henry Newman* (London: Longmans, Green, 1920), pp. 217–218.

HODDER &
STOUGHTON

Hodder & Stoughton is the UK's
leading Christian publisher,
with a wide range of books from
the bestselling authors in the UK
and around the world ranging from
Christian lifestyle and theology to
apologetics, testimony and fiction.
We also publish the world's
most popular Bible translation
in modern English, the New
International Version, renowned
for its accuracy and readability.

Hodderfaith.com   Hodderbibles.co.uk
@HodderFaith   /HodderFaith